THE ROUG

Personal Computers

There are more than two hundred Rough Guide travel, phrasebook and music titles, covering destinations from Amsterdam to Zimbabwe, languages from Czech to Vietnamese, and musics from World to Opera and Jazz

www.roughguides.com

Rough Guide Credits

Text editor: Andrew Dickson **Series editor**: Mark Ellingham
Production: Michelle Draycott, Helen Prior

Publishing Information

This first edition published October 2001 by
Rough Guides Ltd, 62–70 Shorts Gardens, London WC2H 9AH.

Distributed by the Penguin Group

Penguin Books Ltd, 80 Strand, London WC2R 0RL
Penguin Putnam, Inc., 375 Hudson Street, New York 10014, USA
Penguin Books Australia Ltd, 487 Maroondah Highway,
PO Box 257, Ringwood, Victoria 3134, Australia
Penguin Books Canada Ltd, 10 Alcorn Avenue,
Toronto, Ontario, Canada M4V 1E4
Penguin Books (NZ) Ltd, 182–190 Wairau Road,
Auckland 10, New Zealand

Printed in Spain by Graphy Cems.

432pp includes index
A catalogue record for this book is available from the British Library.
ISBN 1-85828-655-7

THE ROUGH GUIDE TO

Personal Computers

written by

Peter Buckley and Duncan Clark

Authors' Acknowledgements

The authors would like to thank: Jonathan and Mark for giving us the green light; Helen for exceptionally patient typesetting; Andy for diligent editing; Amanda Jones for proofreading; Bairbre at Belkin for images; Seb and Andrew for advice; Fran for putting up with it; Adrian for guidance and support; and Rosalie for just being Rosalie.

Picture Credits

The editor would like to thank the following for permission to reproduce images: Belkin Components (pp.63, 64, 226, 306), International Business Machines Corporation (pp.7, 95, 231, 337, 346), the Science Museum/Science & Society Picture Library (p.340); and the US Army (pp.203, 273, 342).

A note about Windows XP

Any book about computers faces the problem of describing an industry in which things have a habit of changing overnight. Despite being produced to the tightest possible deadlines, as this book went to press the final version of Windows XP wasn't yet available – so it's possible that you may notice some minor changes between the pre-release version we describe and the XP that you have.

Contents

Contents

Introduction

where to begin

Over the last two decades, the **PC**, or **personal computer**, has revolutionized the way we go about things. And though the recent high-tech bubble may have burst, a knowledge of computers is more useful and important today than ever before. Not only is computer literacy a prerequisite in many areas of **employment**, it's also a skill that can prove incredibly useful and rewarding at **home**. As well as being invaluable for number-crunching and document editing, the modern PC can also help you stay in touch, be creative and access an unimaginable wealth of information via the **Internet**. And that's not even to mention its potential for music, video and games.

Whether you're thinking of buying your first computer, planning to upgrade an old machine or out to hone your skills, this book is for you. We start right at the beginning and assume no prior knowledge, but cover everything from the basics to the nitty-gritty of how a PC functions – we were surprised, in fact, by just how much we were able to squeeze into such a small book. And where we haven't had room to expand, we've suggested Websites where you can find out more.

What is a PC?

Though in the broadest sense the term PC refers to any personal computer – a computer designed to be operated by an individual – it's generally used in a more specific way. People describe the most popular type of personal computer as the "PC" in order to differentiate it from its only real rival: the **Apple Mac**. We don't cover Macs in this book – they're different enough to warrant their own volume – but we do give a brief summary of how they compare to PCs (see p.12).

PCs come in so many shapes and sizes, vary so much in price and performance and are manufactured by so many companies that it's difficult to imagine what they have in common. In fact they're **all very similar**: they're made from the same sort of components and all can run the same programs. And nearly every PC has **Microsoft Windows** as its **operating system** – the all-important software that defines your user experience. So if you can use one PC, you can use them all.

The modern PC is based on a machine produced by IBM in 1981 which was called, inventively enough, the **IBM-PC**. And in terms of their basic structure, today's PCs aren't actually too dissimilar from that pioneering machine or its immediate successors. But for users the difference couldn't be greater. The modern PC can handle huge volumes of data at an unbelievable speed – we're talking about **millions of accurate computations per second**. This changes everything: playing computer games, for example, no longer means bouncing a small flickering square around a two-dimensional box, but going head-to-head with Pete Sampras in a meticulously detailed 3D cyber-court. Also, PCs are incomparably more user-friendly than ever before.

Gone are the days when using a computer involved learning encrypted languages; today, thanks to intuitive operating systems, it's incredibly easy to harness the power within these plastic shells to do some staggering things. And we're no longer limited by location – with lightweight notebooks and even palm-sized computers, you can do what you want, where you want.

Although technology is moving at an unbelievable pace, R2-D2 is still a long way off – computers can't think for themselves and only operate within strict parameters laid down by us humans. But that's no bad thing: realizing that your PC is just a loyal servant who happens to be rather good at mathematics can be very liberating. And though PCs have come a very long way in the last decade, it's **easier to catch up now than ever before**. So long as you view your computer as an ally and not an enemy, using it should be both productive and enjoyable.

What can you do with a PC?

Modern PCs can do everything you'd imagine and a whole lot more. They're still very good at the kind of jobs they've long been associated with – writing well-presented **letters and documents**, **balancing the books** and so on – as well as other office tasks such as **organizing appointments** and maintaining **databases**. But for most home users, other capabilities are far more important.

First there's the **Internet**, perhaps the most exciting thing ever to have happened in the computing world. More than just a porthole for nerds, the Net can be pretty much whatever you want it to be: newspaper, shopping mall, bank, educational tool or just a pretty cool way to spend a few hours broadening your horizons. You can use the Internet to almost instantly retrieve information on anything from anywhere.

A PC connected to the Internet will also help you to keep in touch. **Email** enables you to communicate swiftly and inexpensively with long-lost friends and distant relations. You could even take advantage of a Webcam and make face-to-face **video phonecalls** to anyone with a similar device anywhere in the world.

Whether you buy a custom-built PC or a family package, the chances are that your system will have astonishing multimedia potential. Perhaps you fancy creating a **home recording studio** and unleashing the pop star within? Or converting your old vinyl collection into an archive of digital music files and burning them onto CD? You could try your hand at multimedia design and **craft a killer Website** to show the world what you're about – or even use your computer as a **video editing suite** and create a Hollywood-style masterpiece complete with special effects and soundtrack. And how about **gaming**? Whether you want to spend long nights trekking through the Amazonian jungle with Lara Croft or blasting chunks of rock in the frozen depths of space, the PC is for you.

With a **scanner** you could create a digital album of all those fading photos in the attic or the stack of your toddler's paintings under the stairs. You could even email them to your friends (not that they'd necessarily thank you for it). And a **DVD drive** would allow you to enjoy your favourite films on your computer in sumptuous digital quality – with the right socket, you could even send the output to a regular TV set.

The PC can also be an amazing **educational** and **reference** tool. Whether you want a second opinion on your aches and pains, a home tutorial on aerodynamics for your nine-year-old genius or lessons on the didgeridoo, there's sure to be a CD-ROM out there with your name on it.

How does this book work?

The first part of this book provides you with everything you need to know when **buying PCs, parts and peripherals**:

where to get them, what to look out for and how to decide what you'll actually need for the kind of computing you're aiming to do. Also in this section you'll find the lowdown on what a PC consists of and how its various components work – before long you'll know your RAM from your ROM and you'll be waxing lyrical about buses, buffers and burners.

Part 2 whisks you through the world of the **Windows operating system**. Whether you're new to Windows or already familiar with its tools, menus and buttons, you're sure to learn a lot. This book covers the basics, but it also introduces you to a barrel-load of tips and tricks to help you get the most out of your operating system. As well as covering the latest version – Windows XP – we also deal with Windows Me and Windows 98. And if you're using Windows 95, most of what we say will still apply.

In Part 3 you'll learn how to set up a **home network** and get to grips with the **Internet**, while Parts 4 and 5 present a roll call of some of the best **software** titles around, tips on keeping your PC working as it should, a **troubleshooting** section to pull you out of deep water should things go wrong and a detailed guide to **upgrading** your machine.

We've tried to keep the book as friendly as possible, but if you do find yourself flummoxed by the odd bit of techie jargon, turn to the **Glossary** (p.350) to get a concise and digestible definition – if nothing else, you'll be much better at Scrabble after reading this book. And if we succeed in whetting your appetite, the **Web Directory** (p.390) will point you towards some of the best, most friendly and most entertaining PC-related sites on the Web. Happy computing . . .

[illegible] to get them, what to [illegible] for, and [illegible] what you [illegible] Control [illegible] computer's system [illegible] [illegible] on what [illegible] [illegible] work [illegible] [illegible] you [illegible] [illegible] change.

[illegible] you [illegible] Windows operating system. [illegible] Windows [illegible] [illegible] more [illegible] [illegible] best [illegible] tricks [illegible] system [illegible] Windows XP [illegible] Windows [illegible] Windows [illegible]

[illegible] to set up a home network [illegible] Internet [illegible]

[illegible] software [illegible] maintaining your [illegible] troubleshooting [illegible] should [illegible] machine.

We [illegible] the book [illegible] [illegible] [illegible] the Web [illegible] [illegible]

from purchase to power-up

1

Buying a PC

what, where, how

If you want to buy a PC, this chapter will help you decide what you want and where to get it. But if you haven't got time to digest all this information – or you're already standing in the checkout queue of your local PC store – there are a few golden rules well worth bearing in mind:

1 Never buy a top-of-the-range PC unless you absolutely need it. And you probably don't.

2 No computer is future-proof, but consider upgradeability.

3 Be suspicious of freakishly good deals. They are probably too good to be true.

4 Avoid packages that include stuff you don't need or peripherals you are likely to replace soon.

5 Where possible, buy with a credit card.

What do you want to do with it?

If you've already decided that you need a PC, you've probably put some thought into what you want to do with your new toy and where you want to do it. And whatever happens, don't let yourself lose sight of these considerations – it's incredibly easy (especially if you go for an all-in bundle) to end up with a load of flash kit and hard drive-clogging software that you probably don't need. If you do, you can always get it later – but for the moment **your money is probably better spent elsewhere**. There are some great multimedia PCs which are ideal for varied family use available off-the-peg, but be aware of common purchasing pitfalls before you buy (see p.27): apparent bargains are often deceptive.

So what will you actually be paying for? Much of the cost of a PC is determined by the speed of the **processor** or **CPU** (the computer's brain: see p.34), the amount of **memory** or **RAM** (which determines how many things the machine can deal with at any one time: see p.40), and the size of the **hard drive** (where programs and files are stored: see p.44). These elements will be of primary concern when choosing a PC, but there are also various other factors to take into account, depending on what you want to do with it.

Computing on the hoof If you're planning to cross the Andes on the back of a llama, you won't want to be carrying a PC tower and a 21" monitor with you. This is where notebooks and palm PCs come into their own – they're ideal for computing on the move or flitting between home and the office. But remember that a desktop PC will give you more machine for your money, so if you're not planning on taking your computer out and about, don't go for a notebook.

Word processing Even advanced word processing is child's play for a modern PC – so if all you want is a twenty-first-century typewriter, don't splash out on a multimedia monster. If you're a serious typist, your money would be better spent on a de luxe ergonomic keyboard, a quality printer and a comfy desk chair.

Surfing the Internet Practically all new PCs ship with a built-in **modem**, so you won't need to buy anything extra to connect to the Internet – except possibly an extension cable to reach a phone socket. You don't need a high-spec computer to surf, but if you plan to get into video phone calls, streaming audio and the like, a slow machine will prove frustrating.

Handling images and video Most modern PCs are fine for messing around with images and photos, but if you want to watch DVD movies or get serious about graphics and animation you'll need a fast **processor**, a **video card** with ample onboard memory and a **monitor** that's up to the job. If you plan to get into video editing, also look out for a large and fast hard drive, an IEEE 1394 port for connecting a digital video camera and a TV-out socket for hooking up to a TV. You may also be tempted by a DVD-R drive for putting your creations onto disc. Does the system come with a **printer**, a **scanner** or a **digital camera**? These may be useful at first, but if you're likely to replace them with better models before too long, look out for systems that don't come with these extras.

Gaming Modern computer games push PCs to the max, so if gaming is something you intend to get into, you'll need a high-end machine. The CPU has to be fast, the RAM plentiful and the video card powerful. You'll also need a **joystick** that you like the feel of, and a decent monitor and **speaker system** will enhance the experience.

Working with sound If audio is going to be your main

concern, you need to think about the capabilities of the PC's **sound card** and **speaker system**. If you're a musician looking to build a virtual recording studio (see p.57), you'll need a powerful machine with a hefty hard drive, and a CD burner will come in handy. You'll also need to ask a few techie questions: is the sound card **full duplex** (capable of recording and playing simultaneously)? Will its inputs and outputs be compatible with your existing equipment?

Future possibilities You'll probably save money in the long run if you get an **upgradeable** system. With a bit of knowledge and sound advice you can ensure that you'll have the option to replace, or enhance, everything from your memory to your processor. A generous selection of **ports, expansion slots, bays and empty RAM slots** will allow you to add both internal and external devices at a later date.

PCs vs Macs

One thing that you have to decide before you buy a new computer is whether to go for a PC or a Mac. But beware – this subject carries a lot of emotional baggage, and you're likely to find yourself on the receiving end of an impassioned rant if you request the opinion of either a PC or Mac devotee. This book only deals with PCs, but for those of you who aren't sure of the difference, or haven't yet decided which way to jump, here's the lowdown.

PCs are manufactured by an endless list of firms, but they all run the same programs and work in the same way. They account for the vast share of the personal computing market, and they practically all use the **Microsoft Windows** operating system. Macs, on the other hand, are made by a particular company –

Apple – and generally run the **Mac O/S** operating system. It used to be the case that PCs and Macs were almost completely incompatible: they ran different software, and you couldn't easily move information from one to the other. These days most popular programs are available for both (though following gaming trends is undoubtedly harder with a Mac), and it's not usually a problem to send information – by email, disk or any other means – from a PC to a Mac or vice versa. So you can write a document on your PC and open and edit it on a friend's Mac, generally without huge problems.

A major difference between PCs and Macs is **what you actually get for your money**. A Mac generally costs about 30 percent more than a PC of the equivalent specs, and the advertised price may not even include a monitor or a floppy drive, let alone a printer and scanner – though you don't always have to go for Apple-made devices when expanding your kit. And if you want to do any serious computing (graphics, sound, etc) steer clear of the much-hyped **iMac**: it's a relatively poor performer with little scope for system expandability.

Macs have for a long time been favoured in certain **industries**, including publishing and graphics, so if you intend to work within these areas, you may want to go with the Apple crowd to save yourself the stress of compatibility glitches.

Things are changing, but it is also important to be aware that the **Internet** has a bit of a PC focus. There are few things more frustrating than surfing with a Mac only to be greeted by a friendly message informing you that the site you are trying to view does not welcome your machine. You can also expect to find it harder to get a Mac **repaired** locally, so it's worth checking out the after-sales service plans: how much will it cost? Will the machine have to be sent away for a year and a day?

And then there are **looks**. Though it shouldn't really be a priority when choosing a computer, there's no escaping the fact that modern Macs – **iMacs**, **iBooks**, **Power Mac G4s** and **G4 Cubes** – look pretty special. You should be able to find one to co-ordinate with any outfit.

Overall, then, unless your job requires it and you don't mind paying a bit extra, you'll leave yourself with many more options if you go with the PC majority. But don't take our word for it – do some research. The PC vs Mac debate is likely to run and run, and eavesdropping on obsessively brand-loyal nerds jousting in Web chat forums can actually be quite entertaining.

Snazzy and space-saving PCs

The PC market is beginning to rise to the aesthetic challenge set by recent Macs. Not all PCs are ugly beige boxes any more – you can now get ugly colourful boxes too. There are also many space-saving PCs available: some simply offer a smaller, sleeker case, while others cram all the guts of the machine into the base of a slimline monitor. These look great, but tend to be very pricey and offer few upgrade options. So unless you can't bear to be without a design classic, beige is (often) best.

Operating systems

A PC can't work without an operating system – a special piece of software that acts as a bridge between the computer's hardware and the software running on it. When you buy a PC, it will probably come with the most recent version of the world's most common operating system – **Microsoft Windows**. Though other operating systems are available,

Windows is so standard that it's the only realistic choice for most PC users. The majority of new computers ship with **Windows XP**, which came out in October 2001: don't accept anything less if your machine is new, as XP is considerably better than earlier versions. If you already own a PC or you are buying one secondhand, it may well have an older Windows version installed. **Windows 95, 98** and **Me** are all absolutely fine for most tasks, though they do have certain limitations – especially Windows 95. If the computer has the necessary specs and you're prepared to foot the bill, you can choose to upgrade to a more recent version. All these issues are covered in much more depth in Chapter 17.

Thinking small: notebooks, handhelds and palm-sized PCs

Portable computers were once the executive toys of high-flyers who wanted to play Tetris on aeroplanes, but as they've become less expensive and more powerful, increasing numbers of people are choosing them. Today, you can get a turbo-charged **notebook** that's less than an inch thick and more than capable of replacing a traditional desktop machine. Or you can complement your home computer with a **palm-sized PC** – a multifunctional piece of kit that will literally fit in your pocket.

Notebooks vs desktops

Though the cost of **notebooks** – which are also commonly referred to as **laptops** – has fallen dramatically in recent years, they're still considerably more expensive than equivalent desktop systems. So why do so many people even give them the time of

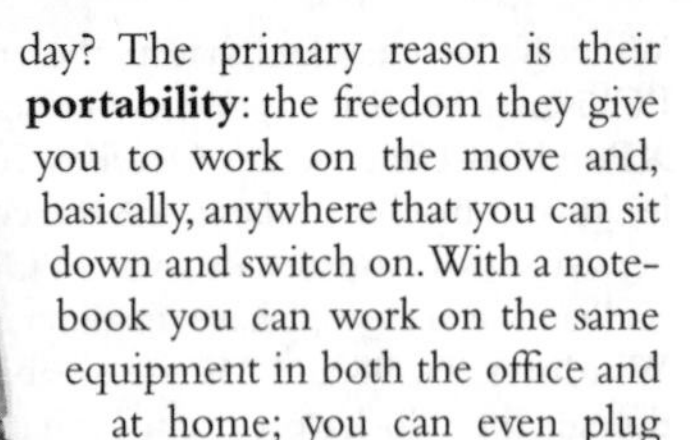

day? The primary reason is their **portability**: the freedom they give you to work on the move and, basically, anywhere that you can sit down and switch on. With a notebook you can work on the same equipment in both the office and at home; you can even plug into a **company network** if you have the appropriate hardware (ask your network administrator what you need).

Much of a notebook's cost can be accounted for by its **flat screen**, so when comparing prices be sure to tally the equivalent desktop setup to include an LCD monitor (see p.70) and the difference won't seem quite as shocking. If you are tempted by a notebook, be sure you're not kidding yourself on aesthetic grounds: yes, they're slick, but if you don't actually require the portability that a notebook offers you're throwing your money away. A desktop will give you more for less.

Here are some trade-offs and considerations you'll have to grapple with when choosing between a notebook and a desktop:

Horsepower and features A notebook is nearly twice as expensive as a desktop machine with comparable performance and features. And because everything has to be made as small as possible, the workings are generally less efficient – so even if the advertised specs of a notebook and a desktop are identical, the desktop will generally be a touch faster.

Hot, hot, hot There's a lot of stuff crammed into a notebook and, as with a desktop, much of it gets very warm, especially with high-performance machines. But cooling a notebook is a tricky business. The fans and vents are small and, depending where they're located on the casing, you may even find that prolonged lap-use is uncomfortable, if not painfully hot. However, there are new liquid-cooling technologies such as IsoSkin on the horizon that may change all this.

Keys, pointers and screens Notebooks have **miniaturized keyboards** and usually come with a small **touchpad** or **rubber pointing device** that you operate with your finger instead of using a mouse. This setup takes some getting used to, and if you also use a regular keyboard and mouse you'll undoubtedly find the notebook controls frustrating. However, it's easy enough to connect a mouse and full-size keyboard to the machine when you're working at a desk, especially if you have a **docking station** (see box). If you're keen on the idea of a notebook but want to work with a big screen, make sure you get a machine that allows you to hook up an external monitor, as notebook displays rarely exceed 15".

Docking stations

If you plan to use a notebook as your main PC and expect to take it out of the home regularly it's worth considering getting a **docking station**. This piece of hardware sits permanently on your desk, with all your peripherals – printer, scanner, mouse, keyboard, monitor, etc – plumbed into it. Whenever you bring your notebook home to roost it simply slots onto the station, giving an instant connection to the rest of your hardware.

Expandability Notebooks, because of their size, leave you with fewer expansion options than desktops, and getting under

PC Cards

PC cards – or **PCMCIA** cards, as they're also known – allow notebook users to add extra pieces of hardware to their computers quickly and easily. Though only about the size of chunky credit cards, all sorts of devices are available in this mini-format – from wireless modems to surprisingly spacious hard drives (allowing large files to be backed up or moved from one machine to another). Many external pieces of hardware such as CD writers can be attached to notebooks via a cable with a PC card on the end. Older notebooks normally have two slots, whereas newer, thinner machines tend to have only one – but they make up for it with an integral modem (see p.57), so you won't have to use up your only slot to get online. You can even get PC card bays that allow you to use these miniature devices with a desktop system. There are three sizes of card: types I, II and III.

the hood is no easy task – so upgrade surgery may not be something that you can do yourself. Having said that, many modern notebooks feature removable hard drives, easily accessible RAM slots and bays that will accept a variety of devices like CD writers and DVD drives, so expanding the kit is far less of a problem than it used to be. Most systems also feature slots for **PC cards** (see box).

Games, Graphics, Video and Music Gaming and image and video editing aren't especially suited to notebooks because of their small screens and inferior graphics potential. Notebooks also used to be unsuitable for music-making, because the lack of PCI slots prohibited the addition of a decent sound card. Recently, though, some rather nice alternatives to the traditional sound card have been developed which you attach with a USB lead, so a notebook studio is perfectly possible. Check out the hardware pages at **http://www.pc-music.com** for more.

Reliability Though they're getting hardier by the month, computers don't particularly like being lugged around, dropped in puddles and restarted while you're navigating rapids in a dinghy. Because of the extra punishment they often receive, notebooks are more likely to go wrong than desktop systems, so make sure the **warranty** is comprehensive and that you regularly **back up your work** (see p.280).

Selecting a machine Because of a notebook's size, a specific brand may have only a certain number of configuration options, and building your own isn't an option. While a desktop system will allow you the freedom to customize a machine to any specification under the sun, you'll really have to shop around to get a best-fit notebook.

Loseability Notebooks are often stolen, and many home-contents insurance policies don't cover them. You may be able to pay extra to get a notebook included, either just in the house or for when you're out and about – though the premiums might make you wince.

Sub-notebooks and handhelds

If a standard notebook is just too bulky for your purposes, you could go for a lightweight, ultra-slim model – but you'll pay a considerable sum for the privilege. The other option, which makes a lot of sense if your portable computer is to be used alongside a desktop PC, is to go for a **sub-notebook**. These save space by having a smaller screen and dispensing with internal CD and floppy drives (these drives are often included, but because they're external you can leave them at home if you want). Usually just over half the size and weight of a normal notebook, sub-notebooks are ideal if you want ultimate portability. Expensive, high-spec models are capable of running the most demanding applications, but less expensive machines are also available – perfect if all you want to do is run a word processor and other not-too-demanding applications on the move.

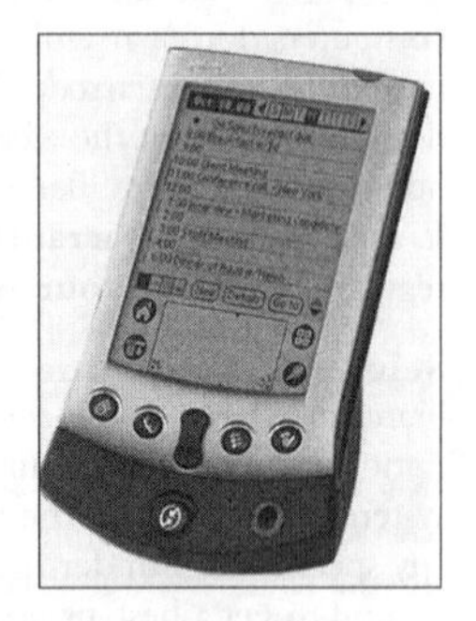

The next step down in terms of size and power is the **handheld PC**, which is small enough to fit in your pocket, but lacks the power of a notebook proper. Many run a slimmed-down version of Windows (called **Windows CE**) as well as tailored editions of popular office programs such as Word and Excel. They're **inexpensive**, and they have a full – albeit small – QWERTY keyboard. Many people use their handheld primarily as a fancy **electronic diary**; you can connect it to your desktop at work, for example, and instantly update your schedule. Also available are mobile phones that fold out to reveal a handheld PC – great for emails.

The smallest member of the PC family is the **palm-sized PC**. About the size of a wallet, a palm-sized comes with a little **pen instead of a keyboard**: you write on the screen and the computer recognizes your scrawl and inserts the appropriate letter. Like handhelds, palm-sized PCs are popular for diary functions, but they're fun for more than just scheduling appointments. You can play games, for example, listen to music and read e-books. And you can hook up a palm-sized to your desktop – via a cable or infrared – and automatically download the news from the Web every morning. You'll never need to buy a newspaper again.

To upgrade, or not to upgrade?

If your existing machine is giving you the blues, before you attack it with a sledgehammer and invest in a brand-new PC, make a list of your current system's problems. It could be that all you need to do is **spruce things up with an upgrade**. Your computer is only as good as its weakest link: it may well be that one thing is holding back its overall performance. But be cautious – you don't want to invest too much money, time and effort in an old machine that has inherent limits. As a general rule, if you're currently running **anything less than a Pentium system**, upgrading might be futile and expensive.

If your system has trouble working with several applications simultaneously, grinds to a halt when faced with a stack of windows, fails to run taxing software or struggles with image editing, the chances are that you need some more **RAM** (see p.40). It could also be the case that your system would speed up considerably with a more powerful **processor** (see p.34), though this may necessitate a new **motherboard** (see p.37). This is a pricier exercise, but could still work out better for your wallet than getting a new machine. Replacing or adding a **video card** (see p.54) may well improve sluggish video and gaming performance, and a better **sound card** (see p.55) should do the trick if your PC's audio is not up to scratch.

If you are **running out of hard drive space** for accommodating software and files, think about getting a second drive to run alongside the first. All these upgrade options are covered in far greater detail in Chapter 22.

Secondhand PCs

PC technology moves so fast that you may be able to pick up a machine that was state-of-the-art a couple of years ago for surprisingly little money. With a bit of luck you can seek out a respectable Internet-ready Pentium II system, for example, for a tenth of the price of an off-the-shelf Pentium IV package. However, buying secondhand from an individual – from an ad in a paper or at an Internet auction – involves a considerable **element of risk**, as you're unlikely to get a warranty or any after-sales service, so you'll have little comeback if it turns out to be a complete turkey. Many professional secondhand dealers and PC refurbishers, though, do offer a guarantee.

Whether you're buying a machine privately or from a dealer, **make sure you see the thing working** before you hand over any money. If you have a friend who's familiar with computers, drag them along: they will help you ask the right questions, spot any obvious flaws and make an informed decision. But even with the best advice in the world, buying a secondhand PC is still a gamble. Here are a few things to look out for:

Check the specs Assuming the PC is running Windows 95 or later, you can make sure that the advertised specs are genuine in the **System Properties** dialog box, which you can open by right-clicking **My Computer** on the Desktop or in the Start menu and selecting **Properties**.

Wear-and-tear Don't judge a book by its cover – you may get a great deal on a machine that is perfectly functional despite a dull screen, suspect mouse or duff keyboard. These components are easy to replace: monitors are quite expensive but new mice and keyboards can be picked up dirt cheap.

Under the hood If you can, have a look inside the machine to find out how much room you'll have for upgrades (see p.303): a little extra memory or a new hard drive could bring an old machine up-to-date.

E-stores, corner stores and superstores

If you've opted to go for a new machine, you need to decide where to shop. It's worth buying a couple of **PC magazines** and browsing the glossy advertisements that litter their pages to get a feel for the things that are available. Read some articles to find out what's hot and what's not, and grapple with the reasoning behind the **reviews and recommendations**. Bear in mind that a PC journalist might rubbish a machine simply because it happens to perform some ludicrous task 0.034 seconds slower than

their preferred system. (In the real world, value for money is a little more important.) Look out for magazines that are doing a comparative test of systems in your price range.

If possible try to **get online**. With a magazine and our Web Directory (see p.390) to hand, you should be able to find the most up-to-date prices. The majority of the big names – like Dell and Gateway – now sell on the Internet without middlemen, but you won't necessarily find them any less expensive than **third party retailers**. Though you may hear horror stories about shopping online and by phone (PCs lost in the post, fictitious customer service departments), **the Web is becoming the preferred channel for PC buyers**. This is in part because of the ease with which the Internet allows you to gather information, compare machines and gawp at cool animations of notebooks opening and closing; but it's also because of the anonymity it provides – you can explore all the options, unhindered by pushy salesmen and sneering jargonites. And if you're concerned about using your credit card on the Web, do your research online and then place the order by phone. In most cases the despatch of your goods will be swift and efficient, though it's worth asking around to see if any of your friends have had good or bad experiences with a particular firm.

Pay with plastic

Where possible, pay for a PC with a credit card. This way, you'll be protected if any damage occurs in transit or the company goes under before the machine reaches you.

If you can't get online or you fancy a test-drive, visit a store. The large **PC superstores** are good places to find all-inclusive deals, though they're not necessarily the best source of advice. **Small dealers**, on the other hand, will be able to furnish you with either a customized machine or a wide range of specific components for upgrades and self-builds (see p.303), and they may be more helpful if things go wrong. If you're feeling brave, go to a **computer fair** – everything from cables to complete systems can be picked up at rock-bottom prices.

Is the brand important?

Certain companies have well-deserved reputations for producing consistently high-quality computers. But with a PC it's the stuff inside the case that's important and with some of these companies you'll pay a bit extra just for the name – an equivalent PC from a smaller retailer might cost you less. Sometimes the extra money will buy you better components – and therefore more impressive performance – but the overall quality can only really be gauged from a comparative review. In some ways, after-sales service is more important than the manufacturer.

After-sales service

When buying, it's also worth thinking about the kind of support you'll get if things go wrong. A **warranty** of one to three years is almost always included in the price, though be sure to check whether it's an **on-site** (OS) or **return-to-base** (RTB) arrangement. With an on-site warranty, the company will come and repair the computer at your home and take it away if they can't solve the problem, but return-to-base means it's up to you to get the machine to wherever it's going to be fixed. This is fine if you bought it from a local shop – you can easily drop the poorly PC off for surgery – but if you purchased it online or direct from a manufacturer you may find yourself having to pack it up and pay for it to be posted across the country, with little chance of getting the thing back within a month.

The **warranty** can speak volumes about the machine and the supplier. If a company is reluctant to throw in at least one year's on-site support, you should wonder why. It could be because they're cutting costs and passing the savings on to you, but perhaps they think the computer is likely to go wrong – or maybe they're determined to sell additional cover at an extra charge.

Most retailers offer some kind of **extended care plan**. These are great if you're after peace of mind, but they are often outrageously overpriced. And do you really need a five-year warranty? You may well have replaced the computer before it even expires.

Technical support phone lines are also usually offered with a new computer. Though the idea of having a number you can call if you need advice on anything from starting up your word processor to serious troubleshooting sounds inviting, many of these services are alarmingly costly – so always **check the per-minute charge**. If you have a patient friend or relative who knows the basics, you'll get a quicker and more sympathetic response if you phone them instead. Besides, with this book in hand, you should be able to cope with most of the difficulties you'll encounter on your passage to PC proficiency.

Building your own

One final option for getting yourself a computer is to buy the ten or so necessary components and put the machine together yourself. If you have the confidence to try this, you can **save some money**, you'll almost certainly **learn a great deal about computers** in the process and you can make the machine exactly to your own specifications using high-quality components. Though not for the technologically shy, building a PC is much **easier than it sounds** – all you really have to do is slot the bits into place. As long as you're quite good at fiddly operations, you have a knowledgeable friend you can call if you get stuck and you don't mind having no guarantee or after-sales support, building your own computer is a serious option – and potentially a highly satisfying experience. If you're considering taking this path for financial reasons, get the components from a mail-order supplier or a computer fair where they can be purchased at rock-bottom prices, otherwise you won't save much money. And bear in mind that you'll also have to get hold of any application software you may want as well as an operating system like Windows, which is usually pre-installed on an off-the-shelf PC. If you're tempted by this option, turn to p.334 to read more.

Purchasing pitfalls

Before you head off to buy a new computer, be aware of a few final things that will help you get the most for your money. Don't get too excited about large bundles of **software** thrown in with a new machine – they're usually advertised as being worth as much as the computer itself, but often consist of such useful programs as a marine encyclopedia. If space is a consideration, you may be tempted by a PC in a small case (a mini-tower or special design), but before you choose such a model, bear in mind that it may not have many spare **bays** or **PCI slots** (see p.38) for expansion in the future. Find out what sort of RAM a machine harbours – anything less than **SDRAM** just won't do and **DDR** is preferable (see p.42). And if you have any interest in multimedia, avoid systems with **integrated graphics and sound**. This means that instead of a separate **video card** (see p.54) and **sound card** (see p.55), these elements are built into the motherboard, and are probably pretty crummy. Theoretically you can always "disable" the in-built sound or graphics and add decent cards in the future, but often this is more problematic than it should be.

Though you may come across a genuine bargain, it's worth being a little bit suspicious of all-in systems at absolutely rock-bottom prices. Corners may well have been cut: the **power supply** or **case** may be poor quality, for example, or you may find the **hard drive pre-partitioned** into more than one separate drive (you can sort this out but it will be a bit of a pain: see p.236).

Don't spend money on things you don't need. This may sound obvious, but it's incredibly easy to get drawn in by fancy gizmos when all you're really after is a simple but powerful PC and the software essentials.

Finally, **a few numbers don't tell you everything about the power of a system**: components and specifications not mentioned in an advert may well have a dramatic effect on performance. A hard drive may be huge, for example, but it may also be slow at reading and writing data. If you really want to get the best computer, you need to understand a bit more about the components themselves – so read on into the next chapter.

2

Anatomy of a PC

take a look inside

This section takes you on a tour inside the belly of the PC, explaining what the various components do and, in the simplest possible terms, how they do it. You'll also find buying advice to help you choose new components for upgrading or building a computer. Though you can easily use a PC without this knowledge (if that's what you want to do, turn to Chapter 4), having a basic idea of what makes a PC tick – quite literally – will make you feel much more in control when using or troubleshooting your system. Also, it's pretty fascinating stuff. Really.

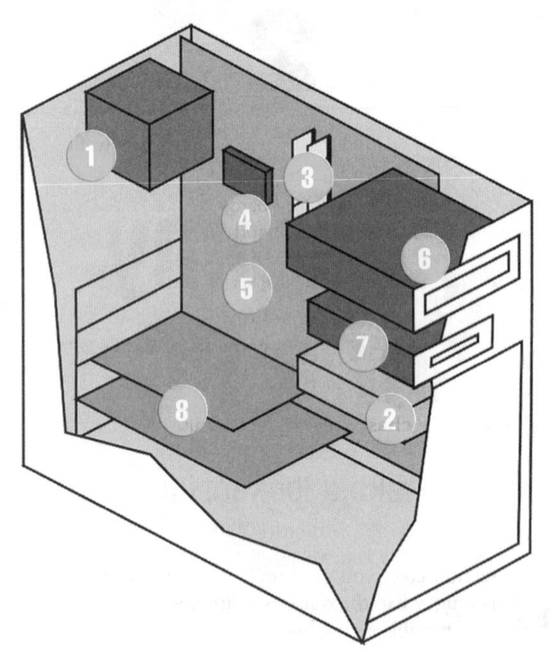

❶ **Case** The box in which all the bits live. Contains a built-in power supply and cooling fan.

❷ **Hard drive** The place where all your programs and documents are stored.

❸ **RAM** The "short-term" memory where programs and documents stay while you're using or working on them.

❹ **Processor or CPU** The brains of the computer, which does most of the actual computing.

⑤ **Motherboard** The large circuit board to which the other components are connected.

⑥ **CD/DVD drive** Reads, and in some cases writes, information to CDs and/or DVDs.

⑦ **Floppy drive** Reads and writes files from or to floppy diskettes.

⑧ **Expansion cards** Circuit boards, such as video cards, sound cards and modems, which add functionality to the system.

Cases

The **PC case**, or **chassis**, doesn't just house all the other components. It includes the **power supply**, which needs to be reliable (cheap ones can fry systems) and powerful enough for the machine (300 watts is essential for most modern setups). The case is also home to the **indicator lights**, those little blinking LEDs on the front of the machine that show you whether the PC is switched on, whether the hard drive is in use and so on. And there will be one or two **fans** to keep everything cool. The main case consideration, however, is size. Most modern PCs come with an upright **tower case** rather that a flat **desktop case**, and there are various sizes of tower: mini, midi and full. Though many people want their PC to be as small as possible, **a small case can limit expansion**. Each case has a certain number of **bays** – parking spaces for internal components – some of which you can see from the outside (DVD, floppy drives, etc), and some that are hidden away (mainly for hard drives). If there are no spare bays, you may end up frustrated if you want to install a new piece of kit a few months down the line. Also, certain modern expansion cards are very long; they simply won't fit in a small case.

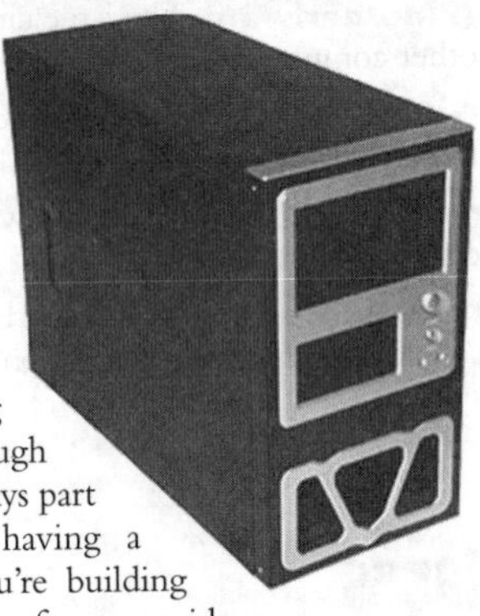

The case also determines **how the machine looks**, and over the last few years PC cases have been appearing in all sorts of shapes and colours – it's no longer a matter of having light beige or dark beige. Though these futuristic cases aren't always part of PC packages, if you're having a machine custom-made or you're building one yourself, you can choose from a wide range (including models which mimic the Apple Mac colour range – tell that to your Apple-obsessed, PC-hating friend).

If you're looking to upgrade an old machine, your current case may well be fine as long as it has enough room to house any new hardware that you want to add. If you're going to change the **motherboard**, however, you'll need to be sure that the case and power supply connection will accommodate the new board's **form factor** (see p.39).

The vital organs

This section looks at the fundamental components of the PC: the bits that deal with actual number-crunching, the short-term storage of information currently being worked on (such as programs that are running) and the distribution of data between all the other internal components. No PC can exist without them.

Tech Info | Tips & Tricks | Try This

Digital information

All information is either analogue or digital – humans see, hear, touch and taste analogue information, but modern computers work exclusively with digital. People often get confused about the difference, but it's actually very simple. **Analogue** information has an unlimited set of values. Take a light bulb with a dimmer switch as an example: when you look at the light bulb and turn the switch, you see infinite degrees of brightness between the bulb being off and the bulb being fully on. What you're seeing is analogue information – a perfectly smooth transition from dark to light.

Digital information, on the other hand, has a limited number of values. You could only describe the same light bulb as digital information if you defined a set number of possible states. You could describe it as having two states (the bulb could be on or off), three states (bright, dim, or off), or a million (really bright, ever so slightly less bright, and so on). Regardless of the number of states, though, the transition from dark to light will be stepwise, rather than smooth.

If you look at a photo stored on a computer it may look pretty convincing, but if you zoom in closely enough you'll find that the picture consists of a certain number of tiny little coloured squares, called **pixels**. The more pixels the photo is made up of, the better it will look. On a traditional printed photo, though, which is analogue, you could keep zooming in and in with a microscope and never find any little squares. Likewise, when you speak, you produce analogue sound, with infinite variation of volume and tone. But the moment you record your voice on a computer it becomes digital information; when you play it back it will still sound like you, but your voice will have been simplified, now having only a limited number of loudness and tone possibilities.

All this paints digital information in a fairly unsympathetic light – as just an approximation of the real world. But it has one huge advantage: digital information can be expressed in numbers. And the numbers can then be copied from computer to computer without ever changing, so the information will never deteriorate – you can copy a digital recording of your voice from computer to computer and it will stay exactly the same. Analogue information, for all its supposed subtlety, changes slightly every time it is copied. If you record your voice onto an analogue medium like a cassette tape, each time you copy it from tape to tape the quality will get worse.

Processors

The processor, which is also known as the **microprocessor**, **chip**, **CPU** or **central processing unit**, is the brain of a PC – the part of the computer that actually computes. It's a silicon chip containing millions of tiny electronic **transistors** that, like switches, open and close, manipulating electronic code according to logical instructions. Everything you do on your PC, from typing a single letter to rendering a high-quality image, is dealt with by the processor.

The speed of a processor – the amount of computations the chip can make in a second – is measured in **hertz**. A processor rated at 500 **megahertz** can make about half a million calculations a second, and a 1.5 **gigahertz** model can handle around three times that. The speed of the processor is perhaps the single biggest factor in determining the power and price of a PC, and it's this hertz tag that's plastered over most computer ads. But be warned: the machine with the fastest processor is not always the fastest computer. There are two reasons for this. First, the specifications of other components are highly significant – the quantity and speed of RAM, for example, and the access time of the hard drive: there's no point having the fastest processor in the world if the rest of the machine can't keep up. Second, the hertz rating doesn't tell the whole story about the speed of a processor: one type of 500MHz CPU might perform tasks faster than a different 500MHz model because of its internal architecture.

When trying to work out which processor to go for, there is one golden rule. Unless money is no object, **never buy the fastest processor on the market**, because you could get something only marginally slower for significantly less cash. And by the time software is available that will utilize its power, the chip will have become annoyingly cheap. Most users will get optimal value in terms of power and future-proofness by choosing something roughly **half the speed** of the fastest available. Another thing to bear in mind is that various versions of the same chip are available. All CPUs advertised as "Athlon 750s", for example, might not be identical. If one was made more recently it may have a faster **front side bus** (fsb), which determines the speed at which data can travel in and out of the processor.

Processors are developing at an alarming rate, and their prices are dropping just as fast, so always check out an up-to-date magazine or Website before choosing a CPU for an upgrade or self-build.

Processor wars – the story so far

Intel (short for **Int**egrated **El**ectronics) have been the biggest name in processor manufacturing since the beginning of the PC revolution. They created the 4004 chip – the first microprocessor – and have been at the forefront of design ever since, dominating from the early Nineties with their flagship range of **Pentium** processors. Their only serious competitor at the time of writing is **AMD** (Advanced Micro Devices). This Texan company was once employed by Intel to produce chips on its behalf, but AMD developed their own processor – based on Intel's design – that was more powerful than anything in their employer's catalogue. The two companies have been head-to-head ever since. AMD tend to offer better value for money, but Intel are still the market leaders, partly thanks to strong customer loyalty and a pretty little jingle.

There are other chip manufacturers around – such as **Transmeta** who produce the energy-saving **Crusoe** range of notebook CPUs – but the market is still basically hosting a two-horse race.

Processors: what's out there

Here's an overview of the most important chips on the market today – newest first.

Pentium 4 (Intel) The turn of the millennium saw a totally new design from Intel: the Pentium 4, which has the capacity to exceed speeds of two gigahertz. It's very good for demanding multimedia tasks such as 3D gaming, streaming audio and video encoding, though the early models were no faster than the Pentium III and the AMD Athlon for many applications.

Athlon (AMD) The first chip to reach a speed of one gigahertz, the Athlon (or K7) was originally released to compete with the Pentium III. However, it can handle much higher speeds, and various new models, such as the Athlon Thunderbird with better cache, have improved on the original, keeping it at the cutting edge. A good-value chip for high-end users.

Pentium III (Intel) The fastest chip available until the Athlon came around, the Pentium III is a powerful all-rounder. The later models with "Copper Burst" technology are slightly better than their predecessors.

Duron (AMD) This is a cheaper and only marginally less powerful version of the Athlon. It is a superbly good-value processor, excelling at everything other than the most demanding applications.

Celeron (Intel) The Celeron is a less powerful version of the Pentium II and III chips, and was designed for use in low-budget machines. It's perfectly capable of most simple tasks, but isn't ideal for multimedia – nor is it as good value as the Duron, the equivalent AMD chip.

Pentium II (Intel) Though firmly superseded by the Pentium III and Athlon, the once cutting-edge Pentium II is perfectly capable of many home and office tasks.

K6 (AMD) The cheapest AMD chip still available, the K6-II can be picked up for little more than the price of a double CD. However, with its "3D Now" enhancement (also found on the K6-III), it's on a par with the Pentium II.

Pentium (Intel) The early Pentiums – such as the Pentium MMX and Pentium Pro – are capable of running most modern applications, but not with much speed. They're fine for word processing and surfing the Web.

Motherboards

The motherboard, also called the **mainboard**, is the large printed circuit board in a computer that everything else plugs into. If the processor is the brain of a PC, the motherboard is the central nervous system, connecting the CPU with all the other

components. Though these large boards don't get mentioned in most computer ads, they are central to a system's **performance and upgradeability**, because they determine what type of hardware can be attached. They also affect **system stability** – computers with decent motherboards tend to crash (temporarily freeze up) less frequently.

The motherboard is full of slots, sockets and ports. There are external ones (see p.89) which stick out of the back of the PC's case for connecting peripherals such as a mouse, keyboard and printer. But there are also internal ones hidden away inside the machine: a slot or socket for the processor, slots for RAM chips (see p.40), a floppy disk drive connector, and various slots – **AGP**, **PCI** and **ISA** – for stuff like sound cards, video cards and modems (see p.53). Hard drives, CD and DVD drives are connected either to **IDE** ports on the motherboard or via a special **SCSI** card (see p.46). At the heart of a motherboard, controlling the flow of data between all these inputs and outputs, is the **sys-**

tem chipset, which acts like a super-complex traffic light system.

As well as all these connections, the motherboard also houses: the **BIOS** (basic input/output system: see p.331), a set of special codes which tell a computer how to start up and interact with the operating system; the **system clock**, which uses a vibrating crystal to control the speed of the PC's operation; and the **CMOS** (complementary metal-oxide semiconductor), which, powered by a little battery, stores the date, time and various bits of information about the hardware setup.

Motherboards come in various different sizes and layouts called **form factors**, and they are only compatible with cases and power supplies of the same form factor. **ATX** is the current standard, though unique form factors are being used more and more for the production of space-saving PCs (see p.14).

If you're buying a pre-built PC, you won't get much choice when it comes to the motherboard – usually you won't even be told what brand or type it is – but there are a few things you should ask. If you're concerned about upgradeability, you should find out what type and speed of **RAM** (see p.40) the board takes and the maximum amount it can hold. And ask about the **maximum processor speed** that the board can handle in case you ever want a faster CPU. Make sure there are a few spare PCI slots – essential for adding all sorts of hardware, from sound cards to network adapters. If you intend the machine to be multimedia-friendly, **avoid motherboards with integrated video or sound**, and make sure there is an **AGP x4 graphics slot** (see p.54).

If you're doing a major upgrade of an old PC or building a machine from scratch, you'll need to make sure that you buy a motherboard which is **compatible with your processor** of choice in terms of model (such as Pentium III or Athlon), connection (socket 7 or slot A, for example) and speed. Also consider the speed of the chipset and the IDE ports. Choose a board made by one of the **big-name brands**; not only will it come with a decent manual and be made to higher standards, but **BIOS upgrades** will be available on the Internet in case any design flaws are discovered in the future. Also, if you want to keep any internal components from your old system, such as an ISA expansion card, make sure there is an appropriate slot to house it.

RAM (Random Access Memory)

RAM is a computer's **short-term memory**, and it allows the machine to get on with its tasks without constantly having to go to the hard drive to retrieve data. Imagine, if you will, that when you open an application such as a word processor your computer is setting the table for dinner: it goes to the cupboard (the hard disk), takes out cutlery and plates (the application) and lays them out on the table (the RAM). When you begin typing your document it's like putting food on the plates. The more RAM your PC has, the more applications and files it can handle at any one time – so using a computer with inadequate RAM is like trying to serve a banquet on a coffee table.

The amount of RAM that a computer has is measured in megabytes (MB), and is usually a multiple of 32: 64MB, 96MB, 128MB, etc. For a computer to run a modern operating system such as Windows XP, 64MB of RAM is a minimum, but 128MB is much more reasonable. Still more – 256MB perhaps – is preferable for taxing applications.

Tech Info | Tips & Tricks | Try This

How RAM works

Let's say you're typing the letter "D" into a word processor. The instant this happens, your computer sends tiny bursts of electricity to one of the millions of grid locations within your RAM via microscopic strands of conductive material etched onto the chip. At each of these "address points" is a minuscule **transistor** switch, which when turned on allows the electricity to charge an energy-storing **capacitor** – this charge represents **1 bit**. When your computer retrieves the data, it recognizes the capacitors' states as either 1 or 0 bits: a charged capacitor represents 1 bit, while an uncharged capacitor represents 0 bits. This binary information is grouped into eight-digit strings to represent a single **byte** of data. Our letter "D" is memorized across eight capacitors that read 01000100 (this equals the decimal number 65, which in the globally-shared ASCII language represents D). When your computer is turned off, the RAM is returned to its blank state – all the charges drain away and the **data is lost**.

RAM stands for **Random Access Memory**, which describes the way in which any bit of information can be accessed immediately – unlike with a **sequential access** system, such as a video cassette, where you have to go through the data in sequence until you reach the bit you want. RAM is neatly packaged onto small circuit boards about the length of your finger. Along one edge is a row of little metal teeth, or **pins**, which slot into the motherboard (see p.37).

Nearly everything you do on a PC involves data being transferred between the RAM and the processor, and the faster the data moves back and forward, the more powerful the system can be. You can have the fastest processor in the world, but if the RAM and the motherboard can't keep up then you won't be able to exploit its full potential. Accordingly, various types of

RAM have been developed over the years, capable of coping with ever-increasing transfer rates.

Most old PCs use a type of **DRAM** (Dynamic RAM), such as **EDO** and **FPM**. The majority of more recent systems use **SDRAM** (Synchronous Dynamic RAM), which is much quicker than the older types and comes in three standard speeds – 66, 100 and 133 megahertz, referred to as PC66, PC100 and PC133 respectively. In the last couple of years two even faster RAM technologies have been developed. The first, **DDR SDRAM** (Double Data Rate SDRAM), is very similar to standard SDRAM but effectively doubles the rate that information can be transferred. The second, **RDRAM** (Rambus DRAM), which is often just referred to as "Rambus memory", is a whole new type of design that can achieve very high speeds, though it hasn't always performed in tests as well as the theory would suggest. If you want a really fast PC for gaming, working with video and so on, one of these two RAM types is definitely advantageous.

If you want to improve your PC's performance, adding more RAM is a cheap and effective way to do it – especially if your system is struggling to run big programs or many applications simultaneously. It's surprisingly easy to install RAM yourself, though you have to make sure you select the correct type of RAM for your system. For a full discussion of RAM types and upgrades, turn to p.307.

Tech Info | Tips & Tricks | Try This

Binary, bits and bytes

Humans tend to use the **decimal number system**, which has ten different figures: 0, 1, 2, 3, 4, 5, 6, 7, 8 and 9. The basic language of computers, however, is **binary**, which uses only two figures: 0 and 1. Any number can be expressed in either system, but it will look different. In decimal, a three-digit number consists of three "columns", which (from right to left) represent how many ones there are, how many tens and how many hundreds. The decimal number 132, for example, represents one hundred, three tens and two ones – one hundred and thirty-two in total. In binary, however, the columns mean (from right to left) 1, 2, 4, 8, 16, 32, etc. The binary number 1101, therefore, represents one eight, one four, no twos, and one one – thirteen in total. So binary 1101 is the same as decimal 13.

There are various reasons why computers work in binary. First, computer memory and processors work with transistors, which are effectively little electronic switches which can be "on" (charged with electricity) or "off" (uncharged). These states can be used to represent the 0s and 1s of binary. Also, the binary system leaves less room for error. Electronic signals sometimes get a little bit "fuzzy" or "dirty"; if an electronic signal meant to represent "1" comes in with a little bit more or less power than it should, the computer can have a pretty good guess that what it meant was "1". But if there are more numbers (such as 0, 1, 2, 3, 4 and 5), a dirty signal that was meant to mean 4 could be confused for a 3 or a 5 relatively easily.

The size of a piece of computer data is described in terms of the number of 0s and 1s it takes up. A single 0 or 1 (a single "column") is described as a **bit**, and eight bits make one **byte**. The size of a document or program is always described in terms of bytes.

1 kilobyte (1KB) = roughly 1000 bytes

1 megabyte (1MB) = roughly 1000 kilobytes

1 gigabyte (1GB) = roughly 1000 megabytes

1 terabyte (1TB) = roughly 1000 gigabytes

So if a hard drive has a capacity of ten gigabytes, it means it can store ten billion bytes, which is eighty billion zeros or ones – thirteen for every person in the world.

Chapter 2

Disk drives and storage

Now it's time to look at the bits of the PC that are used for storing and reading information. Some, like floppy drives, read from and write to removable disks, while others, such as the hard drive, use special internal disks that cannot be taken out. Both store and read data as **magnetic charges**, but there are also various types of **optical drive**, which use light to read from and write to CDs or DVDs. Every PC should have a hard drive, a CD drive and floppy drive as a minimum, but most machines don't have all the disk drives and storage devices discussed below – but they can all be added relatively easily. Though they're most commonly found inside the PC, all these devices are also available as **peripherals**: external devices that plug into your PC via a cable rather than being housed within the case (see p.61).

Hard drives

The hard drive or **hard disk** (referred to as **C:** in Windows) is the storage depot of a computer – where all the programs and documents are kept. Generally, hard drives are pretty reliable components, providing safe accommodation for your valuable data, but things can go wrong – so it's worth regularly **backing up your files** (see p.280). If you already own a computer and have run out of space to save documents or programs, you could opt to add an extra hard drive to a PC or replace your old one with something a bit more spacious (see p.324).

If you're looking to buy a new hard drive, the most obvious and significant consideration is **capacity**. Usually measured in **gigabytes** (often abbreviated to **gigs** or **GBs**), this tells you how much data a drive can hold. Whether you need a high-capacity drive depends on the kind of documents you usually

work with. Text documents take up barely any space – a 10GB drive, for example, could hold the complete texts of around 10,000 novels – so if you're only going to use your computer as a glorified typewriter, you won't need a massive hard drive. Bear in mind, though, that software also occupies space and that you'll probably end up using your machine for more than you thought, so don't settle for anything less than 10GB and go bigger if possible. If you're the sort of keen computer-user who likes to install every program or game you can get your hands on, a decent-sized hard drive is essential. Other drive-fillers are image, video and sound files – so if you intend to store the family photo albums or an MP3 music library, you can't really have too much room.

A standard **internal drive** – designed to live permanently inside a PC – is relatively inexpensive and doesn't require an extra power supply. Installing a new one isn't generally that difficult, but it can be tricky and it does require you to take the case off the machine and perform some minor surgery (see p.324). If you don't feel up to this, any computer shop will do it for you relatively cheaply. Unless your computer has a special SCSI adapter, you should go for a drive with a standard **IDE** – or **EIDE** – connection.

Tech Info | Tips & Tricks | Try This

IDE versus SCSI

IDE (also known as **ATA**), and SCSI (pronounced "**scuzzy**") are the two common ways of connecting internal hard drives and CD/DVD drives to a PC, and there is much debate about which is better. IDE devices are inexpensive and can be attached to the IDE ports found on all modern motherboards. Most motherboards have two ports, each of which can hold two devices, making a total of four – and more ports can be added with an expansion card if required. In ready-made PCs, the hard drive and CD/DVD drives are invariably connected via IDE. A single SCSI port – internal or external – can handle many more devices than an IDE port. But there are no SCSI ports built onto standard motherboards, so you need a special expansion card to attach a SCSI device, and this makes everything a bit more expensive. SCSI is faster than IDE in terms of maximum data transfer, but the difference is small, so you'll need very high-speed drives and a fast system to notice any improvement in performance. Also, IDE technology has got much better over the years, and fast-transfer versions like **Ultra ATA**, or **UDMA**, almost match SCSI for speed (though only new motherboards exploit the full speed of Ultra ATA hard drives). Overall, for home PC use, it's easier and cheaper to stick with IDE.

If there's no room left inside your PC or you want to be able to move your hard drive between computers, you could consider an **external drive**. These are more expensive, need their own power supplies and generally come with either a USB, IEEE 1394 or SCSI connection (see p.63). Here are the other factors to consider when choosing a new hard disk:

Physical size Also called **enclosure size**. This one's simple: 3.5" internal drives are standard for desktop machines and 2.5" internal drives are standard for laptops.

Tech Info | Tips & Tricks | Try This

Inside a hard drive

The hard drive is one of the few components in a modern PC which is actually mechanical – it consists of moving parts – and this makes the speed and accuracy with which it works all the more incredible. Despite the term "hard disk", a PC hard drive usually contains not just one disk but three, four or more, all stacked up like records in an old-style jukebox. On each side of each disk, or **platter**, is a **read-write head**, which looks like a little record-player arm and stylus. The disks spin about 100 times per second (hence that whirring noise when you open a file) and the heads hover somewhere in the region of a millionth of an inch away from their surfaces, moving back and forward with phenomenal precision to read and write the files. Data is stored as tiny **magnetic charges**, which are created on the special ultra-fine coating of the disks. The amount of information stored on a standard modern hard drive is remarkable, but prototypes are currently being developed which can store as much as 100 gigabytes – around 20 billion words of text – on one square inch of disk surface, so expect pocket-sized reference libraries soon. A hard drive is completely sealed in its own metal box, because even the tiniest dust particle could play havoc with its delicate mechanism. The bottom of the box is a printed circuit board called the **logic board**, which controls the action inside.

Data access time Measured in milliseconds (ms), the data access time is a general measure of drive performance: a shorter time means the drive can read and write information more quickly. It is affected by various factors including **seek time** (the average time the drive takes to find a file), **spindle speed** (the speed at which the disks spin around) and **data transfer rate** (the rate at which the drive can send and receive information). A high speed makes a PC a bit faster and more efficient, especially for those who like to challenge their PC with real-time tasks such as live audio recording.

Cache Measured in megabytes (MB). This little memory chip stores the information most recently recovered from the drive, so it can be re-accessed almost instantaneously. The more the better.

Floppy drives

Almost all PCs come with a floppy drive, which takes handy little 3.5" disks called **floppy disks**, **floppies** or **diskettes**. The disk itself is housed in a square plastic case, which makes it pretty sturdy but far from indestructible. Floppies aren't particularly roomy as storage devices go – a standard **high-density** (HD) disk can hold 1.44 megabytes of data on its magnetic surface, which is enough for quite a few text documents but not for a single high-resolution digital photo. Once a floppy is formatted (see p.290), which prepares it for duty, it can be used again and again – you can write files to the disk and delete them at will.

There are other high-capacity diskettes on the market that have built upon floppy technology, like the Imation Corporation's **SuperDisk** drive and the more commonly used Iomega **Zip** drives (see p.77).

CD-ROM drives

Most PCs built in the last decade have a CD drive for reading information from **CD-ROMs**, usually referred to simply as "CDs" because they look identical to ordinary music compact discs. Unlike the information on a floppy disk, data on a CD-ROM cannot be altered – hence the name ROM (Read Only Memory). A single CD, though, can store over 500 times more than a floppy. Software usually comes on CDs, and you can also buy discs containing everything from encyclopedias and works of fiction to gardening manuals and foreign language courses. Also, CD drives can read standard audio CDs – so you can listen to your favourite tunes whilst working on your computer (see p.172). If you have a very old PC it may not have a CD drive, but you can add one very cheaply and without too much hassle. Drives are advertised as being of a certain **speed**, expressed as how much faster they are than a conventional audio CD player – **32x** faster, for example. A speedier drive can read information more quickly, though in reality you're unlikely to notice much of a difference in performance unless you regularly copy huge files from CD. Even so, don't go for anything less than 24x. Most drives connect to one of your motherboard's IDE ports, and also have a **digital audio output** that links directly to your PC's sound card for music playback.

CD burners

CD burners – which are also called **CD writers, CD-R and CD-RW drives** – can not only read normal CD-ROMs but also write, or "burn", information onto special types of CD. Burners used to be expensive luxuries, but prices have fallen so dramatically over the last five years that they're now shipped as standard in most middle- to high-end PCs. They're great for backing up data and transferring large folders between computers – and you can even burn music onto a CD and play it back on a conventional CD player. Most CD burners can write information onto two different types of disc. With a **CD-R**, the data cannot be altered once it's been written. With a more expensive **CD-RW**, you can write data and "rewrite" over it again and again; standard CD-RWs cannot be read by an audio CD player, though special music CD-RWs are available.

When buying a CD burner there are quite a few considerations. First, the speed, which is described similarly to a regular CD-ROM drive but with three figures instead of one: something like **12x 8x 32x**. Usually the first number refers to the rate at which the drive can **write** onto a CD-R, the second refers to **rewriting** onto CD-RW and the third refers to **reading** from a CD-ROM. Occasionally these numbers are the other way around, but the biggest figure is always the reading speed, and the smallest the CD-RW writing speed. To give you an idea of what the numbers actually mean, a 12x writing speed drive will take around five minutes to burn an average album-length audio CD. Here are a few other things to consider:

Internal/External Though most people go for an internal drive with a standard IDE connection (see p.46), you could consider an external drive. Though they're more expensive and not as fast, external burners can be used with a notebook, or moved between PCs.

BurnProofing If you can afford the extra, go for a drive with BurnProofing. This greatly reduces the likelihood of a CD being ruined halfway through recording because the flow of data has been interrupted – especially useful if your PC is quite slow.

Buffer size If a writer hasn't got BurnProofing, check the buffer size – 4MB or more is preferable. This allows the drive to think ahead a little, reducing the chance of errors.

Text enable This feature allows you to store song titles along with the tracks on an audio CD, which will be displayed when you play the disc back on a PC.

Overburning Allows you to squeeze a tiny bit more information onto each CD.

DVD drives

Though they look similar to normal CDs, DVDs work in a different way and can store approximately thirteen times more data – up to 17 gigabytes on a single disc (that's over 10,000 floppies). DVD stands for **digital versatile disc**, though the phrase **digital video disc** is often used because at the moment these high-capacity, double-sided discs are primarily used for storing and playing back movies. As the DVD gradually takes over the territory of the video cassette, more and more modern PCs are being shipped with a DVD drive. For the time being, you won't get much use out of it other than watching films, but in the future DVDs are likely to eclipse CDs as the primary storage device for software and large files.

If you already have a PC, you can buy a DVD drive cheaply and fit it relatively easily (see p.318). But check the speed of your computer's processor before buying – if your machine's processor is slower than around 500MHz you'll probably need a special **DVD playback expansion card**. When choosing a drive, the things to look out for are **speed** (the faster the better, and don't go for anything slower than 6x) and **buffer size** (the more the better). DVD drives can read standard CDs, and there are also **combo drives**, which combine a DVD player and a CD burner in a single unit. These are ideal if you don't have much room inside your PC.

With a DVD drive installed you can watch movies on your computer monitor, but many people prefer to hook their PC up to their television. This is only possible if you have a **TV-out** socket on your PC's video card – have a look on the back of your machine next to where the monitor plugs in.

DVD burners

In the past year or so, **DVD burners** have started to appear on the market at prices realistic for home users. These drives are great not only for storing movies to play back on computers and conventional DVD players but also for backing up data – you can store a huge amount on a single disc. There are various types of DVD burners, each of which writes to different types of disc. DVD-R drives burn discs which can only be written to once, but can be played back in conventional DVD drives and players – great if you're working with video on your PC and want to be able to share your work with others. More expensive and less common DVD-RW drives take discs that can be written and overwritten but can't be played back on a standard DVD player. However, the future will also see DVD+RW drives coming onto the market, offering the rewrite capability of DVD-RW with the compatibility of DVD-R. The final type of DVD you may come across is DVD-RAM. These delicate discs often come in protective plastic cases (a bit like floppies), and can only currently be used in DVD-RAM drives. There is no limit to the number of times a DVD-RAM disc can be rewritten to.

Internal backup devices

An internal backup device is a useful addition to any PC. Once it's installed, you can set Windows to automatically back up your files while you're asleep in case anything happens to the work stored on your primary hard drive. Backing up is discussed further in Chapter 20 (p.275), but for now here's a quick look at the internal backup hardware options.

Perhaps the option that will give you the most for your

money is an **extra hard drive**, which will be permanently hidden away inside your PC. But if your computer is ever stolen, flooded or set on fire, you'll lose both the original and the back-up files. One way around this problem is to get a **removable caddy** for the drive to live in. You fit a special unit into one of the expansion bays on the front of your machine, and the caddy holding the drive can be removed and stored away from your PC for safe-keeping. When buying a second hard drive, you'll have to decide whether to go for one big enough to back up all your data and programs, or something smaller for essential files only.

Alternatively, you could go for a **tape drive**, which stores data on a tape that looks like a small audio cassette. Most tapes have a large capacity, allowing you to back up the whole of your hard drive onto something compact, light and robust. However, they have the disadvantage of being **sequential access devices**, meaning that your system has to go through the tape in sequence to find the relevant data (unlike with a hard drive, where the read-write heads can skip to the correct areas of the disks almost instantaneously).

Expansion cards

Expansion cards are rectangular pieces of circuit board that slot onto a computer's motherboard. They usually deal with a specific type of task such as graphics, sound or Internet connections and frequently have a rear panel that protrudes from the back of the PC in order to provide **ports** (sockets) for attaching relevant devices. A video card has a port for attaching a monitor, for example, whilst a modem expansion card has a port for connecting a telephone cable. Some cards are very common and found in most modern PCs, such as **modems**, **video cards** and **sound cards** (though video and sound functions are sometimes built into the motherboard). But there are many other types that you could choose to add if and when you require them, such as a **TV card** to let you view television on your monitor, or a **network card** to let you hook up to another computer. There are also cards that exist just to add extra sockets to your system (such as **USB**, **IEEE 1394** or **SCSI**, see p.63). For information about fitting a new expansion card, turn to p.314.

There are three types of expansion cards, and each fits into a different type of slot on the motherboard: **AGP**, the fastest, is specifically for video cards; **PCI** is used for all types of cards; and **ISA** is an older type which is pretty much obsolete today. The most common types of expansion cards are described below. Equivalent devices are also available as external units, or as **PC cards** for use with notebooks.

Video cards

A PC's video card, also known as the **graphics card** or **video adapter**, is the piece of hardware that translates computer data into a picture signal and sends it to a monitor. Though this was once a relatively simple task, today's three-dimensional graphics-intensive games and applications require a powerful piece of kit capable of handling enormous amounts of data.

Video cards traditionally slot into one of the motherboard's **PCI slots** (see p.38), but because of the sheer volume of data that passes between the card and the processor, most modern cards use a newer slot-type called an **Accelerated Graphics Port** (**AGP**). Before you rush out and buy an AGP card, make sure your motherboard has the necessary slot.

If you're buying a new PC, ensure that it actually has a video card: some lower-end computers come with **integrated video** (video capability built into the motherboard), which is generally pretty pathetic and sometimes a hassle to upgrade. When choosing a card you will need to consider several variables. First, **video memory**: a card with more memory can display more colours, at a higher resolution and with a faster refresh rate (the speed at which the image on the screen is replaced). Go for a card with no less than 8MB of onboard memory, but if you intend to do any serious 3D gaming or watch DVD movies, 32MB is desirable. When it comes to choosing a particular model, you should also focus on the card's **chipset**, its built-in processor – the difference between two cards made by different brands but with the same chipset is often quite slim. Check out the latest magazine reviews to find out which card is best suited to your needs and price range.

If you want to use your PC to view DVD movies on a regular television, be sure the card has **TV-out** (though if not, special external devices are available for turning your monitor socket into a TV-out). Other special features found on some video cards include built-in **TV receivers** (see p.60), ports for connecting **digital camcorders** (see p. 81) and **double-display outputs** for attaching two monitors to a single PC simultaneously.

Sound cards

The sound card is responsible for the sound both coming out of and going into a PC (except the little beep that the machine makes when it starts up). It turns digital data from the computer into an analogue sound signal to be sent to speakers, and turns analogue sound from an input – such as a microphone – into digital computer data. The basic spec of a sound card is expressed as a number of **bits**, which refers to the quality of the digital to analogue converters, or **DACs**; the higher the number of bits, the higher the sound quality. Two other considerations are whether a card is **Sound-Blaster compatible**, important if you want to play games, and whether it's **full duplex** (can record and play back sound simultaneously), which is useful for internet phone calls and music-making. Also, check out the type of **synthesizer** a card uses to create sounds – **wave table** is better than **FM** – and look at what **input and output sockets** it has. Most have three "minijack" sockets for speakers, headphones and a microphone, but some high-quality cards have many more.

For most users a simple sound card will be perfectly adequate – especially if you plan to listen to the sound it makes through the tinny little speakers which come as standard with most PCs. But those who are seriously into music or gaming may want to go for one of the many higher-quality cards on the market. Gamers could opt for a card with **3D audio**, which can be connected to a **surround-sound speaker system** to bring certain games to life. If you want high-quality music reproduction from CDs or MP3 files, go for a 16-bit card, and consider whether there's a **line out** to connect the PC to a hi-fi, or an **optical out** for digital connection to a MiniDisc recorder. If you think you'll be regularly connecting and disconnecting things to and

Building a home recording studio

If you plan to make your PC the hub of an effective home recording studio, you'll need a powerful PC with lots of RAM and a high-quality, 16-bit or better, full-duplex sound card. When choosing a card there are many considerations to take into account. You'll probably want **MIDI ports** to hook up an electronic keyboard, and possibly **SP/DIF** sockets for connecting to a DAT recorder or effects rack. And **phono-lead outputs** make for easy connection to a hi-fi. If you want to deal with samples, get a card with lots of onboard RAM, or consider buying a card that utilizes your system RAM. If you're more interested in recording a whole band, go for a **multi-in card**. These are pretty expensive, but they allow you to record several microphones or instruments simultaneously onto separate tracks. You can then edit the tracks individually just like in a real recording studio. Many multi-in cards, and some others, come with a "breakout box" of inputs that sits on your desk, saving you from having to dig around behind the PC whenever you want to plug something in. Finally, you'll need some **music software** – see p.263 – though decent sound cards often come bundled with a pretty good selection. For more on PC music hardware, visit **http://www.pc-music.com**.

from your sound card, you may want to invest in a card with a **front panel unit**, which lives in one of the bays on the front of your PC's case, providing easy access to many of the sockets.

Modems

Short for **mo**dulator-**dem**odulator, a modem is the piece of a PC used to connect to the Internet. It translates digital information into an analogue wave, and vice versa, so that computer data can be transmitted down a telephone line. The speed with which modems relay information is measured in **bits** – not to be confused with **bytes**, see p.42 – and the standard modems

Digital connections

If you want a really fast Internet connection so that pages will load almost instantaneously and downloads won't take ages, you should consider getting a digital connection. There are various types of digital connection, such as **cable**, **ISDN**, **DSL** and **satellite**, but you won't be able to receive these services through a standard modem. For more on digital Internet connections, see the *Rough Guide to the Internet*.

found in today's PCs can theoretically download (receive) information at a rate of 56,000 bits per second (56Kbps) and upload (send) information at a rate of 33.6Kbps. However, in reality most regular phone lines struggle to shift this amount of data, especially at peak times when telephone networks are busy.

If you're buying a modem, make sure you don't go for anything less than 56Kbps. Also, avoid cheaper **soft modems** (or software modems); these parasitic devices skimp on hardware by using your main processor to do some of the work, and if your system's not up to the job everything might slow down.

Standard **internal modems** look like any other piece of circuit board and connect to your motherboard via a **PCI slot**. Once installed, the only part of it you'll see is the little panel on the back of your machine with a socket for a phone line. A perfectly functional internal modem comes pre-installed in practically every new PC, but if you're upgrading an old machine or you want to use a modem with several different computers, it's worth considering an **external modem**. These require their own power supply or battery, but they're effortless to install and easy to swap between machines, especially if they have a USB connection (see p.63). Also, they usually feature a little set of flashing lights that display the status of the phone connection – keeping your cat amused for hours.

Notebook modems

Most new notebooks also come with a built-in modem and a socket for hooking up to a normal phone line. If your notebook doesn't have one, a standard external modem will work fine, or you could go for a credit-card-sized **PCMCIA** modem, which will fit into a **PC card slot**. These can be taken in and out at will, and they don't need an extra power supply. If you want to get online without being tied to a landline, however, you can connect via a suitable **data-compatible mobile phone**. As well as the phone, you'll need either an appropriate PCMCIA modem or a serial or USB data cable with a software modem. Though more expensive, the neatest option for surfing whilst out and about is to get a **PCMCIA modem-phone**, which looks like a regular PC card with a little antenna sticking out of the side. This way no phone or cable is required – you can even plug in a hands-free kit and use it to make voice calls. Charges can be paid monthly or added onto an existing mobile phone account.

Network cards

Network cards, or **NICs** (network interface cards), are expansion boards that connect via a PCI slot – or a PC card slot on a notebook – so that the machine can be connected to a network. If you're intending to link your PC to a specific network, at work for example, check with the system administrator to find out exactly which piece of hardware you need: each NIC is designed for a particular type of network.

For home or small business networking, you'll need to get hold of a networking kit, which will come with all the cabling and network cards you need. For more on home networking, see p.224.

TV cards

A TV card, which shouldn't cost you too much, allows your computer to double as a multi-functioning television. They usually come as standalone PCI or AGP expansion cards, though video cards with integrated television capability are available. You plug a TV aerial into the socket at the back of the PC, a built-in tuner finds the channels and the card adjusts the picture signal to make it suitable for a computer monitor. With a decent screen and card, the resulting picture quality is excellent – equal to or better than most televisions. And if you have a good speaker system, you can achieve high-quality stereo, or even Dolby surround-sound.

As well as giving you a high-quality image, most TV cards also allow you to do loads of fun things: record clips or still images onto your hard drive, plug in a video camera or watch lots of channels at once. They can even be used to receive music in MP3 format. If you get a card with a digital receiver, you can watch digital stations without a special decoder box (one reason for their increased popularity is the presence of illegal software which allows the user to unlawfully receive TV stations that should be paid for).

3

Peripherals

stuff that plugs in

Peripherals are computer devices that live outside the PC's case, and they come in all shapes and sizes – from the diminutive mouse to the giant A1 printer. Regardless of which device you're buying, there will be a huge selection of brands and models available, with a price-range to match. And thanks to Plug and Play technology (see box overleaf), once you've chosen a peripheral it's likely to be incredibly easy to install: take it out of its box, plug it into the appropriate socket and away you go. If your installation experience isn't quite this smooth, you may want to refer to the Troubleshooting chapter (see p.285).

In this chapter you will learn about the special software that comes with peripheral devices, the various types of connections and cables you are likely to encounter and the devices themselves.

What's on that CD?

In addition to an instruction manual, peripherals almost always come with one or more CDs or floppy disks. These contain

Tech Info | Tips & Tricks | Try This

Plug and Play

Plug and Play (**PnP**) is a computer industry-wide standard introduced to combat the problems faced by PC users trying to get their systems to accept new internal components or peripheral devices. The idea is that your PC detects the new device, regardless of the brand or type, and configures everything so that you can literally plug it in and start to play – without having to worry about techie things like jumper settings and software installation. PnP first appeared in the mainstream as part of Windows 95 and was rapidly nicknamed "Plug and Pray" because of its less than impressive success rate, but the system has improved hugely since then. Today it's pretty reliable, and the majority of PC devices, as well as all the major operating systems for both PC and Mac, support the protocols. This, combined with the advent of USB and IEEE 1394 connections, has made adding extra kit to PCs easier than ever before.

software to make the device work: **utilities** that allow you to operate it and **drivers** to tell your operating system how to control it. For simple peripherals you may not need to use the disks at all, as Windows has many software drivers built-in – though you may need to install the software if you want your new toy to perform all its functions. For example, if you buy a mouse with a **scroll wheel** and two extra buttons, you should be able to plug it in and use it straight away with the Windows default settings. But if you want to set the buttons up to execute other tasks, you'll need the extra software. Sometimes you'll also get some free applications with a peripheral, either on separate CDs or bundled in with the utilities and drivers.

Ports and plugs

Peripheral devices connect to PCs in many different ways, using different types of cable and attaching to different types of port (sockets on the computer) – you will often have to decide which kind of port connection to opt for when you choose a device. In some cases it will make very little difference, but in other cases it pays to think carefully about the type of connection because some are faster and more convenient than others. Always make sure you have the necessary ports for a device before you buy it, but if you do find yourself with a connection problem, don't fret: the cable or adapter you need is almost certainly out there somewhere, and expansion cards are available to add extra ports to your PC. Some peripherals use a dedicated port (mouse port, monitor port, etc), but you can also expect to be faced with a choice between one or more of the following connection types:

USB (Universal Serial Bus) This clever little connection allows you to attach up to 127 peripheral devices to your machine via a single port, either through a hub (like a junction box) or a multi-head cable. Major advantages are that you can **hot swap** hardware – add and remove devices without shutting down your system – and that all recent PCs have the necessary ports. The bad news is that standard USB connections are pretty slow (12 megabits per second), which is fine for most devices but not ideal for high-speed peripherals such as DV camcorders and external hard drives. The newer **Hi-Speed USB** is 40 times as fast, but to take advantage of it you'll need a Hi-Speed USB port.

IEEE 1394 (Also called **FireWire** by Apple, and **iLink** by Sony) IEEE 1394 is similar to Hi-Speed USB, shifting data at up to 400 Mbps. It has become a standard connection for digital video devices, and is ideal for external hard drives and backup devices.

SCSI (Small Computer System Interface) The various flavours of SCSI are mostly for high-spec devices, and one 50-pin port can control quite a few **daisy-chained** peripherals (devices strung together in sequence like a chain of flowers). SCSI doesn't come as standard in PCs, so you'll need a internal SCSI **interface card** to get the port. This adds to the price, though some devices do come with a SCSI card (or kit) thrown in.

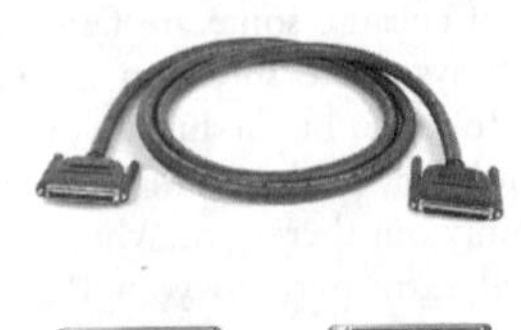

Parallel The standard for printers until USB came along, parallel leads have long, flat 25-pin plugs secured by two little screws. They're a bit bulky and awkward but do the job perfectly well.

Hubs, switch boxes and plug adapters

There are numerous products on the market – many of which are inexpensive – that can turn a single port into a multi port, or convert one type of plug into another (adapters). **Powered USB hubs** are great for running several devices simultaneously through a single USB port, while **parallel switch boxes** let you

Hot swap safely

Even though USB "hot swapability" means that you can add and remove devices without having to turn off your system, Windows XP and Me still expect you to follow certain procedures when unplugging USB devices so that they know to stop trying to communicate with them. In the Notification area on the Taskbar, look for the little icon which displays a diagonal green arrow hovering over a grey slab. Right-click it to reveal the **Safely Remove Hardware** dialog box, which contains a list of unpluggable devices. Select the device you want to unplug and then click the **Stop** button. You'll soon get a message giving you the all-clear to pull the plug.

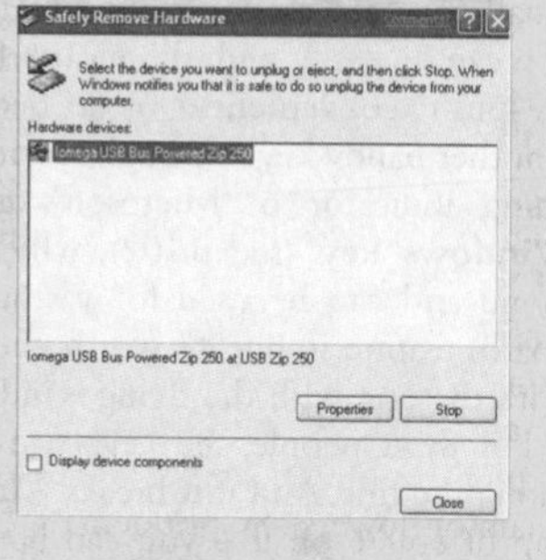

alternate the usage of a single port between two or more peripherals. In short, for practically every wiring conflict you encounter there's sure to be a small plastic solution.

Keyboards

Until recently, all PC **keyboards** looked much the same: tilted grey-beige panels with a specific set of keys. But in the last few years they've become much jazzier, coming in all sorts of shapes and colours. They still feature the same basic set of keys – which includes a number pad, a row of function keys and a QWERTY letter layout – but many also now have **hotkeys** for common tasks such as controlling the computer's CD player, opening an email program or connecting to the Web. These are all things you can do easily with the mouse, but many people like the single-push convenience of a dedicated keyboard function. Another handy key – though, if you're feeling paranoid, a frightening indicator of Microsoft's global domination – is the **Windows key** (see p.102), which opens the Windows Start menu and can be used for various shortcuts. Most new keyboards feature it, but it's worth checking to make sure it's there – it's the one with the flying window icon on it.

For most people, the keyboard that comes with a new PC should be fine. And if it breaks – usually when someone spills a cup of coffee on it – you can buy a new one very cheaply. If you're a serious typist, however, you'll probably want to invest in something more comfortable to use and which has appropriately springy keys. You may also want to try out an **ergonomic split keyboard**, which has keys for the right and left hands separated and angled to allow for a comfortable arm position. If you're a pathological wire-hater, you may consider spending extra and getting a **cordless keyboard**. You plug a little receiver into the back of the PC and the keyboard, powered by a bat-

tery, beams your keystrokes to the receiver unit by infrared or radio waves – making your desk that little bit tidier. These are often sold in a set with a cordless mouse.

Keyboards attach to the back of a PC through either a 6-pin keyboard socket (old PCs have a slightly bigger socket, but cheap adapters are available for fitting a new keyboard) or a USB port – there's no particular advantage to either.

Mice and more

The **mouse** is a brilliantly simple PC input device. You hold it in your hand and manoeuvre it around on a desk or mouse mat, and a little on-screen pointer matches your movements. The standard mouse has two little buttons on its top, which you "click" to select something on the screen. To make your rodent do what you want you'll need to become fluent in the simple language it understands: that of **left-clicks**, **right-clicks**, **drags** and **double-clicks** (see p.98). Many newer mice also come with a **jog wheel** for "scrolling" through documents, and **extra buttons** that can be set to perform specific tasks in different applications: you could use them, for example, to "copy" and "paste" text (see p.181) or move forward and back between Web pages.

The mechanics of a mouse are uncomplicated: as you move it around, the heavy rubber ball that pokes out from the underside moves too, and that motion is transformed into an electronic signal which is sent to the computer. This arrangement means that over the hundreds of miles it travels across your desk the ball can get rather grimy, making the mouse sluggish and unresponsive. This is easy enough to solve with a good scrub (see p.286), but if it keeps happening you might consider upgrading to a ball-free **optical mouse**, which bounces a laser around to track the mouse's movements – no mechanical parts to get clogged with dirt and you don't even have to use it on a horizontal surface. You could also opt for a **cordless mouse**, which sends an infrared or radio signal to a little unit that plugs into the back of the PC. These are great if you don't want your desk cluttered up with wires, but they require batteries, they're relatively pricey and, well, they're easy to lose.

Mice usually connect to either a **PS/2 mouse port**, a **USB port** or (on older machines) a **serial port** – all of these are equally good. Some mice come with an adapter that allows you to connect to different ports.

If the humble mouse doesn't float your boat, there are other pointing devices on the market that do pretty much the same thing:

Trackballs These come in various shapes and sizes, and to all intents and purposes are mice lying on their backs – you use your fingers to move the large protruding ball. Though some people swear by them, trackballs are not as intuitive as regular mice, so try before you buy.

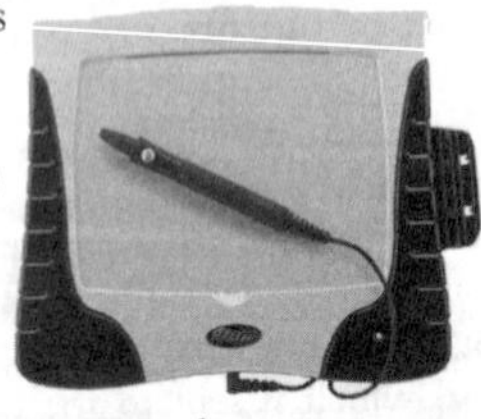

Graphics tablets Also known as **drawing tablets** or **digitizing pads**, graphics tablets look similar to a rectangular mouse mat but are able to read the movements of a stylus (like a pen) and a puck (a multifunctional mouse used for tracing). These high-tech devices are often used by graphic designers, cartographers and illustrators, but aren't especially suited to general PC use.

Light pens As intuitive as your own finger, a light pen is used directly on-screen, and with many such pens any screen will do. The device plugs straight into the back of your PC and allows you to guide the pointer around the monitor, putting pressure on the pen's soft tip to "click". Again, try one out before you decide to buy, and consider a setup with an angled screen as they're a nightmare to use with a regular near-vertical one.

Touchpads On notebooks (see p.15) the primary input device is a small touch-sensitive pad, though most machines also come with a standard mouse port. So if you find the touchpad a little too fiddly, you can always buy a mouse instead. It's not a very popular choice, but you can also purchase touchpads for use with a desktop PC.

Monitors

Choosing a computer **monitor** (also a **display** or **screen**) is a serious business, because this is the thing you are going to be staring at for hours on end. If it's too small, dull or flickery you could end up straining your eyes, and you won't be able to realize the graphics potential of the rest of your system.

In years gone by monitors were either **monochrome** – displaying a single foreground colour against a darker background – or **greyscale**, like a black-and-white TV. Today, however, nearly all computer monitors are capable of displaying millions of colours. Your PC's **video card** (see p.54) tells the monitor what to display at any given time, specifying the **resolution** (the number of points that make up the image horizontally and vertically), the **refresh rate** (how fast it wants the points to change) and the **colour** each point should be. There's no point in pairing a high-quality video card with an inferior monitor: the card may be able to generate a resolution of 2048x1536 dots, but if your screen can only handle 1280x1024 you're going to miss out. Choose a monitor that can refresh the image at a rate of at least **85MHz or higher**, but don't go crazy – anything faster than 100MHz will make little difference for most tasks. And try to have a look at some monitors displaying the kind of programs you intend to use, so that you can decide what resolution and physical dimensions you actually need. Higher resolution often represents a trade-off against sharpness and refresh rate, so never look at a single spec in isolation and always try before you buy.

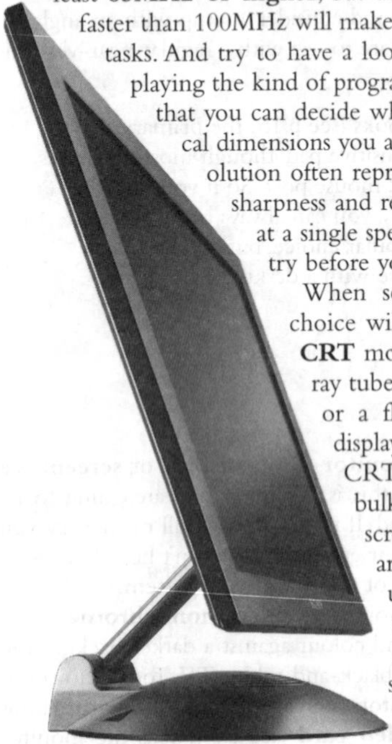

When selecting a monitor, the choice will be between a standard **CRT** model, which has a cathode ray tube like a traditional TV set, or a flat **LCD** (liquid crystal display), as used on notebooks. CRT monitors are extremely bulky compared to their flat-screened cousins, but they are much cheaper to buy, usually have larger screens and can handle higher resolutions than similar-sized LCDs. Also, LCDs generally have quite a limited angle of view: as you move to your left or right, the image will become harder to see. On the other hand, LCDs look neat, take up less space (their "footprint" is smaller), consume much less power and emit far less brain-melting radiation. These days, nearly all flat displays have **TFT** (thin film transistor) screens, which are even more compact than older LCDs, and boast impressive resolution capabilities – so these are the sort to go for.

When buying a CRT screen, you'll be told the monitor's **nominal size** (15", 21", etc), which refers to the diagonal distance from corner to opposite corner; but beware, the **viewable image size** is usually around an inch less. Some dealers quote both specifications, so when comparing screens, double-check to see exactly what you're comparing. Also, try to get a **Trinitron** or **Diamontron** tube; these have flatter screens and boast superior image quality and minimal glare. When it comes to LCDs, you need to choose between an analogue or digital signal. Digital monitors are arguably better, but they're pricey and require a compatible video card (see p.54). Whichever type of monitor you go for, you'll also need to decide whether you want any fancy extras. Built-in speakers and microphones aren't anything to get excited about, though a USB hub (see p.64) built into the monitor's base may prove very useful.

Despite all this techie stuff, the most important thing is how comfortable you feel in front of a screen: does it seem bright and sharp enough? Are lines crisp and curves smooth? And remember that bigger isn't always better – you may find that a smaller screen is easier to work with.

Printers

Printers allow you to bring documents, images and Web pages from your computer into the real world, so you can scribble on, fax, post or frame your work, just like in the bad old days. Unsurprisingly, these are among the most popular of all

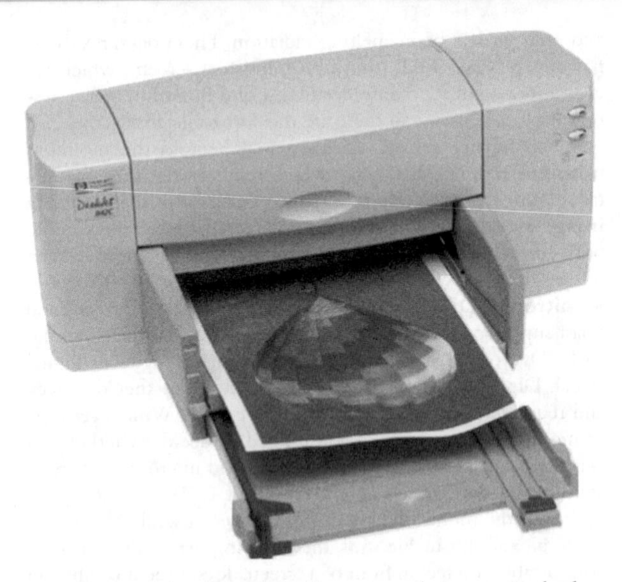

computer peripherals, and they've come a long way in the last couple of decades. Choosing a home printer no longer means deciding between a **daisywheel** and a **dot-matrix** – today, for relatively little money, you can buy something capable of producing high-quality colour photographs or churning out over 500 pages of text an hour. There are so many brands and models on the market that the choice can seem daunting, but once you've asked yourself a few basic questions about what you want to use the printer for, everything becomes much clearer. If you only intend to print the occasional letter, you can pick up something suitable for the price of a meal for two; most PC packages come with such a model thrown in. But if you plan to create photos, produce documents in large quantities or print onto large sheets of paper, you'll need to invest in something better.

The first decision is whether to go for an **inkjet** or a **laser** printer. Practically all home users opt for an inkjet: they're cheap, small and good for a variety of uses; practically all of them print in colour; and many can produce photo-quality images. However, if you want something capable of handling an intensive workload you should have a look at laser printers – the fast, smudge-free, high-quality machines used in most offices. Colour lasers are prohibitively expensive, but black-and-white models have become significantly cheaper over the past few years, making them a realistic option for home and small business use. They still cost more than inkjets, but could save you money in the long run because they're very durable and the cost per page usually works out cheaper. Those with big budgets who are keen to achieve professional-quality photographs might also want to consider a more expensive **dye sublimation** printer.

Once you've decided which type of printer you're after, you'll need to weigh up the specifications and prices of various models. One consideration is **printing speed**, which is usually measured in **ppm** – pages per minute. Generally a faster figure means a faster printer, but you should always take these numbers with a pinch of salt as they tend to describe a best-case scenario. When it comes to image quality, the specification you'll see most commonly is **resolution**, usually measured in **dpi** (dots per inch). A high dpi rating is a good sign, but resolution alone is not an accurate measure of image quality: other factors, such as the **number of ink colours**, play a part. Most printers mix all their colours from the four "CMYK" inks (**c**yan, **m**agenta, **y**ellow and blac**k**), but printers with six or more produce truer and sharper colours – important if you're printing photos. And then there's the quality of the **printing heads**. Inexpensive printers often have inferior heads, which can create uneven textures and inconsistent colours. The only way to judge a printer properly is to see an example of its printout. If shops in your area don't have examples on display, reading reviews in magazines or on the Internet is the best way forward.

As well as speed and quality of image, it's worth considering what extra features a printer offers. Some can handle lots of different paper sizes, for example, or come with a **feeder reel** so you can print uninterruptedly onto a long sheet of paper. Photo enthusiasts may want a printer with **edge-to-edge capability** or a **memory card slot**, which allows you to print the pictures from your digital camera (sometimes even preview them on a little LCD screen) without even switching on your PC. If you're prepared to foot the bill, you could even go for a printer that can handle A3 paper or larger.

Before you make your final selection, check out the **ink cartridge** situation. Practically all printers have one cartridge for black ink and one for colour, but some budget models don't hold both at the same time, leaving you with the inky-fingered hassle of swapping cartridges depending on what you want to print. Also, be sure to investigate the price of replacement

Tech Info | Tips & Tricks | Try This

How printers work

Inkjet and laser printers work in totally different ways. An inkjet moves a printing head over the page line by line, using heat or force to push tiny quantities of ink from minute nozzles onto the paper. Laser printers, on the other hand, work like photocopiers. They use a laser (or other form of light) to produce a charged image of a page on a cylindrical drum. The drum is rolled through a pool of special toner, which only sticks to the charged areas of the drum. Heat and pressure are then used to transfer the toner from the drum to the paper.

cartridges: an apparent bargain may be expensive in the long run if you have to fork out lots of cash every time you run out of ink. If you intend to regularly print out multiple copies of colour images, consider getting a printer that has separate cartridges for each colour, an innovation introduced by Canon. This way, if you print out ten copies of a photo dominated by a rich blue sky, for example, you can replace the blue ink without having to throw away whatever is left of the other colours.

Scanners

A **scanner** (or **optical scanner**) is a device that allows you to copy photos and printed documents into your PC so that you can email them to friends, create archives or just mess around with them using a graphics application (see p.259). A scanner **digitizes** (translates) whatever is on a piece of paper into a **bitmap** – an image made up of a grid of points, or **pixels**. Using **optical character recognition** (OCR) software, which most scanner packages now include, you can even turn printed type into computer text and edit it in a word processor. The more points the scanner uses to represent an image, the higher its resolution; this is quoted as a number of dots per inch (**dpi**) along two axes – 600x1200 dpi, for example.

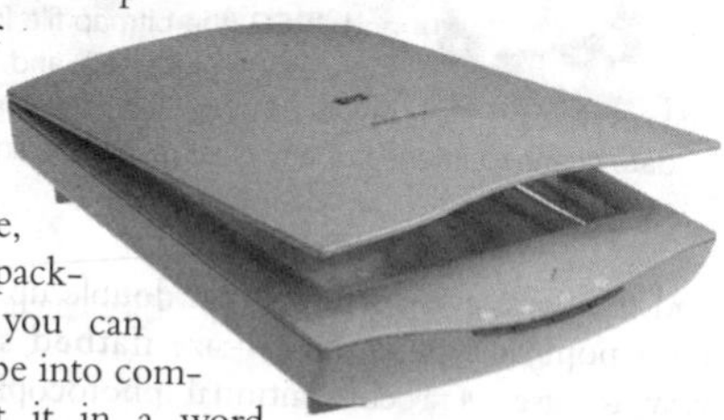

You can get handheld scanners that look and work like highlighter pens, saving the text as they're passed over a line of type,

Tech Info | Tips & Tricks | Try This

Bitmaps

Digital cameras and scanners are used to transfer images into a format understood by computers. They work by translating a "real" analogue image into a **bitmap**, a digital image consisting of a grid of points. How realistic a bitmap looks depends on its **resolution** (the number of points on the grid) and the number of colours and tones recognized (the **colour depth**). A **monochrome** bitmap is the simplest type, each point being represented by just one piece of data: 1 bit means the point is filled, 0 bits means the point is empty. **Greyscale** and **colour** bitmaps, however, are more complex, as each tone and shade needs its own unique string of 1s and 0s to distinguish it from every other. The more colours that can be recognized, the longer the strings need to be – a bitmap in **true color** uses 24 bits (0s and 1s) to describe each point. The

bitmap files that you'll come across most frequently will have the following **file extensions** (see p.122) on the end of their names: **BMP** (the Microsoft Windows bitmap format), **GIF** and **JPEG** (the bitmap file formats commonly found on the Internet), and **TIF** (the format favoured by professionals, as it can accommodate scanned images of any size, resolution and colour depth).

and there are even printers that double up as scanners. But the most popular type is the A4-size **flatbed scanner**, which is as easy to use as a conventional photocopier: you place your document on the flat glass scanning bed, close the lid, press the button and off it goes. Flatbed scanners are inexpensive and are regularly included in PC bundles. Cheap or thrown-in models are fine for most tasks (they nearly always have the standard 600x1200 dpi resolution) but versions offering higher quality are available. As with other devices, try to see a scanner in operation before you buy it to be sure it produces a good image and isn't excruciatingly slow. It's also worth checking that it doesn't have a raised lip around the glass bed – this can make it hard to scan magazines and sections of documents that are larger than A4. If your PC has a spare USB port, go for a scanner with a USB connection as they are more convenient than models with a SCSI or parallel interface (see p.63).

Removable storage

Removable storage media generally tend to be large cartridges that look like conventional floppies and work in a similar way, though they can hold a lot more data and each one requires its own class of drive. The most popular types – **Zip**, **Jaz** and **Peerless** drives – are built by Iomega, and you'll see them pretty much everywhere.

Not to be confused with the **zipping** process of file compression (see p.134), the **Zip** disk is a high-capacity floppy diskette. It's thicker and broader than the conventional floppy, and comes in two formats: one that holds 100MB of data and another that will take 250MB. Zip disks are great for backing up files and transporting large amounts of data, and you can reuse them as many times as you like. To use Zip disks you need a Zip drive, of which there are two varieties: the original **Zip 100** drive (for use only with the 100MB disks) and the newer **Zip 250** (which can use both types of disk). Though a Zip drive can be installed as a fixed device in one of your PC's expansion bays, they are more commonly bought as external devices, recognizable by their distinctive blue plastic casings. They usually come with a USB connection, though parallel and SCSI versions are also available (see p.64). Like floppy disks, Zips are robust and very easy to use.

The **Jaz drive** takes 2GB and older 1GB cartridges. These cartridges are chunkier than Zips and more expensive, but they are great for storing or backing up large amounts of data such as image and sound files. Jaz drives use a SCSI connection to give them very fast data transfer rates (up to 8MB per sec), which means you can use them like a hard drive. If you don't have a SCSI card (see p.64), you can get adapter cables to link the drive to most other types of port, though some of these will significantly limit the speed of data transfer.

The newest addition to the Iomega family is the capacious **Peerless drive** – an external, futuristic-looking base unit that connects to your PC via either a USB or IEEE 1394 (FireWire) cable, and which takes 5GB, 10GB or 20GB removable disk cartridges. The company claims that as well as offering oodles of data storage space, the IEEE version is fast enough to make light work of such taxing tasks as digital video editing and backing up hard drives. However, you can achieve basically the same results with an IEEE external hard drive – so compare prices and read a few magazine reviews before you buy. For more, see: **http://www.iomega.com**

Digital stills cameras

Most **digital stills cameras** look similar to any other camera: they are generally of a comparable shape and size, with a lens at the front and sometimes a zoom. And just like standard cameras, they have the power to make otherwise sane individuals grin like lunatics or dive under the table. But where regular cameras record analogue images onto film, digital cameras store them as – yes, you guessed it – digital information. The digital images, which are known as **bitmaps** (see p.76), are stored in either a fixed internal memory or on removable, reusable cards, commonly called **Flash memory cards** or **SmartMedia cards**, which are available with various capacities such as 4, 8, 16 or 32MB. When your memory or card is full – or whenever you fancy it – you hook up the camera to your PC (usually via a USB port) and download the images to your hard disk. If you like the results, you can store, edit and print your pictures; if you don't, simply delete them.

Only the most expensive digital cameras can really compete with analogue cameras – you won't find many professionals wielding digital models yet. But with a middle-range digital camera, a decent printer and some photo-quality paper you can produce very impressive results. And digital cameras have the advantage of lots of extra features. Most have a little **LCD display** on their back, which allows you to set up the shot without using the viewfinder and to review the photos as you take them, deleting the duds as you go. And because you're not wasting any film, you can be as trigger-happy as you like; you can even use your digital camera as a visual notebook when you're out and about – great when buying a house, for example. Some stills cameras will also let you record **short video sequences** or add sound to individual images, though if you want to do any serious filming you should go for a DV camcorder (see p.81).

When choosing a digital camera, the most important consideration is **resolution**, which is usually measured in megapixels – the number of dots, in millions, which make up the maximum-quality image. A million dots sounds like a lot, but only cameras of around 2.5 megapixels or more come anywhere near analogue picture quality. Read reviews wherever possible (see p.390), as digital cameras are highly complicated, and the advertised resolution isn't enough to predict the image quality of a model. Most digital cameras have some kind of zoom function, and you will often be quoted magnification specs for both an **optical zoom** and a **digital zoom**. Don't get too excited about digital zoom – all it does is enlarge the pixels in the centre of the image to generate a new picture with a lower resolution; the optical zoom figure is the one to look out for. The number of pictures that you can store on a device depends not only on the memory or card, but on the resolution of the images: the higher the resolution, the more memory is needed to store a single image. Most cameras will offer several different picture qualities, so when you compare image capacity claims be sure you're comparing like with like. Also check for extra features such as self-timers, remote controls, manual modes for aperture-control and the availability of different lenses.

Webcams

Webcams are little digital cameras designed to sit on the top of your monitor, staring unremittingly at you while you work. They are primarily used for making video phone calls – streaming images of you onto the Internet – but they can also be used to record photos and video pictures straight onto your PC's hard drive. Some even have their own **Flash memory**, allowing you to take them out to be used just like a regular digital camera. When shopping for a Webcam, check out resolution and if possible see various models in action to judge the quality of the images generated on-screen. They often deliver rather grainy pictures, especially those with a zoom function. Like other digital cameras, most connect to your PC via a USB port.

Digital video (DV) cameras

The final member of the digital image capture family is the **DV camcorder**. Though these are still pretty expensive items, prices are dropping fast. You can record in one of two ways: either via a cable plugged into your PC (which passes information straight into your hard drive) or straight onto a **mini-DV tape** in the camcorder, to download later or play back through a regular television.

When choosing a DV camcorder find one that has **DV-in** capability, which gives you the option to export footage from your PC back to the camcorder's DV tape. This is really important, because digital video will fill your hard disk very quickly if you have nowhere else to put it – 90 minutes of digital video will eat around 20GBs. Also look out for a model with a decent-sized colour LCD screen, good sound quality (12-bit or better), a variety of both analogue and digital ports, the capacity to take stills photographs and a **digital image stabilizer**: this will help to keep your footage wobble-free while you stumble around with all the grace of Spielberg in stilettos.

If you intend to get serious about digital video, you'll need a high-spec PC with a decent video card and a sizeable hard drive. For fast transfer between camera and computer, go for a camera with a **bi-directional IEEE 1394 (FireWire) port** (if you don't have an IEEE 1394 port on your PC, you'll need to add one with the appropriate interface expansion card). You should also consider what kind of **editing software** you want to use (see p.262).

Speakers

Until fairly recently, a computer's audio output consisted of little more than the occasional beep and the whirr of a hard drive, but as multimedia capabilities have increased sound has become a serious concern, and PC **speaker systems** have grown to reflect this. As more and more users are playing games, music and movies, tinny little speakers are rapidly giving way to impressive surround-sound systems.

The speakers that come with most systems will be fine for most basic needs, so if you can't be bothered with all this high-fidelity stuff, stick with them. And even if your PC didn't come with any you can buy a budget pair for the price of a decent bottle of wine. But if your primary concern is **playing music** – either from CDs or downloaded MP3 files – and you have a decent hi-fi nearby, you should consider hooking it up to your computer. As long as the hi-fi has a spare input (usually labelled **Aux**), this is the cheapest way to get quality sounds out of a PC. All you need is a cable to make the connection: usually a stereo minijack-to-phono lead will do the job. Serious gamers and DVD fans may not be satisfied with the paltry two channels that stereo provides, however, and should consider a **surround-sound speaker system** instead. Sometimes thrown in with multimedia packages, these systems have a number of small speakers (between two and six) with a subwoofer for bass, and they do an impressive job of reproducing the cinema experi-

ence, with bullets flying past your face and explosions rocking your swivel-chair. These setups usually come with an amplifier that doubles as a **Dolby Digital decoder**, turning the PC's signal into multichannel sound to distribute between the speakers. Before you spend loads of money on speakers, however, bear in mind that the sound quality is limited by the capabilities of your sound card (see p.55).

Microphones

Computer systems often ship with a **microphone**, which can be used with **voice recognition software** (you speak and the computer types) or for recording snippets of sound to play back or email to friends. Most computer microphones are pen-sized devices on little stands and can be plugged into the appropriate socket on the back of your machine, though sometimes they're built into a headset or integrated into another component such as a monitor or a Webcam. Most are pretty low quality and can be picked up very cheaply. There's little point in buying anything more expensive unless you want to use it for recording music – in which case bear in mind that the quality of the sound will be limited if you have a poor sound card (see p.55), and expensive mikes may require an adapter to connect to the PC.

Joysticks and gaming devices

If you want to get into gaming and you don't fancy hammering away with just a keyboard and mouse, you'll need either a **joystick** or some other device like a **gamepad** or **steering wheel**.

These come in a variety of shapes and sizes: some discreet, others outlandish.

Joysticks attach to your PC using either a USB or game port (which, if present, can be found on the back of your sound card). They both work fine, but USB devices are preferable because they can be hot swapped (see p.63). When you buy a joystick, look out for **Force Feedback** features, which deliver vibrations and jolts through the joystick handle. Also take note of the number of buttons a unit has, and how useful they actually are: pricier bits of kit may have throttle levers, a special pointer-button for panoramic views and so on. Most importantly, make sure the thing feels comfortable in your hand and looks as if it'll stand up to some punishment.

The other main option available is a **gamepad** – more commonly associated with consoles like the Sony PlayStation. PC gamepads connect to your system in the same way as joysticks, and there are a bemusing variety of styles, colours and button configurations on the market. Again, look out for Force Feedback devices, or you could even consider getting a unit with a built-in gravity sensor – such as Microsoft's Sidewinder Freestyle Pro – that detects the tiniest of tilting movements that you make with your hands: great for flight simulation games.

If driving games are more your thing then you should consider investing in a **wheel**. As before, Force Feedback is well worth checking out, as are units that come complete with foot pedals – though make sure the device looks solid enough to handle the pounding it'll most likely receive.

This is by no means the whole story, however. There are new

types of device coming onto the market all the time: some specifically designed for first-person action; others for strategy games; still others that come with a headset allowing you to trade insults with your multiplayer enemies. The list is endless.

MP3 Players

Today, more and more personal computers are functioning as music libraries, and with the ever-increasing size of standard hard drives it's possible to build up a respectable collection of digital music while leaving plenty of room for all your applications and other files. But the fun really starts when you get an **MP3 player**: a small Walkman-like device that can store a selection of your favourite tracks and play them back when you're on the move. Most devices will hold at least two hours (that's around 64MB of memory) of music downloaded from your PC, but others can store considerably more. You might consider a device that takes removable Flash memory modules to increase the amount of music you can transport, and you should also look out for units that accommodate a variety of compressed music formats – MP3 and WMA are the formats you're most likely to encounter. If you're on the move a lot you can get devices that are small and light, but you may well end up losing out on memory and battery life. Two of the best brands to look out for are Rio (**http://www.riohome.com**) and Sony (**http://www.sony.com**).

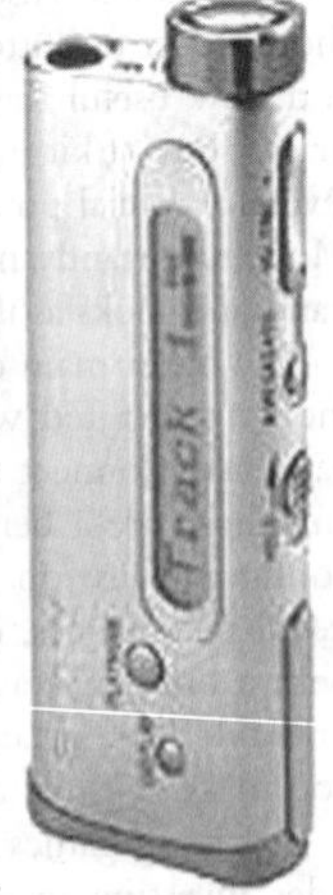

4

Setting up and switching on

turning on for the first time

So you've decided which machine to go for, parted with your money and carted the thing home. Now it's time to worry about setting up and switching on. In years gone by this was a complicated affair: ports and plugs required fiddly little screws, cables were unlabelled and the PC didn't so much spring to life as slowly stagger to its feet as you fed it a bewildering platter of floppy boot disks and encoded commands. These days everything's easy to plug in and machines generally come with their operating systems pre-installed, so all you need to do is turn the thing on. In fact, everything's so simple that there are only two things that you really have to concern yourself with before switching on: where are you going to put your PC? And what on earth are you going to do with all that polystyrene foam?

Finding your PC a home and settling it in

Chances are you've already decided where you want your computer to live, but there are a few things that you need to bear in mind when choosing a location for your new system. It may seem obvious, but make sure your PC sits on a flat, stable surface with an electrical power point nearby. If you plan to connect your PC to the Internet, you'll also need to be near a phone socket, though you can use a standard telephone extension cable to reach one further away if necessary. Also try to find a position for your computer with a constant (and preferably cool) temperature, out of direct sunlight and away from damp walls or condensation-prone windows.

A surprising number of computers get damaged by electrical surges caused by anything from dodgy wiring in the home to a bolt of lightning. To protect your machine it's worth getting a **surge protector** – these prevent spikes in the electrical flow reaching your kit, and can be bought from most computer stores built into a **4-way plug** especially suited to PC usage.

If your PC has arrived on a particularly cold day, give it some time to reach room temperature before switching on. And whatever the weather, make sure the vents and fans on your PC's case aren't covered: your machine will generate a lot of heat when running and even a few sheets of paper left over an air vent can cause a potentially damaging rise in temperature inside the case.

Plugging everything in

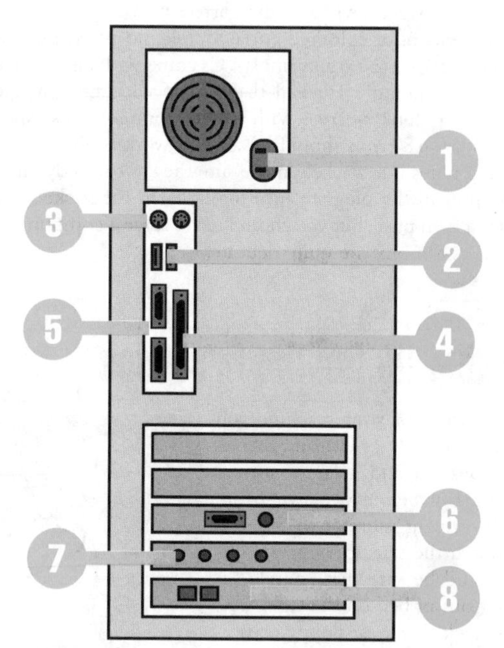

1. AC Power
2. USB Ports
3. Mouse and Keyboard Ports
4. Parallel Port
5. Serial Ports
6. Video Card Ports
7. Sound Card Connections
8. Modem

Plugging the monitor, keyboard, mouse and any other peripherals into a PC is surprisingly simple. Many of the sockets are labelled with little pictures and colour-coded to help you match the correct devices to the correct ports. And even if you don't have icons or coloured ports, connecting everything properly shouldn't be too tricky: most PCs come with an instruction manual containing a labelled diagram of what goes where. If yours didn't, don't worry – with a bit of common sense and the diagram on p.89 you should be able to work it all out. When inserting plugs into sockets, make sure they're correctly aligned, so the pins in the plugs fit into the holes in the sockets. Some require a firm push, but you should never force a computer connection as the pins are quite delicate.

Booting up for the first time

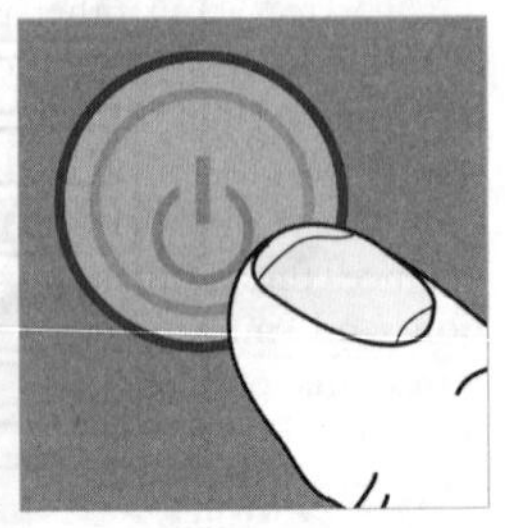

On the front of your machine you will see a couple of buttons: a small **reset button** and a larger **power button**. But before you switch on, switch on your monitor so that you can watch the startup sequence onscreen and be sure that your PC is getting out of bed on the right side. And check that your floppy drive is empty before lift-off, as a disk in the drive will confuse the PC when it tries to start up.

When you push the power button, you'll hear beeps and clicks and a whirring sound as the hard drive starts to do its thing. The cooling fans will be up and running, producing a continuous hum, little lights will be blinking and you'll see figures and specifications scroll by on-screen as your PC checks that all its components are present and correct. What you see next depends on whether or not you have Windows pre-installed. If you don't, all you'll see is some white text on a black background and you'll have to install the operating system yourself. Your computer should have come with instructions on how to do this, but if not, turn to p.238. If Windows is present, you'll see a welcome screen inviting you to follow a series of simple self-explanatory instructions to get your machine going for the first time. You'll need to read each instruction and then proceed by clicking the left mouse button where it says **Next** or **OK**. At some point you'll be asked to enter your name, and in Windows XP the names of any other people you want to register as "users" (you can always add more later). Type in the name you want the computer to know you by: it could be John, John Smith, King Arthur – it's your call. You'll also be given the option of entering a password. If you do enter one you'll have to type it in every time you turn on your machine, but if you're not worried about other people in your house accessing your files you may choose not to bother (and don't worry, all this can be changed later). After a couple more simple steps, you might also get a little tune and a box prompting you to "take a tour" – click **OK** if you want to and **Cancel** if you don't.

Once these instruction and information boxes are out of the way, everything should settle down and you'll see the basic Windows screen, which will look something like this picture:

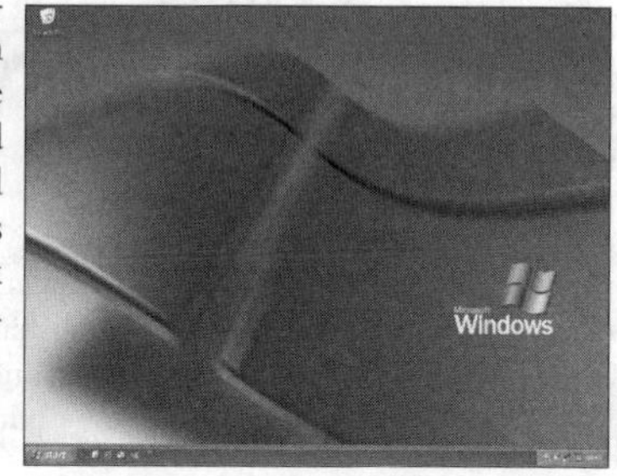

If you've got to this stage, then it's time to start exploring a brave new world of boxes, menus and icons – all of which is explained in Chapter 6 (p.104). But first, here's a couple of things you should know:

1 Shutting down In the same way that your system needs to unpack itself when you turn it on, it also needs a few seconds to put everything away before the power is switched off. This is why your PC should be **turned off via the Start menu** (see p.115), and not simply by using the power button or mains socket.

2 Activating Windows XP If your PC came installed with Windows XP, you will be required to **activate** it within fourteen days of switching your machine on – otherwise it will stop working until you do. This is a Microsoft anti-piracy initiative to stop any copy of XP being used by more than one per-

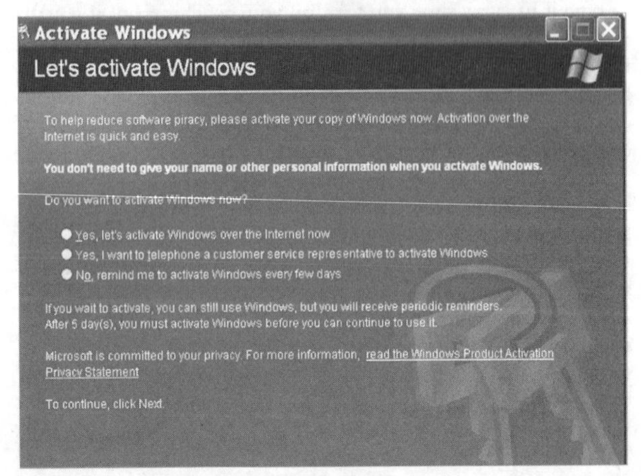

son. Activation doesn't require you to provide Microsoft with any personal information – not even your name – though during the activation process you can choose to register your details in order to receive updates and the like. To activate Windows XP, go to the **Start** menu, select **Programs** and click **Windows Activation**. If you have a phone line connected to your modem, you can just follow the wizard, and the in-built dialling program will connect to Microsoft and make the activation. If you don't have a phone line connected to your PC, click the **Telephone option** and you'll be given a phone number to call, allowing you to activate your copy with a real human being.

3 A floppy spanner in the works Sometimes when you start your machine you might be confronted by a foreboding message questioning the validity of the "system disk" in drive A (the floppy drive). Don't panic: this simply means that you left a floppy in the drive last time you used the machine. The PC gets confused because it detects the disk and assumes that it's found part of the bootup information, when in fact it's probably nothing more than a letter to Great-Aunt Edith. All you need to do is eject the disk, press the **Enter** key on your keyboard and the computer will continue as if nothing had happened.

4 It's stopped working! Computers can be rather temperamental, and sometimes they **crash** – temporarily freeze up and refuse to do anything at all. This can be very annoying, but don't worry: all PCs crash every so often and usually it's not the result of anything serious. Occasionally these problems can be resolved by pressing the **Esc** button on your keyboard, but usually you'll have to press the **Ctrl**, **Alt** and **Delete** keys simultaneously. This brings up a box with a list of all the things your PC is currently doing; if you've crashed, the top item on the list will probably have **Not Responding** written next to it. You'll be given the option at the bottom of the box of clicking **End Task**. Usually this will close the application you were using last; you may lose any unsaved work, but your machine will be back in action. Sometimes, though, this technique won't work, and you'll have to **reboot**, or **reset**, your PC – start up from scratch. This can be done either with the **reset button** on the front of the machine, or by pressing the magic **Ctrl+Alt+Delete** combination twice in quick succession. If you crash regularly, it could be that you have insufficient memory for the programs you're running. You could add some more RAM (see p.307), but there are also a few other tricks you can try first. See the chapter on Troubleshooting (p.297) for more information.

part two

working with Windows

5

Know your tools

using a mouse and keyboard

Now that you've got your system booted up, it's time to explore the Windows environment. Windows operating systems are pretty intuitive, so you can master the basics very quickly. In this part of the book you'll learn how to find your way around Windows, manage your programs and files, change the appearance of your work area, get online and much more. But before you dive in, you'll need to familiarize yourself with the tools that connect you to your PC: the mouse and keyboard.

The mouse

Whether you've got a basic two-button rodent or a sportier creature with a scroll wheel and extra buttons, all mice have the same basic function – they move a little arrow, or **pointer**, around the screen. But to get your pointer to do anything useful, you'll need to master some simple left- and right-button manoeuvres.

Left button

The most common move you will make with your mouse is the humble **click** – point to an item, like the Recycle Bin icon which should be on your screen, and quickly press then release your mouse's left button. The icon changes colour to show that it has been selected. Be careful not to move the mouse as you click, or you might select the wrong thing or accidentally move something. Now try a **double-click**. This is two clicks performed in quick succession, and generally makes an item spring into life. If you double-click the Recycle Bin icon, for example, it will expand to become an active window (to close it again click on the small "**x**" in the window's top-right corner). The left button is also used to **drag-and-drop** stuff. Point to an item on-screen, press and hold down the left mouse button and the object will stick to your pointer, allowing you to move it around. When you release the button, the pointer loses its stickiness and the object is released. Try dragging the Recycle Bin icon into the centre of the screen.

Right button

A few years ago the right button was pretty useless, but these days it's a powerful ally. The basic **right-click**, as if you hadn't guessed already, is a single click of your mouse's right button. Doing this almost always brings up a small menu of options, called a **mouse menu** (also known as a "shortcut" or "context"

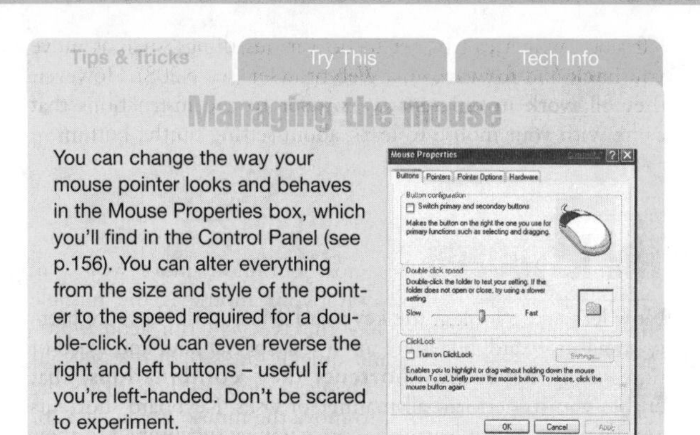

Managing the mouse

You can change the way your mouse pointer looks and behaves in the Mouse Properties box, which you'll find in the Control Panel (see p.156). You can alter everything from the size and style of the pointer to the speed required for a double-click. You can even reverse the right and left buttons – useful if you're left-handed. Don't be scared to experiment.

menu) relevant to the icon or place where you clicked. Try right-clicking the Recycle Bin icon, for example. This will yield a menu of options including **Open**, **Explore** and **Search**. You can either choose something from the menu by pointing to it and clicking the right or left button, or you can get rid of the menu by left-clicking anywhere else on the screen. You can also perform a **right-drag**: this is similar to a regular left-drag, but when you release your finger a mouse menu will appear asking you what you want to do with the object you've moved: **Copy Here**, **Move Here** and so on.

Scroll wheels and extra buttons

Many modern mice have a scroll wheel protruding from their tops, between the left and right buttons. This can be rolled and clicked to scroll down through the contents of a window (especially good for Web pages – hence they're often called "Web wheels"). Some mice also have extra buttons on their right and left sides, which can be set to do various things, such as move you **back** and **forward** in a Web browser (see p.208). However, they all work in different ways: refer to the instructions that came with your mouse to learn about setting up the buttons.

The keyboard

Now let's take a look at the keyboard. Most of the keys are pretty straightforward, but there are a few special keys and loads of time-saving **keyboard shortcuts** (**key combinations**) that enable you to perform all manner of tasks. Keyboard shortcuts are definitely worth learning – once you've succumbed to their charms you'll find it hard to believe you ever managed without them. To learn all the most useful shortcuts, check out the Tips and Tricks chapter (p.193). For now, let's take a look at the individual keys in the diagram on pp.102–103.

Notebook keyboards

Space is saved on notebooks by having a small keyboard, and by doubling-up the functions of certain keys. The numeric keypad, for example, is usually found among the regular alphanumeric keys rather than having its own distinct section. Normally, you hold down the **Fn** (Function) key if you want to use these numbers rather than the letters. Notebook keyboards can be rather fiddly to use, and many people find the touchpad even more annoying. For this reason, keyboard shortcuts (see p.193) can be are especially useful for notebook users.

1 **Esc** (Escape) Backs you out of whatever task you are currently performing. This is your first line of defence if your PC appears to have frozen or crashed.

2 **F keys** (Function Keys) These perform different shortcuts in different programs. F1 usually opens built-in "help" pages.

3 **Backspace** Deletes the previous character in a line of text.

4 **Delete** Banishes selected items to the Recycle Bin in Windows, and, in a line of text, deletes the character to the right of your "insertion point" (the vertical flashing line that shows you where you are in a document).

5 **Enter** or **Return** Opens a selected item; selects the highlighted button in a dialog box; and moves your insertion point down to start a new line of text.

6 **Cursors** These "arrow keys" allow you to navigate through menus, text, lists, tables, etc.

7 **Num Lock** (Number Lock) Transforms the number pad into a set of cursor and navigation keys (not, as it happens, a great deal of use). A little light on the keyboard will tell you whether Number Lock is currently on.

8 **Home** and **End** Moves you to the beginning or the end of a line of text – very useful when word processing.

9 **PgUp** (Page Up) and **PgDn** (Page Down) Lets you skip up and down a document in chunks, often page by page.

10 **Numeric Keypad** A calculator-like section useful for dealing with numbers. (Behaves like the cursor key section when Num Lock is off.)

11 **Ctrl** (Control) and **Alt** (Alternative) When held down in conjunction with various other keys on the keyboard, these

little gems can trigger more shortcuts than you can shake a stick at. **Ctrl+A**, for example, selects all items or text in a window or on the desktop – try it. (See p.193 for more.)

⑫ **Windows Key** Found on most modern keyboards, this key launches the Windows Start menu. It can also be combined with other keys to trigger a bunch of shortcuts (see p.193).

⑬ **Mouse Menu Key** Similar to a right-click of the mouse, this relatively new key yields a floating mouse menu (or "shortcut menu") for any object or word that your pointer is hovering over at the time.

⑭ **Shift** When the shift key is held down, any letter key will yield a capital letter, while a number or symbol key will result in whatever symbol is on the top half of the key.

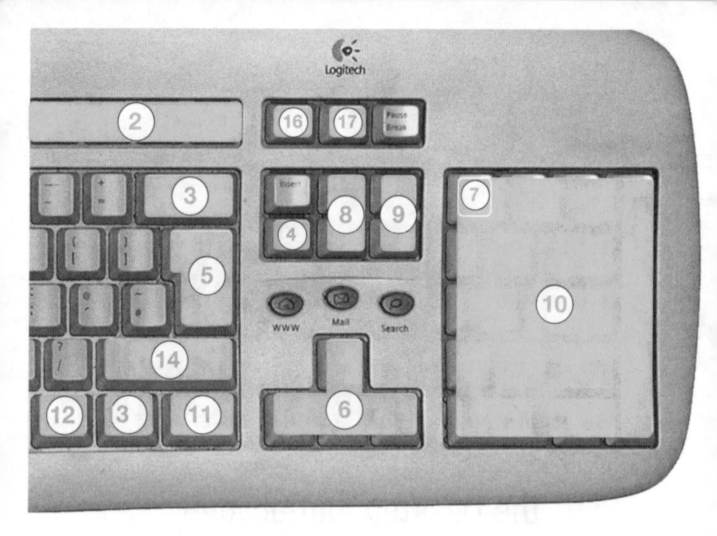

⑮ **Caps Lock** If you press this once, all the letters will come out as capitals until you press it again. Usually there's a little light either on the key or above the number pad to show you whether Caps Lock is currently on.

⑯ **Prt Sc SysRq** (known as the Print Screen button) Sends an image of whatever's on the screen to the Windows Clipboard (see p.183), which can then be pasted into a document or email.

⑰ **Scroll Lock** Turns Scroll Lock on and off. In certain programs, such as Microsoft Excel, if it's on it means that the arrow keys will move the whole page around. As with Caps Lock, there's usually a little light above the number pad to let you know whether it's selected.

6

The Windows environment

the Desktop and beyond

So there it lies before you, the Windows work environment. It may look unhelpful or intimidating, but the fact of the matter is this: if you can get your head around the basic principles of Windows – it's a metaphor for the way things are laid out – then everything else becomes relatively straightforward.

The Desktop

The main section of the screen is called the **Desktop**. Depending on which version of Windows you are running, it

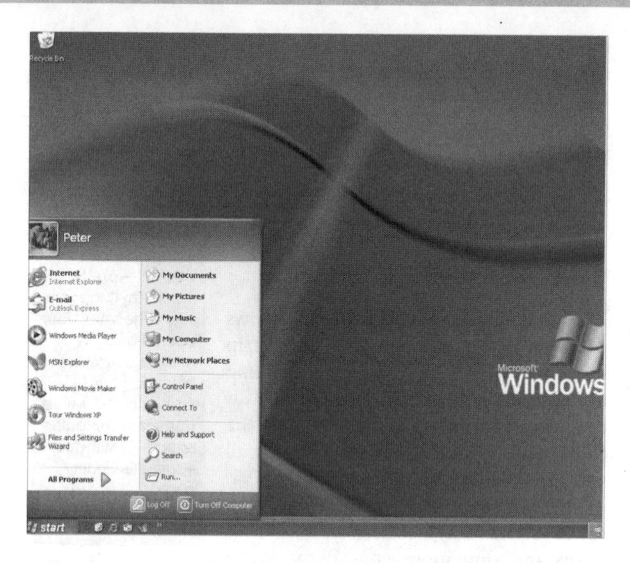

will either be a big blank space or a colourful image (to learn how to change the image, see p.136). The Desktop on a PC isn't that different from a real desktop: it's an open space, with tools nearby, on which you can spread out your work. And just like in the real world, some people have very tidy Desktops, while others' are cluttered and messy. On your Desktop there will be one or more **labelled pictures** called **icons** – which are like ignition buttons that, when double-clicked, start a program or open a document.

Icons on the Desktop can be **dragged-and-dropped** – moved around the screen as you see fit. Try it: click and hold your left mouse button over the Recycle Bin, for example, move it to a blank area in the centre of the screen and let go of the button. Should things get too messy, a right-click on any blank section of the Desktop will yield a mouse menu of options to help you realign and arrange your scattered flock.

> **What is a window?**
>
> Just like those things made of glass, windows on a PC offer you a view: of a document, a photo, a page on the Internet – pretty much anything you like. Whenever you open a document or start a new piece of work, your PC presents you with a framed rectangular space – a **window** – that fills either part or all of the screen.

The Taskbar

The most important part of the Windows environment is the grey or blue strip known as the **Taskbar**, which runs along the bottom of the screen. At its left end is the **Start button** – click this to open the **Start menu**, which contains icons for all your programs and more. At the right end of the Taskbar is the **Notification area** (or **System tray**), where you'll see a **clock** and some more icons. Between the two you'll see areas for **Quick Launch** icons and **window buttons** (one for each open window). Let's look at these elements in turn.

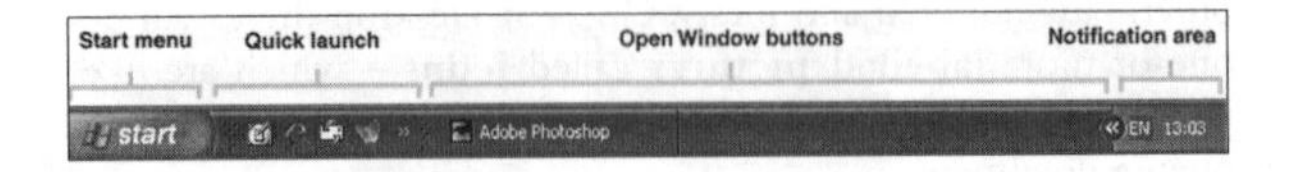

The Start button and Start menu

The Start button is, as you might imagine, a good place to start. Click on it and up pops the all-powerful **Start menu**, which is

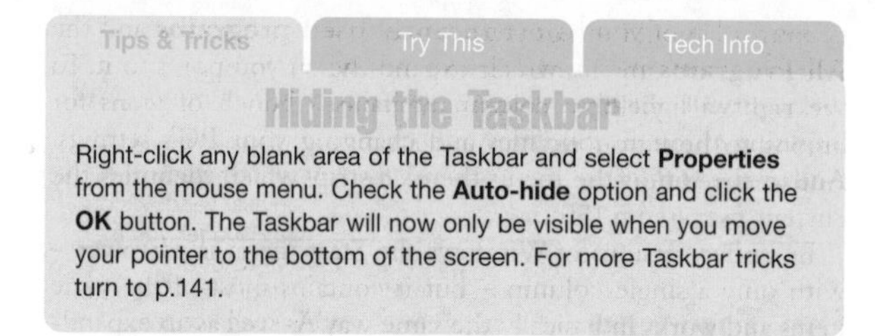

Hiding the Taskbar

Right-click any blank area of the Taskbar and select **Properties** from the mouse menu. Check the **Auto-hide** option and click the **OK** button. The Taskbar will now only be visible when you move your pointer to the bottom of the screen. For more Taskbar tricks turn to p.141.

full of icons for programs, document folders and so on. You simply move your mouse pointer to the item you want and click to select it. If you hover over an item with an arrow to its right, you will be offered a further submenu of choices – and so on, until you run out of arrows.

The Start menu is different in Windows XP from all other versions of Windows. In XP, programs are dealt with in a white column on the left, which includes **Internet** and **email** appli-

cations, a list of your **most recently used programs** and the **All Programs** menu, which expands when you point to it. To the right, a light-blue column contains a bunch of icons for browsing through your files and changing your PC's settings. And at the top of the menu there's a strip, which identifies the current user (see p.150).

In earlier versions of Windows the Start menu is narrower – with only a single column – but it contains most of the same items and works in basically the same way. As well as an expanding menu containing all your programs, you'll find three others, including **Documents** – which houses icons for the files you most recently worked on.

Quick Launch

Next along the Taskbar, you'll see the **Quick Launch area**. Because the Taskbar – unlike the Desktop – is always visible, it makes sense to use a section of it to store icons for your most commonly used programs or files. Some program shortcuts are here by default, but you can add and remove items at will (see p.143). When you open Windows for the first time you will most likely see: a blue-cornered square, which usefully minimizes all the windows currently open to let you view the Desktop; a blue letter "**e**" that launches Microsoft's standard web browser, **Internet Explorer** (see p.208); and a little envelope graphic that starts the **Outlook Express** email program (see p.218). You may also find a colourful butterfly that launches Microsoft's new easy-to-use **MSN Explorer browser** (see p.209).

Open window buttons

Any window that you have running will be assigned a corresponding button on the Taskbar. This is what the Taskbar is all about, really: letting you see what tasks, windows or programs are currently running. Try opening **My Computer** (don't worry about what it's for just yet) from the Start menu or Desktop. Not only does a window spring open, but a button appears on the Taskbar. Now summon another window by opening **My Documents** from the Start menu or Desktop - and another button will appear on the Taskbar. The My Documents window will probably obscure some or all of the My Computer window, and its button on the Taskbar will be indented to show that it's the **active window**, ready to receive instructions. Here's where the Taskbar comes into its own. To bring the My Computer back into view simply click on its Taskbar button: it will rise to the surface and become the active (or "foreground") window.

In Windows XP, when the Taskbar becomes full of window buttons they are automatically **grouped together by type**. For example, if you're surfing the Internet and you have lots of Web page windows open, you may suddenly find that they are all represented by just one button on the Taskbar. Click it and a little menu will pop up containing a list of all the separate windows – select one to bring it to the front.

Notification area

The final stop on our tour of the Taskbar is the **Notification area** – traditionally referred to as the **System tray**. This section contains a **clock** and a selection of icons (in XP you'll need to click the little button with the double arrow to see them all). Many of the icons represent system utilities, such as a virus checker, and they let you know that – while you can't see them running like normal programs – they're doing valuable work somewhere in the background. Usually you can interact with the items in the notification area by single-, double- or right-clicking the icons.

What does this do?

If you do fancy investigating a mysterious icon on the Taskbar – or almost any element of the Windows environment – just let the mouse hover over it and a small message, called a **Tool Tip**, will pop up. In the case of an icon you'll be given its name, while other objects deliver either a clue to their purpose or some other handy snippet of information – hover over the clock, for example, and the date will appear. Also try right-clicking an item you're not sure about. This will bring up a menu of choices, generally with one highlighted in bold type. This is called the **default** choice, and tells you what will happen if you double-click on the item.

The window

So, a window is a rectangular space that fills some or all of your screen, displaying anything from a list of files to a Web page. And once a window is open there are all sorts of things you can do to it.

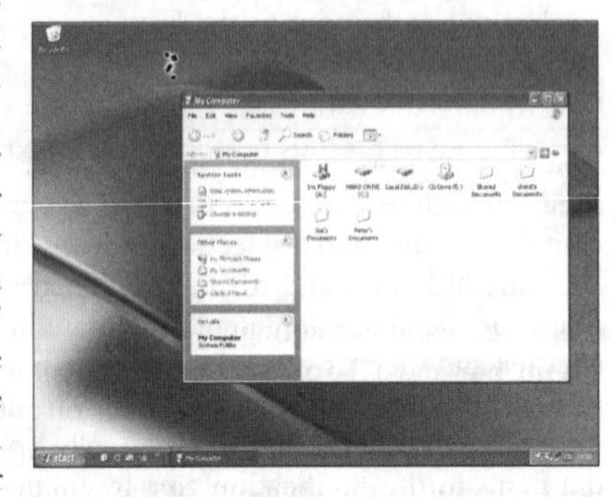

Try opening **My Documents**, for example. A window will appear with "My Documents" written on the **Title bar** – the blue strip at the top. You can move your window around the screen by **dragging**: move your mouse pointer over the Title bar, press and hold the left mouse button, and off you go. And try pointing to one of the window's corners or edges: your pointer will become double-headed, allowing you to resize and reshape the frame.

In the top right-hand corner of your window you'll see three little buttons. The left one **minimizes** the window – press it and the window will vanish, but its button on the Taskbar will remain. Though you can't see it, the window hasn't actually closed, it's just been hidden – and a single click of the Taskbar button will bring it back into view. The middle button **maximizes** the window to fill the screen, and then becomes a **restore** button that will return the window to its previous size and shape when clicked. You can also maximize, or restore, a window by double-clicking its Title bar. The final button – the one with the "**x**" on it – **closes** the window.

If a window isn't big enough to display all its contents, you will see **sliders** (or **scrollbars**) along the bottom or down the right-hand side. Click their little arrow buttons or drag the grey sliders to reveal more.

As already mentioned, you can open many windows on the screen at once – and as you open them they stack up on your Desktop like sheets of paper on a desk. You can click on any part of a window, or press its button on the Taskbar to bring it to the top of the pile.

Toolbars, Menu bars and Address bars

Nearly all windows contain two sections under the Title bar: a **Menu bar** and a **Toolbar**. The Menu bar contains a number of words, each of which yields a menu of options when clicked. The Toolbar contains buttons and icons for performing various tasks relevant to the contents of the window.

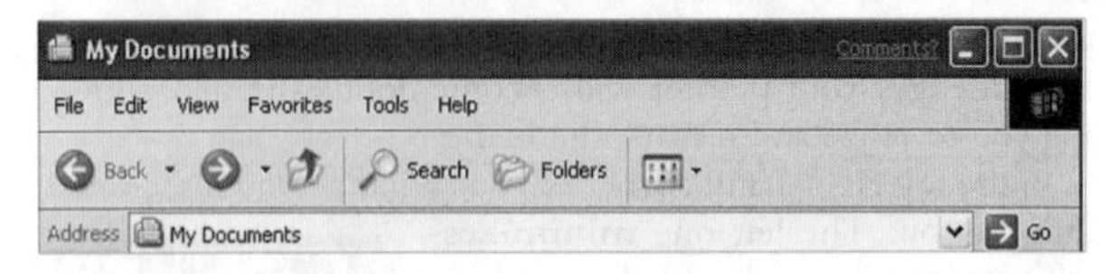

Windows for navigating the Internet or the contents of your PC also include a third "bar", called the **Address bar**. This provides information about the location of whatever the window contains: an **Internet address** if you're viewing a Web page, and a **name** or **pathname** (see p.219) if you're viewing the contents of a folder or disk drive.

Basic elements

Now you understand the architecture of Windows, let's take a look at some of the items you'll come across on the Start menu or the Desktop.

My Computer

This essential item, which resides on the Start menu in Windows XP and on the Desktop in older Windows versions, opens a window displaying an icon for each of your computer's disk drives, allowing you to browse through all the files on your system. For more on browsing files and using My Computer, turn to p.123.

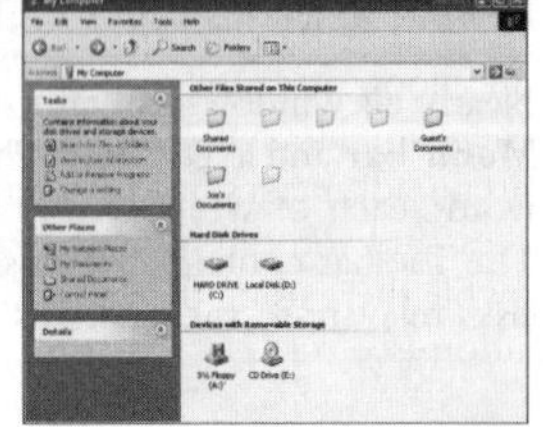

XP's classic view

If you're a Windows XP user who pines for the good old days, you can choose to view your Start menu with its "classic" single-column look. Right-click the **Start** button and select **Properties**. When the dialog box appears, select the **Classic Start menu** option and hit **Apply**. This will also return various icons – like My Computer and My Documents – to the Desktop, where they lived in years gone by. If you want the icons back on the Desktop but like the new XP Start menu, right-click the Desktop, select **Properties** and under the **Desktop** tab click **Customize Desktop**. In the **Desktop Items** box that appears you can choose exactly which icons you want displayed. For more on changing how Windows works and looks, see p.136.

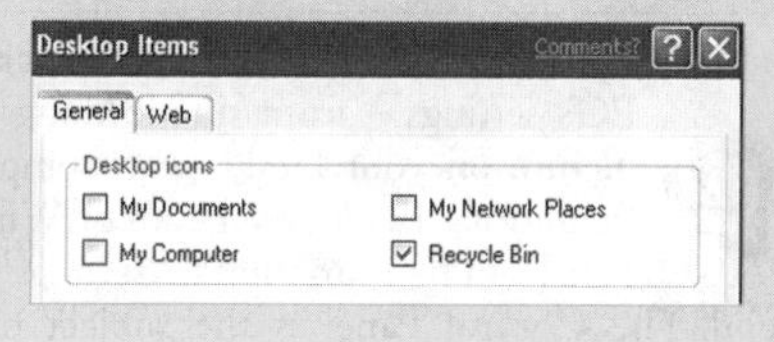

My Documents

My Documents is the suggested home for your filing system – a place where you can organize and keep tabs on all your work, pictures, letters, music or anything else. Though you can choose to store your files anywhere you like, My Documents has certain advantages: it's very easy to access and you can instantly "send" any file there using the right mouse button (see p.132).

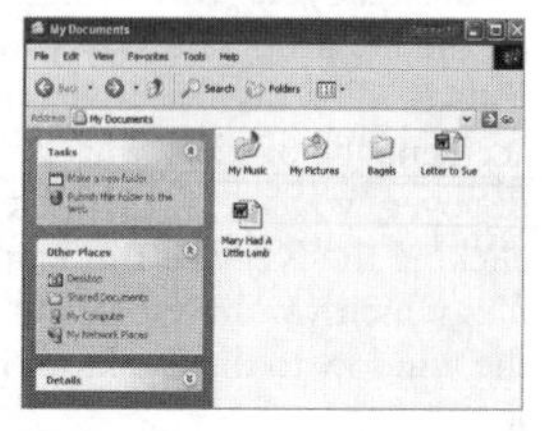

My Music and My Pictures

These folders live within My Documents, but because they're so useful, icons for them also appear on the Start menu in Windows XP and Me, allowing quicker access. Again, you can store music and picture files wherever you like, but these folders are very handy – and in XP they include links for various relevant tasks such as playing music files, shopping for music online and sending digital photos away to be printed.

Control Panel

The Control Panel is where you go to make changes to your PC's settings – from simple things like changing the picture on your Desktop to complex hardware configurations. In older versions of Windows, the Control Panel can be found in the Settings section of the Start menu. The Control Panel is the subject of Chapter 10 (see p.156).

Recycle Bin

When you delete a file on your PC it generally doesn't disappear completely, but is instead banished to the **Recycle Bin**, which lives on the Desktop. This way, you can recover files that were erased accidentally or that you later discover you need. Double-clicking the Recycle Bin icon opens a window displaying all the files which you have deleted. To rescue a file, simply drag it from the window to the Desktop or somewhere else. Alternatively, you

Recycle Bin

Recycle Bin

can use **Restore** to move some or all of the files back to wherever they were when you deleted them. You'll find this function in the mouse menu when you right-click a file.

If you find that you are running out of room on your hard drive, emptying the Recycle Bin might free up some space. To do this, open the Recycle Bin window and select **Empty Recycle Bin** from the file menu or link on the left. You can also right-click the bin's icon on the Desktop and select Empty Recycle Bin from the mouse menu, though this way you don't get a last chance to check which files you're permanently deleting. When the bin contains files its icon is full of rubbish and when it's empty, so is the icon – nice touch.

Turn off and Shut Down

At the bottom of the Start menu is **Turn off computer,** or **Shut Down** as it's called in older versions of Windows. This is where you go to switch your computer off, giving Windows a chance to pack everything neatly away – turning off your machine by any other method is a bad idea. Click this button and you'll be presented with a few choices. As well as choosing to **Turn off**, you can select **Restart** (which turns off then restarts your computer) or **Stand By**, which puts your PC into an energy-saving mode until you press any key to get things going again.

In Windows Me you'll be offered the option to **Hibernate** – this shuts downs your system but retains a memory of all the programs and windows you were using, so that next time you switch on you can pick up where you left off. And in Windows 98 you could choose **Restart in MS-DOS mode**, an old-school techie option that yields a black screen with a **command prompt** (see p.166) awaiting your instructions.

Log Off

If more than one user is set up to use your system (see p.150), clicking here lets you close or hide your tasks and settings to allow another user to log on. In XP this process is pretty quick thanks to the **Fast User Switching** feature (see p.153), but in earlier Windows versions the machine basically has to shut down and restart before offering a new user the chance to log on. If you're the only person who uses your computer, you need never worry about this option.

Help and Support

This feature – just called **Help** in earlier versions of Windows – launches the Windows help pages, which you can browse or search for information about using and troubleshooting Windows.

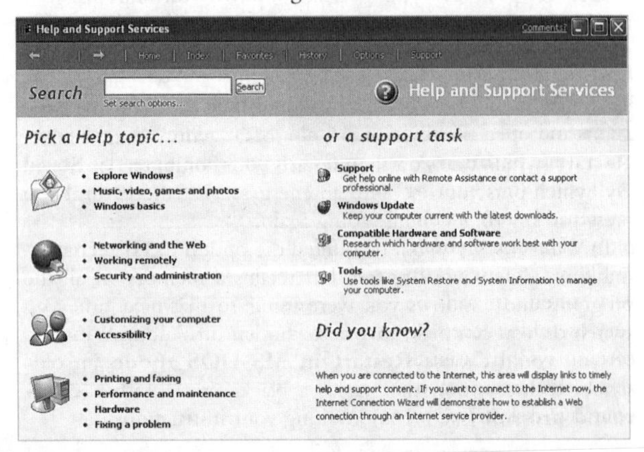

Search

Search - or **Find** in some earlier versions of Windows - helps you find files on your computer (see p.127). You can even use it to look for pages on the Internet (see p.211), though it's not necessarily the best way to go about it.

Connect to

This XP icon takes you directly to the section of the Control Panel that deals with network and Internet connections. For more on networks see p.224, and for the lowdown on Internet connections turn to p.205.

My Network Places

If you have home network set up, use this icon to browse the other computers. For information about setting up a network, turn to Chapter 16.

Run

This Start menu item opens a box in which you can start programs and open files by either typing their address on the computer (the **pathname**: see p.129) or in some cases by typing their name (try entering "notepad", for example). Though you're unlikely to use Run very often, it can be very useful for accessing certain system utilities and kick-starting uncooperative disk drives.

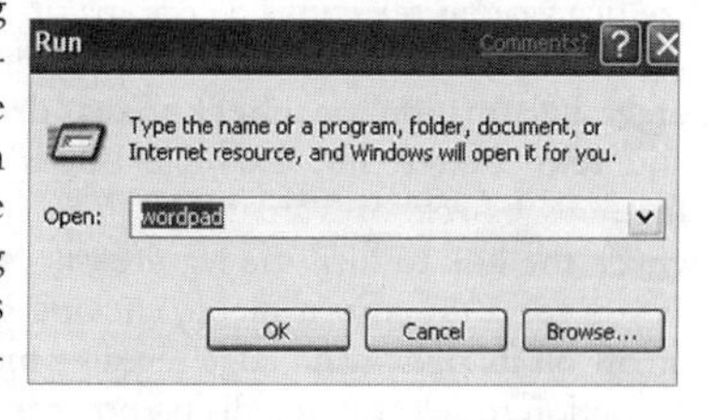

Dialog boxes

Computers, being essentially pretty stupid, can't figure out too much without your help, so they often need to ask questions: "Are you sure you want to do that?" "Do you want to save your work before turning off your computer?" "Where do you want to save the file?" And so on. But computers aren't very good at having verbal conversations – yet – so Windows uses another method to talk to us: the **dialog box**.

The most basic dialog boxes simply pass on information. They pop up, tell you something, and all you have to do is click the **OK** button. Most, however, are **question dialog boxes**, like the one shown here. These present you with a question and a number of answer buttons, most commonly **OK**, **Yes** and **No**. Often the dialog box will have a **Cancel** button as well; this closes the box and takes you back to where you were before it appeared. Some dialog boxes also have an **Apply** button, which sets in motion any changes that you've made in the box without actually closing it. This is very useful if you want to try out various selections before making a final decision.

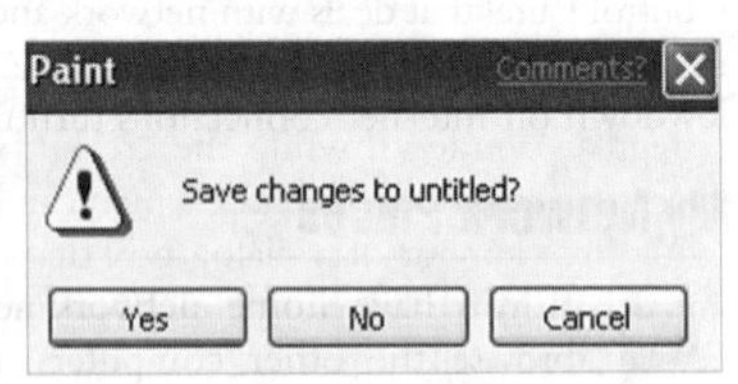

Some dialog boxes are more complicated, allowing you to enter information via **checkboxes**, **dropdown menus**, **tabs** and **text boxes**. The example opposite displays all of these methods. Checkboxes are used to turn certain features on or off: check the box to turn the feature on; uncheck it to turn it off. If you see a dropdown menu, clicking the downward-pointing arrow on its right-hand edge reveals a menu of options; click on an option to select it. If a dialog box has tabs at the top, each tab brings up a different "sheet" of options.

Tips & Tricks | Try This | Tech Info

Answer with keys

In any dialog box, one of the option buttons is highlighted – either by a little dotted line or a dark edge. Hitting **Enter** on the keyboard is the same as clicking the highlighted option. You can highlight the other option buttons in turn by repeatedly pressing the **Tab** key. If you hold **Shift** while you press Tab, you'll cycle through the options in the reverse order.

Many dialog boxes also have two buttons in their top-right corner. The one marked with an "**x**" closes the box (just like in a regular window), while the "**?**" button will add a question mark to your mouse pointer which can be used to get extra help with any element of a dialog box that's puzzling you. Just click on the thing you're not sure about and a frame containing an explanation will appear.

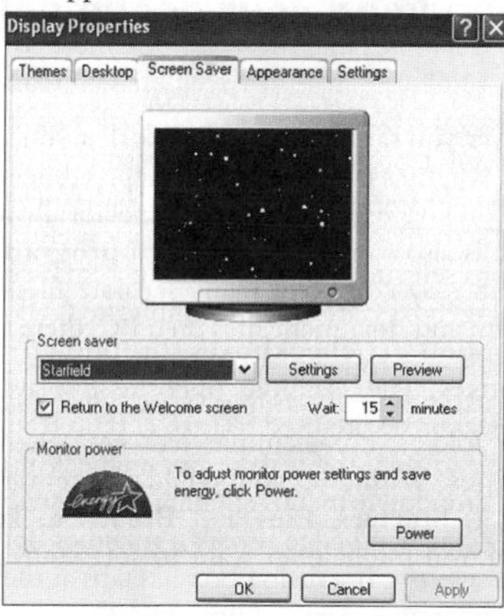

7

Files and folders

managing your documents

Whenever you save a piece of work that you've created on a PC, whether it's a letter, photo, spreadsheet or anything else, you save it as a **file** – more specifically, a **document file**. Software is also stored in files, called **program files**, but a single program may consist of many separate files. If you listed all the program and document files on a PC, there would be literally thousands – so to keep everything tidy, files are organized into **folders**. And to make things even tidier, folders can live within other folders. For example, let's say you have a folder named **Recipes**. Within it you could create various further folders such as **Starters**, **Pies** and **Breads** to keep all your recipe files in. You might then want to sort your bread recipes into folders for **Bagels** and **Loaves**. You will soon have developed a multi-layered folder system, which can be browsed like a family tree.

In this chapter you'll learn all about working with files and folders – how to browse through, find, open, save, move, copy, arrange and delete them. With this knowledge your PC will be a tidier, more efficient and much less confusing place to work and play.

Folders

Most folders are represented by icons that look like plain yellow paper folders, though some have little pictures on them. Double-clicking on any folder icon displays its contents in a window.

The folder that you will probably have the most contact with is **My Documents** – a convenient place to keep all your document files. This folder can be accessed via the Start menu or the Desktop, depending on your version of Windows.

Files

File icons often look like pieces of paper with folded corners, but they come in all sorts of colours and styles.

When you double-click a file, Windows attempts to open it, and to do so requires the help of a program: if you try to open a music file, for example, Windows will need to open a suitable music application to play it back. An icon's appearance gives you some clue about the type

Tech Info | Tips & Tricks | Try This

File extensions

Every file has a special identification tag as part of its name – like a surname – called a **file extension**, though in Windows they're frequently hidden to keep things tidy. Image files from digital cameras, for example, are usually bitmaps (see p.76), identified by the extension **.bmp**. So if you save a digital photo as "Picture of George", your computer will actually save it as "Picture of George.bmp". You can choose to unhide extensions in the **View** tab of **Folder Options**, which you'll find in the Control Panel (or under **Settings** in Windows 98's **Start** menu). This dialog box also has a **File Types** tab; click here and you can change the default program you want Windows to use when opening different types of files.

of file you're looking at and what program Windows will try to open it with – a Media Player file features the Media Player icon, for example. But if you want to know exactly what type of file you're looking at, right-click it and select **Properties** from the mouse menu. (If you're looking at a list of files in a window, selecting **Details** from the **View** menu will also display the file types.) Some types of file are very common and are recognized by many applications, while others will open only in the program that created them.

Anonymous files

If you try and open a type of file that isn't associated with a particular program you'll probably be presented with the **Open with** dialog box, which asks you to select a program for Windows to try opening the file with. If you know the file contains an image, try a couple of image programs from the list – but you might not get very far. One possible solution is to drag the file onto an open Web browser window such as Internet Explorer (you don't have to be online to do this). You won't be able to edit anything, but you may be able to view any text or images in the document.

Exploring your computer

Among the most important elements in Windows are the special **Explorer** windows, which, in their various guises, can be used to browse the contents of your computer. Every window that displays files, folders or disk drives is in fact an Explorer window – for example, the windows you get by opening My Computer, My Documents or the Recycle Bin.

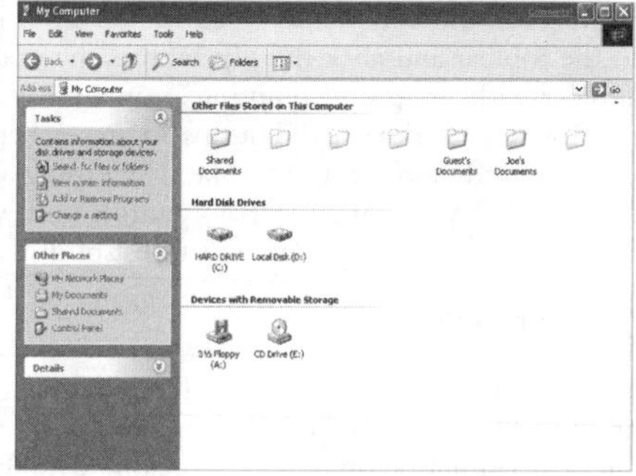

To get used to Explorer windows, open **My Computer** from the Start menu (or the Desktop in older versions of Windows). A window will pop up containing icons that represent all the disk drives on your PC and possibly some folders too. The number and type of drives listed depends on your system, but you'll most likely see a floppy drive labelled **A:**, a hard drive labelled **C:**, and a CD drive labelled **D:**.

In Windows XP you'll also see a section on the left of the window that contains links to other places on your computer – such as My Documents and the Control Panel – and various information and "tasks" relating to any item selected in the window.

Double-clicking any one of the drive icons or folders will display its contents. Try double-clicking **C:** to view the contents of your hard drive, which is also known as your **Local Disk** (if XP questions your selection, click **Show the contents of this drive** from the blue **System Tasks** menu on the left). You'll probably see a number of folders, including **Program Files** and **Windows**. Again, if you click on these folders, their contents will be displayed in the window.

To "back out" of a folder – go up one level in the tree – go to the toolbar and click the **Up** button, the one that looks like a folder with an upward-pointing arrow on it. You can also click the **Back** and **Forward** buttons to move between windows you've already looked in (just like when using a Web browser – see p.208). Try clicking the Back button until you get back to the My Computer window with its list of disk drives.

Different views

When you're looking at a list of files or drives, various options are available to change how they are displayed. From the toolbar click the last button on the right (the one with the little coloured square on it), and a menu of options will drop down offering such items as **Icons**, **List**, **Details**, **Tiles** and **Thumbnails**. Try clicking the various options to see which you prefer.

The folder tree

In any Explorer window you can choose to view another column down the left-hand side of the window. Called the

Explorer Bar, this column can perform various tasks, the most useful of which is displaying the folder tree (or "directory tree"), which provides an overview of everything on your system. To view the folder tree, click the **Folders** icon on the toolbar – or in earlier versions of Windows click the **View** menu and select **Explorer** Bar then **Folders**.

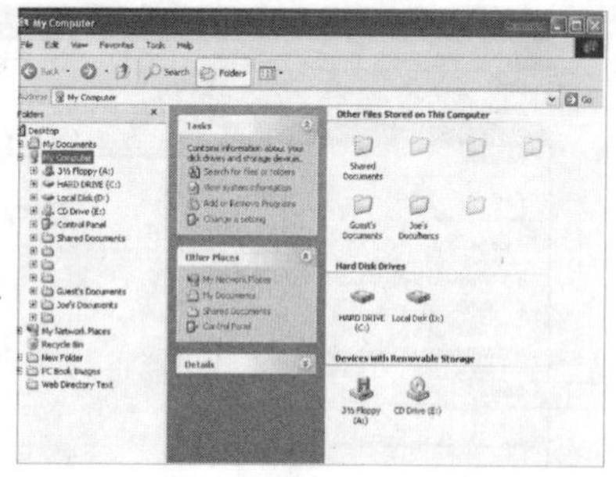

The folder tree is a graphic representation of your folders and drives, and it works a little like a family tree. Any folder or drive that contains other folders is known as a **parent folder**, and will have a little plus sign next to it. Clicking on the plus sign "opens up" the folder or drive so that you can see its contents; once open, the plus sign turns into a minus symbol which can be clicked to "collapse" the folder. If you click any folder in the folder tree, its contents will appear in the main section of the window. And if you click the Desktop icon that resides at the top of the tree you'll see all the items on your Desktop.

The folder tree is great for seeing the bigger picture, and it's also very handy for moving files around (see p.131).

Saving files

When you open a program and start working on a new document, it doesn't actually become a file until you **save** it. In

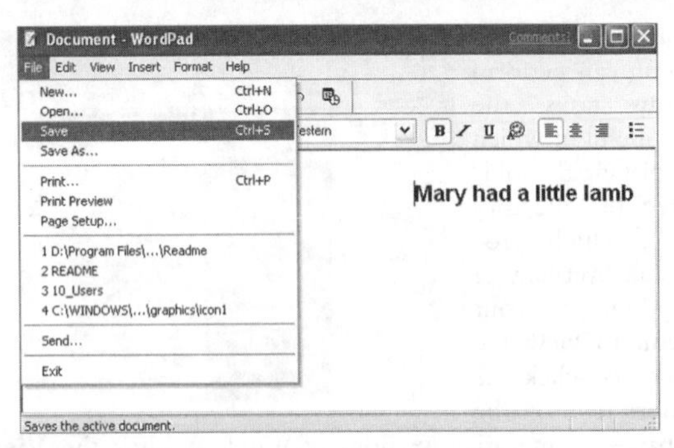

practically all Windows applications you can save a new document by clicking **Save** in the dropdown **File** menu on the Menu bar. This will bring up a **Save As** box.

This little box allows you to choose where you want to save your piece of work and what you want to call it. You navigate to the place where you want to save in the same way that you browse through files in Explorer windows – double-clicking on folders and using the **Up** button – or by using the **Save in** dropdown menu. Once you've found the place where you want to save your document, give it a name by typing in the **File name box** and click the **Save** button.

In the Save As window you'll also usually see a **Save as type** dropdown menu, which allows you to choose a file format from a list of the file types supported by the program you're using. You won't need to use this menu for most saves, but it sometimes comes in very handy. For example, if you write a document in a modern word processor and include some pictures, you could choose **Text Only** from the **Save as type** menu. This would lose the pictures, but the document could then be opened on any computer – including one without a decent word processing program.

Tips & Tricks | Tech Info | Tips & Tricks

Create and save a document

Go to **Start**, **Programs** then **Accessories** and click **WordPad**. This will open the simple word processor that is built into Windows. Type yourself a message and then select **Save** from the **File** menu. From the **Save in** dropdown menu, select **Desktop**, type "Trial Document" as the **File name** and then press the **Save** button. Close the program, and you should find your Trial Document sitting on the Desktop. Double-click it and the document should open again.

Save vs Save As

If you open a file that you saved earlier and make some changes to it, you'll have two saving options – **Save** or **Save As** – both of which you'll find in the **File** menu. If you click **Save** you'll overwrite the old version with the new version. But if you want to save the altered document without replacing the older version, click **Save As**: this will open the Save As box, and you can save the new version with a new name or a different file type.

Searching for files

Sometimes you may want to open a file but have no idea where it is – if you saved a document as "Letter to Sue", for example, but you can't remember where you put it. Don't worry: you can get Windows to search for it. To open the Windows search utility, open the **Start** menu and click **Search** (**Search** then **Files or Folders** in Windows Me; **Find** then **Files or Folders** in Windows 98). You can alternatively click the Search icon on the toolbar of an Explorer window, which looks like a little magnifying glass hovering over a globe.

The search utility looks different in the various versions of Windows, but they work in a roughly similar way – you enter information about the file, usually its name, and click the **Search** (or **Find**) button. If you can't remember what the file you're searching for was called, explore the various other search options. You could use the **Containing text** option to search for a word or phrase contained in the document itself (be warned, though – this can take some time), the **date** the file was created or modified, or look for its **type** or **size**.

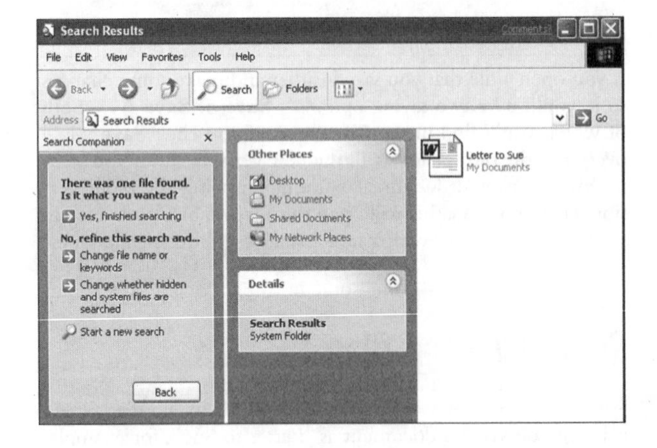

Windows will start trawling through your files, displaying each one that matches any part of the name you typed, along with its location (expressed as a **pathname**: see the box below). If the locations don't appear, select **Details** from the **View** menu.

Tech Info | Tips & Tricks | Try This

File locations

Though you usually select a file by clicking on icons until you reach it, you may sometimes be asked for the **pathname** of a file – its exact address. For example, when you use Windows to search for a file, the location of each item found will be displayed in a format similar to this:

C:\Windows\Desktop\Letters\Letter to Sue.doc

The letter at the beginning tells you the drive where the file is located, and each backslash refers to a folder. In full, then, the above address tells you that the file **Letter to Sue.doc** is in the folder **Letters**, which is in the folder called **Desktop**, which is in the folder **Windows**, which is on the **C** drive (the hard drive).

If the file you're looking for is found, you can double-click it to open it from there – though you may want to make a note of its location so you can find it more easily next time or move it to a more sensible place.

Doing a full search of your hard drive can take quite a while, so you can limit your search to a particular folder or drive in the **Look in** dropdown menu (sometimes part of the **advanced** options in Windows XP).

Organizing files

Just because a file is saved in one place, it doesn't mean it's stuck there for ever. You can delete files, move them around, duplicate them or create a new folder to put them in – and all with a few clicks of the mouse.

Renaming files

You can change the name of a file or folder very easily: simply right-click it and select **Rename** from the mouse menu. Type in the new name, hit **Enter** and the job's done. Alternatively, single-click the icon, click its name and you're ready to type.

Deleting files

As was explained in the previous chapter, when you delete a file you don't usually get rid of it completely but instead send it to the **Recycle Bin** – which is where it will remain until you either decide to retrieve it or "empty" the bin, erasing the files within (see p.115). There are four main ways to send a file to the Recycle Bin: you can drag it there using your mouse; you can right-click on it and select **Delete** from the mouse menu; you can select the file with a single-click and then press the **Delete** key on your keyboard; or you can select it and press the **Delete** button on a window toolbar. If for some reason you don't want to send a file to the Recycle Bin but decide to erase it completely, you can select the file and press the **Shift** and

Tips & Tricks | Tech Info | Try This

Selecting multiple files

It is often useful to select more than one file at the same time – once they're selected you can move, delete or open them all in one go. This is easily done with your mouse and the Control key on your keyboard: hold down **Control**, click on each of the files you want to select and then release the key. Another technique, useful if you're selecting lots of files that are next to each other, is to hold down the **Shift** key on your keyboard and click the first and last files that you want to select – all the ones in between will become highlighted too.

Delete keys on your keyboard simultaneously. Either way, you will be presented with a dialog box asking you to confirm the action.

Moving files around

Moving files and folders around is almost as easy as deleting them. One technique is simply to drag a file from one place to another. This works fine, but only if you can see the file and the place you want to drag it at the same time. This is no problem using the **folder tree** view (see p.124): you can view the file you want to move in the right-hand section of the window and drag it over to its new location on the left, as shown in the illustration.

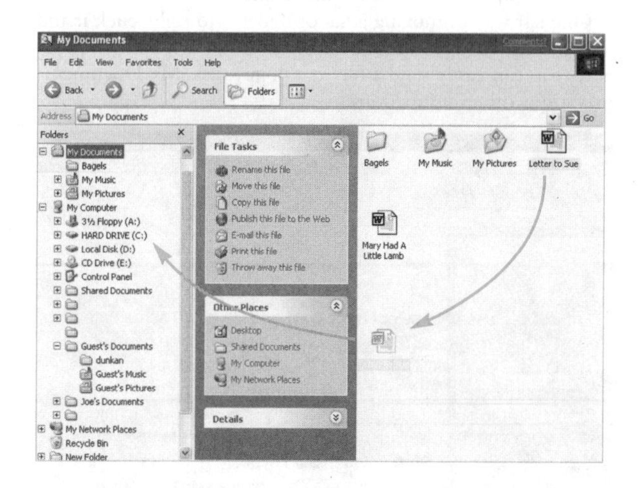

There are various other ways to move files around. In Windows XP you can select one or more files in an Explorer window and click the **Move this file** link on the left-hand side: a box will pop up in which you can navigate to the folder where you want the file to go. Alternatively, you can use the **Cut**, **Copy** and **Paste** commands, which you'll find in the **Edit** menu or toolbar of an Explorer window or in the right-click mouse menu. Select one or more files, click **Cut** and the selected file icons will become faint. Then navigate to wherever you want to put them (by double-clicking on folders and using the **Up** button) and click **Paste**. The file will appear in its new location. If you want to duplicate a file or folder, simply select it and click **Copy**. Then navigate to the point where you want the duplicate copy to appear and click **Paste**.

One last way of moving a file or folder is to right-click it and select **Send to** from the mouse menu (as shown below). From here, you can easily send a file to a floppy disk, My Documents or various other destinations.

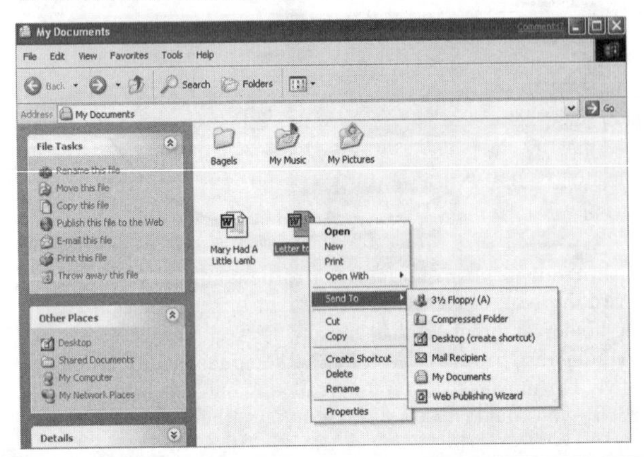

Creating folders

In order to keep all your files organized it's essential to create folders to keep them in. For example, you might create some sub-folders in My Documents to separate office work from personal work, or to keep all the files associated with one project in the same place. You can do this in a number of ways, but the easiest option is to open **My Documents** or wherever you want the new folder to appear, then right-click in some empty space and select **New** then **Folder** from the mouse menu. (You can also find the New command in the **File** dropdown menu on the menu bar.)

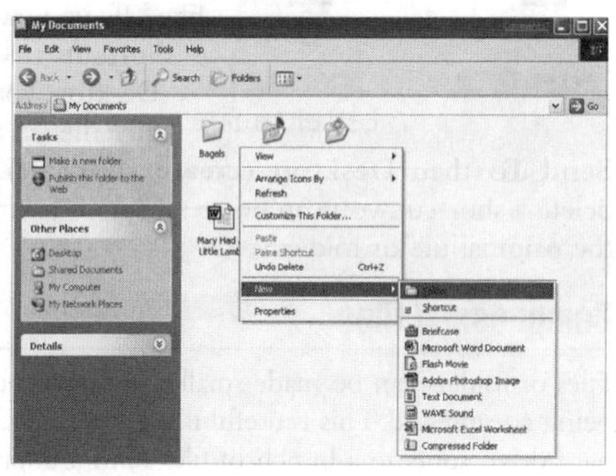

The folder will appear, its name highlighted in blue and surrounded by a box. Type in the name for the folder and press **Enter**. You can always rename it later by right-clicking it and selecting **Rename** from its mouse menu.

Shortcuts

A **shortcut** (or icon shortcut: not to be confused with a keyboard shortcut) is a special type of icon that acts as a link to a file, folder or program that actually lives elsewhere. This can come in very handy. Say you have a document within a folder in My Documents that you use frequently but which is a trek to reach – you could create a shortcut to it on the Desktop for easy access. The same goes for programs: if you use them regularly, create shortcuts to save you going through the Start menu every time you want to use them.

With a few special exceptions, shortcut icons look identical to the file or folder they lead to, but they have a little arrow on their bottom-left corner and they are named **Shortcut to...** when created.

It's easy to create a shortcut: simply right-click on any file or folder and select **Create Shortcut** from the mouse menu – the shortcut icon will appear, and you can drag it wherever you like. If you want to make a shortcut to live on the Desktop, you can right-click any file or folder, and select **Send To** then **Desktop (create shortcut)**. If you want to delete a shortcut, you can do so safely: no harm will be done to the original file or folder.

Compressed files

Files or folders can be made smaller – in terms of disk space – by being compressed. This is useful if you want to save space on your hard drive, squeeze a bunch of files onto a floppy disk or email a large file to someone and reduce the time it will take to download. There are various compression programs available: the most commonly used is **WinZip** (which can be downloaded from the Web at **http://www.winzip. com**), though if you want an excellent and completely free alternative try PowerArchiver (**http://www.powerarchiver.com**). If you have either Windows XP or Me you can open and create compressed files without any extra programs. Simply place the files you want to compress

Tech Info | Tips & Tricks | Try This

How compression works

File compression works in an ingenious way. Let's say that you've saved a document containing the text "every land and every sea: here, there and everywhere". The compression program would look for recurring patterns, and notice that "here", "every" and "and" occur more than once. It would make itself something like a key, where **every** = !, **and** = *, **here** = ^. Then it could write the same sentence as: **! l* * ! sea: ^, t^ * !w^**. (Compression is actually much more complex, but this gives you the idea.) The bigger the document is, the more it will compress – though certain types of documents compress much better than others.

in a new folder, right-click it and select **Send To** then **Compressed File**. A new folder will appear decorated with a zipper graphic which denotes it as the compressed version.

8

Customizing Windows

personalizing your PC

Windows is a cinch to customize: you can change the way everything looks and works with a few clicks of your mouse. Whether you want bigger icons, purple windows or a picture of your pet rabbit on the Desktop, customizing your PC is fun, useful and a good way to explore the Windows environment.

Dressing-up the desktop

As the big space that you see when you start up your PC, the Desktop is crying out to be customized. This is easily done in

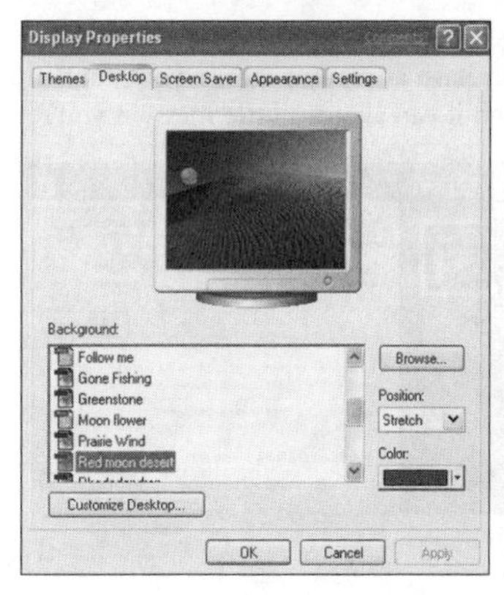

the **Display Properties** box, which you can reach either via the **Control Panel** (see p.156) or by right-clicking any empty space on the Desktop and selecting **Properties** from the mouse menu.

The thing you'll probably want to play around with first is the **wallpaper** – the image or pattern that fills some or all of your Desktop. To do this, click the **Desktop** or **Background** tab. The white box at the bottom presents you with a list of built-in patterns or pictures – select one and you'll get a preview on the little screen at the top. Alternatively, click **Browse** to select any other image on your computer (a photo from a digital camera, for example). There is also a little drop-down menu called **Position** or **Display**, where you can choose whether you want the picture to be in the middle of the screen, stretched to fill it, or to be tiled across it (repeated over and over).

Bringing the Web to your Desktop

If you have an Internet connection you can download Web pages and place them straight onto your Desktop (this is when the so-called **Active Desktop** gets active). The content you choose will sit on your Desktop even when you're offline, but if you use a Web page that is continually updated – such as a stock teller or sports results service – you can set Windows to refresh the content as frequently (or infrequently) as you like. Once a Web page is on your

Desktop, click on its top edge: you can resize or close it just like a normal window. And you can have as many pages as you want in view at any one time – though it can all get a little messy if you're not careful.

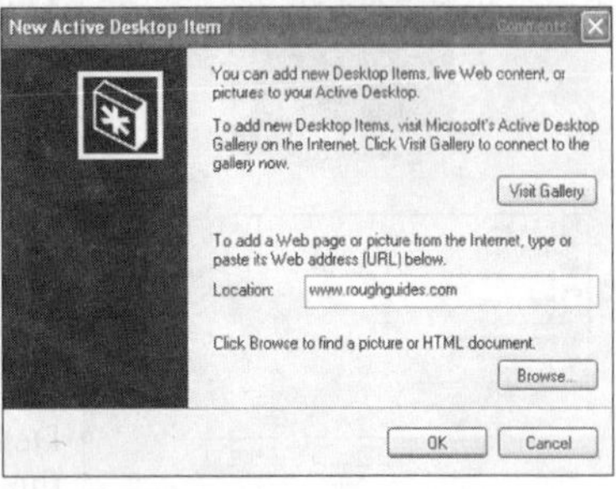

To add Web content to the Desktop, right-click it and select **Properties**. Then click the **Web** tab if you use Windows 98 or Me; in Windows XP, select the **Desktop** tab, click **Customize Desktop**, and choose the **Web** tab. Press the **New** button and type in the address of the page you want (you'll also be invited to visit the Microsoft Content Gallery where suggested pages are available). If you have a Website or HTML page saved on your hard disk, you can press the **Browse** button to locate and select it. Give it a try.

All the content currently available for use on your Desktop is listed in the white box in the Web tab – you can display or hide each item by clicking its checkbox. If you select an item and then click the **Properties** button you'll be presented with further options including **Make Available Offline**. This is where you get to download the page (complete with all its links) and tell your PC to refresh the content online at a certain time every hour, day or week.

For more on the Internet, see Chapter 14.

Windows, icons and the rest

If you don't like the way that the windows on your PC look, right-click the Desktop and select **Properties**. Then select the

Appearance tab: you'll be presented with various dropdown menus for altering how the whole environment or individual components look.

If none of these options take your fancy, consider adopting a Windows **theme**, which will change the way in which your entire work area looks and sounds. In Windows XP, right-click the Desktop, select **Properties** and click the **Themes** tab to see what's available. In earlier versions of Windows select **Desktop Themes** from the **Control Panel**. You can then choose from various themes, including "Science", "Nature" or "Sport". Should you select "Nature" in Windows 98, for example, you'll see a selection of stones and leaves as your Desktop wallpaper, a butterfly for My Computer, a log fire for the Recycle Bin and stone-coloured windows. You'll also hear the sound of a wind blowing when you turn on your machine, and your screen saver will crawl with hairy caterpillars. You can go for a partial theme by unchecking some of the options on the right of the box, or return to your previous settings in the Theme dropdown menu.

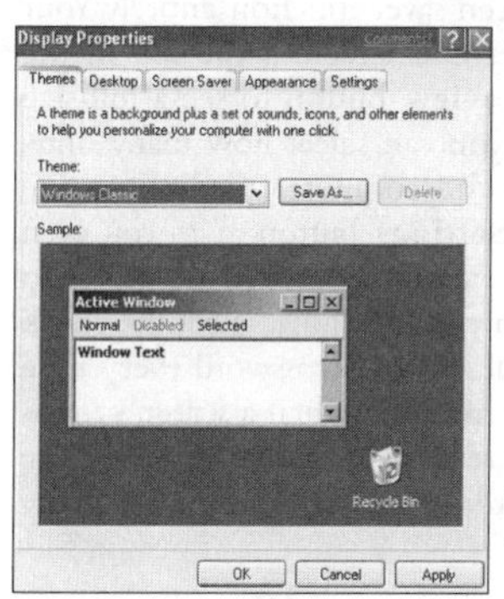

Screen savers

Screen savers are the animations that appear on your monitor when you haven't pressed a key or moved the mouse for a certain period of time. They were originally designed because screens would be damaged (or "burned") if the same image was present for too long, but these days monitors are a little hardier and screen savers are primarily just for fun.

To choose one, right-click the Desktop, select **Properties** and click the **Screen Saver** tab. You can choose from whichever screen savers are installed on your system via the **Screen Saver** dropdown menu. Windows comes with a selection built-in and you can download others from the Internet. You can also choose **none** to disable the screen saver function entirely. Your selection will be shown on the little screen at the top of the frame, but you can press the **Preview** button to see a full-size version. With the **Wait** option you can select how many minutes of inactivity will result in the computer turning on the screen saver, and a click of the **Settings** button gives you even more options. If you're worried about others having access to your PC when you're away from your machine, select the check box. This way, the computer will ask for a password every time someone tries to re-activate the machine when a screen saver is running. In Windows XP, the screen saver password will be the same as your Windows password; in earlier editions, click the **Change** button to choose one.

Try This | Tips & Tricks | Tech Info

Text screen savers

If you want to create a unique screen saver (or leave a surprise message on a friend's machine), try selecting 3D text in the Screen Saver dropdown menu and then click Settings. Enter any message you like in the text box and it will be animated as a screen saver. You can also change the speed and way in which it moves around the screen.

Screen area and colour depth

The screen resolution is the number of pixels your screen image is made up of. With a high setting, you can squeeze a lot of information onto your screen, but everything will appear very small; with a low setting everything will be bigger, but less will fit. It's worth experimenting with various settings to get the best balance. Right-click the Desktop, select **Properties**, and click the **Settings** tab. Then use the **Screen resolution** slider (labelled **Screen area** in earlier versions of Windows) to change the settings. The maximum available resolution depends on the capabilities of your monitor and video card.

Also in this tab you'll see a **Colors** dropdown menu, which determines the maximum amount of colours you can see on the screen at any one time. A high setting such as **True Color (32 Bit)** or **High Color (16 Bit)** is preferable if your video card and monitor are up to it.

It's worth noting that these two settings are dependent on each other – if you select a very high resolution, your maximum number of colours may drop, and vice versa.

Tweaking the Taskbar

If you're reworking your Windows environment, don't forget the Taskbar, which can be customized in various ways.

Moving and resizing

The first thing to experiment with is where you want the Taskbar to live – instead of being stuck at the bottom of the screen you can place it on either side or at the top. Click and hold the left mouse button over a blank space on the taskbar and drag the whole bar to one of the other screen edges. Give it a go: you can always move it back again. The second thing to decide about the Taskbar is whether you always want it in view. After all, if you want to maximize your screen area for a certain task, it can get in the way. Go to the edge where the Taskbar meets the Desktop, and your mouse pointer will turn into a double-headed arrow with which you can drag the whole Taskbar to make it as small or as big as you like. To restore it to its original size, simply drag it back again.

Taskbar Properties

Another option is to have the Taskbar automatically hide itself, only appearing when your pointer drifts close to the edge of the screen where it lives – or when you hit the **Windows** button on your keyboard. To do this, right-click on any blank portion of the Taskbar and select **Properties** from the mouse menu to bring up the **Taskbar and Start Menu Properties** dialog box. Click the **Auto-hide** checkbox and then click **Apply**.

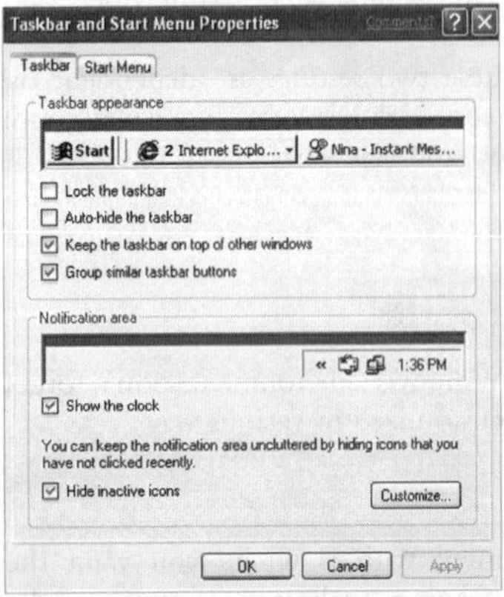

While you have this dialog box open, browse the other options. You can also choose to hide the clock, set it so that windows can go "on top" of the Taskbar, and so on.

Notification area icons

In Windows XP, unused icons in the Notification area – sometimes called **tray icons** – are automatically hidden unless you turn this option off in the Taskbar and Start Menu Properties dialog box (see above). In older versions of Windows this option isn't available, but you may be able to hide some of them. Try double-clicking a few icons. Some will launch a program, while others will present you with a Properties window. Search around and you may well find a **Display tray icon** checkbox; uncheck it and off goes the icon. If you don't find this option, or if you get fazed by some techie-looking stuff, just press **Cancel** – don't alter any settings you're not sure about.

Quick Launch area

The chances are that next to your Start button you have a number of little icons on the Taskbar for Outlook Express, Internet Explorer and so on. As you learnt in Chapter 6, this is the **Quick Launch Toolbar**, which is designed to house shortcuts for some of your most commonly used programs. If there's an icon here for a program that you never use, feel free to right-click it and select **Delete** – the icons are only shortcuts (see p.133), so deleting them won't do any harm to the actual program. And it's just as easy to add a program to your Quick

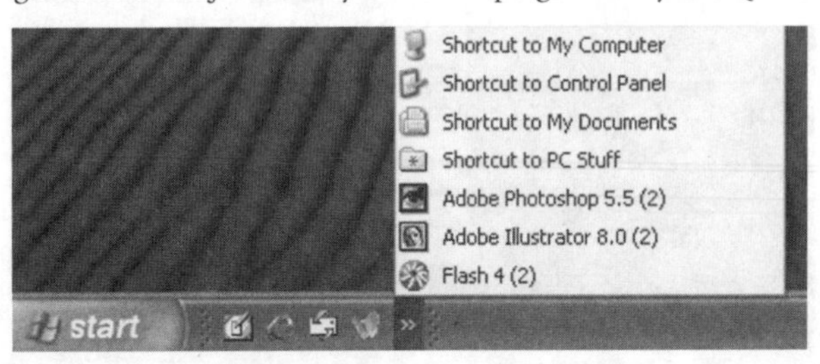

Launch area. Browse through the programs in your Start menu until you get to the one you want to add. Right-click it and select **Send To** and choose **Desktop (create shortcut).** A new icon labelled **Shortcut to...** will appear on the Desktop, which you can drag straight onto the Quick Launch toolbar. You can put shortcuts to files or folders in the Quick Launch area in the same way.

If you have a little double arrow sign on the edge of the Quick Launch area, as shown below, click it and further icons will be revealed. Or you can drag the little embossed vertical line to expand the section along the Taskbar until all the icons are visible.

Taskbar Toolbars

The Quick Launch area is only one example of a toolbar that can reside on the Taskbar; you can create a toolbar out of practically any selection of files or folders, and there are a number of ways to do it. Click on any blank portion of the Taskbar and select the **Toolbar** option from the mouse menu. You can either click one of the ready-to-use options (there is one, for example, that shows all the icons on the Desktop) or choose **New Toolbar** to select a folder, such as **My Documents** or **Control Panel**. When you've made your selection, the new toolbar will

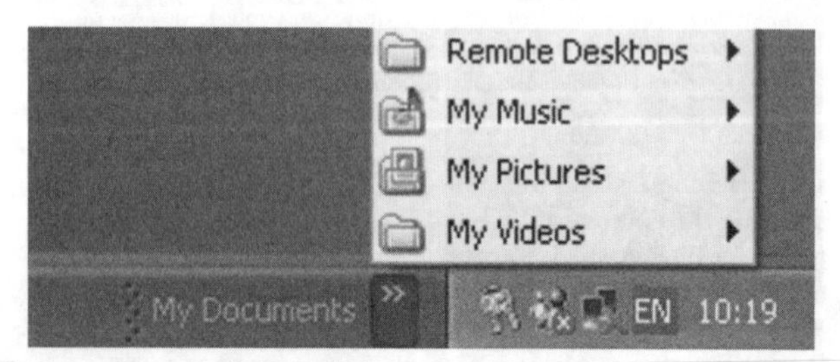

Try This | Tips & Tricks | Tech Info

Giving folders a face-lift

As well as changing how Windows looks overall, you can also customize specific folders. In Windows XP, you can select a picture or photo to appear on the folder icon when you're in thumbnail view. Open the folder, select **Customize This Folder** from the **View** menu, select **Choose Picture,** navigate to your image of choice and click **OK**.

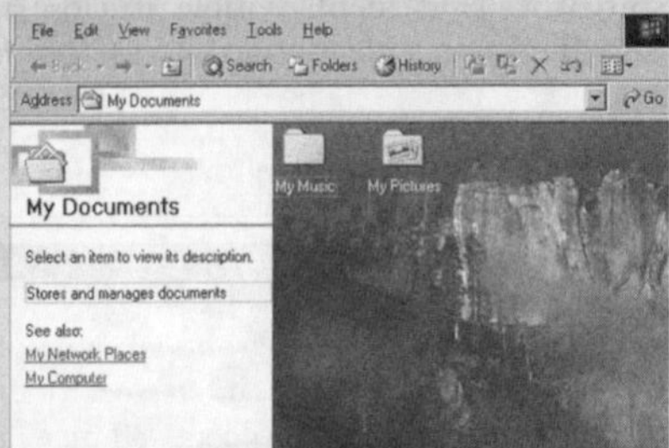

In Windows 98 or Me, you can't add pictures to folder icons but you can add a background to a folder, as shown above. Double-click a folder (**My Documents,** for example) and select **Customize this Folder** from the **View** menu. Then select **Choose a background picture**, click **Next** and you'll be presented with a dialog box offering you various pictures and a **Browse** button, which allow you to select any suitable picture on your computer. You may want to change the text and background colours too – go on, live dangerously. Click **Next** when you're done, and your folder will be customized. To delete the new look, click **View/Customize this Folder**, select **Remove customization** and click **Next**.

appear on the Taskbar. You can rearrange the various toolbars by dragging the embossed Taskbar dividers back and forth, but they may be a bit squashed unless you drag the whole Taskbar up a bit to make enough room for an extra row of toolbars. Alternatively, drag your new toolbar as far to the right as possible and click the arrow that appears to browse its contents as a pop-up menu, as shown on p.144.

If you right-click on the left-hand edge of a toolbar, you can change how it looks by selecting or deselecting **Show Title** and **Show Text**. You can also drag a toolbar around on the screen by its left edge so that it floats like a mini-window. Then try right-clicking its Title bar and selecting **Always on top** so that it's permanently visible. To close a toolbar, right-click its left edge or Title bar and select **Close** from the mouse menu.

Spicing up the Start menu

In Windows XP you can make lots of tweaks to the Start menu to make it work exactly the way you want it to. Most of these are done via the **Taskbar and Start Menu Properties** box, which you can reach by right-clicking the **Start** button and selecting **Properties**. Here you can choose whether to stick with the fancy XP Start menu or revert to the "classic" single-column variety found in earlier versions of Windows. Whichever one you choose, you can click the **Customize** button to make various changes to how the menu looks and works. The tweaking options for the XP Start menu are pretty good: as well as options for smaller icons, a longer recently used programs list and so on, you can click the **Advanced** tab and make all sorts of changes to what appears on

Tips & Tricks | Tech Info | Try This

Exploring the Start menu

If you want to move lots of things around in your Start menu or create folders to live in your Programs menu, it's easiest to use Windows Explorer. Right-click on the **Start** menu and select **Explore**. An Explorer window will open with the Start menu selected. You can then move files around and create folders as you would anywhere else.

the right-hand side of the menu. And you can choose whether you want the icons to act as links that open a new window or as expanding menu (similar to the **More Programs** menu). This is especially useful for **My Documents**, allowing you to browse through your filing system and open files without opening a window.

The other XP tweaks you can make are also possible in earlier versions of Windows: you can rearrange the items in your Programs list either by dragging and dropping them or by right-clicking in the list and pressing **Sort by Name**. And you can add shortcuts to programs or files to the top section of the menu by dragging any file or folder onto the Start button.

Doing away with the double-click

Part of Microsoft's strategy to make Windows look and feel more like the Internet is to give you the option of ditching the double-click so that you can browse through and select your files in the same way as you surf the Web – by single-clicking on underlined links.

If you want to try this option, open an Explorer window such as **My Documents**, select **Folder Options** from the **Tools** menu and select **Single-click to open an item**. (In Windows 98 or Me, select **Folder Options** from the **View** menu, and select **Web style**.)

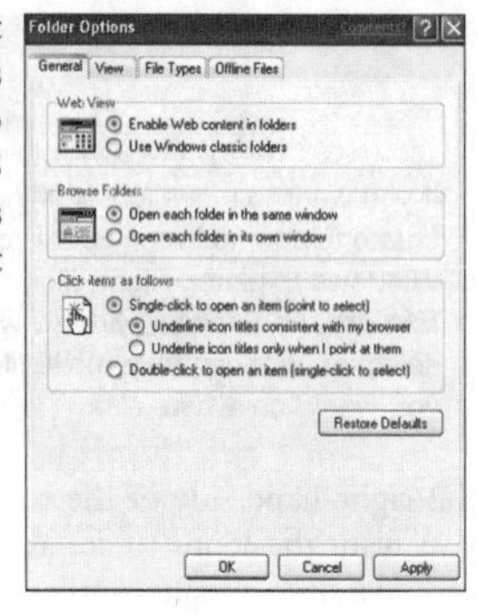

Sorting out your sounds

One final thing you might want to customize in Windows is the selection of sounds that occur when you start up, shut down, try something the system doesn't like and so on. To change or turn off some or all of these sounds, open the **Control Panel** and select: **Sounds, Speech, and Audio Devices** followed by **Change the Sound Scheme** (in Windows XP); **Sounds and Multimedia** followed by the **Sounds** tab (Windows Me); or **Sounds** (in Windows 98). Towards the top of the dialog box you'll see a list of actions. A little speaker icon next to any one indicates that a sound will occur when the action is carried out. Click on an action to select it, and pre-view the relevant sound by clicking on the triangle-bear-

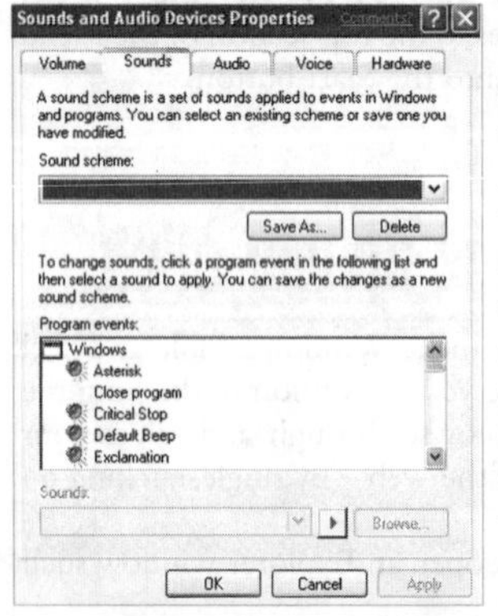

ing **Play** button. If you don't like what you hear, you can use the dropdown menu to select a different sound (or no sound at all) for that action; alternatively, click **Browse** to choose any other sound file you may have on your computer such as a recording you've made with Sound Recorder (see p.173).

The **Schemes** section allows you to save your customized selection of sounds as a "scheme" alongside the various schemes (like "Robotz") that come as part of Windows.

9

Users

sharing your computer

If your PC is used by various people within your home or office, you can configure Windows to recognize each individual as a **user**. This way, when someone sits down at the machine they'll be able to work within their own special setup – protected by a password if desired. Each user has their own My Documents folder, their own Web favorites (see p.214), and can customize Windows in any way they like. All these individual files and settings constitute a user's **account** or profile.

The user options in Windows Me and earlier versions are rather limited and not very secure, but can be useful nonetheless (see p.155 for more). In Windows XP, they're much more comprehensive: there are various different types of user, and each can choose to make their files private so that no one else can access them.

Users in Windows XP

Either during the Windows XP installation or the first time you use your machine, you will be prompted to enter the names of the people you want to set up as users. All you need enter is a **username** for each person – it could be a first name, a full name or an imaginary moniker of your choice – and choose what type of user you'd like them to be. The primary user of the computer is the **Administrator**, while others can be registered as additional Administrators or as **Limited** users. Each type of account allows the user a different level of control within the PC:

❒ **Administrators** have control over all system-wide settings, they can install hardware and software and they can create, change and delete other users' accounts. They can also access all files not protected by a private password.

❒ **Limited users** have even fewer powers, though they still maintain their own password, private files and Windows settings.

Each time you start your computer, all the users will be listed in a Windows welcome page – simply click on the appropriate username to log on. Next to each name on the Windows welcome page you'll see a little picture. Windows assigns a default image – such as a cat, flower or soccer ball – to each user when the accounts are created. But you can easily change the pictures to something more to your taste or a little more personal (perhaps a picture of yourself if you have a digital camera or scanner). A user's image is also displayed at the top of the Start menu when they're logged on.

By default you won't need to enter a password to log on, but

you can add a **password** to your account in the User Accounts window (see p.153). This is also where you go to add and delete users or alter individual user settings.

Guest users

If someone wants to use your machine but they're not registered as a user, they can log on as a **Guest** at the Windows welcome page. They'll be able to work within your computer, but will have no access to any user account settings or the documents of other users. If, as the Administrator, you don't want anyone accessing your machine without a personalized account, you can turn the Guest account off by going to the **Start** menu, then **Control Panel,** then **User Accounts**, clicking the **Guest** icon and then selecting **Turn off the guest account** from the list of tasks.

Logging off and switching user

Windows XP features "**fast user switching**", meaning that users no longer have to actually log off when a new person wants to use the machine, as was the case with earlier Windows versions. Now the current user has two choices after selecting **Log Off** from the Start menu: first comes **Log Off**, which shuts down all their settings to make way for the next user; then there's **Switch** User, which preserves all their settings and active programs in the background while the new user does their thing. This feature means that you can quickly move between different user setups without ever having to close the programs or documents you have open.

User Accounts window

Only an Administrator can add a new user or change the settings of the current users – Limited or Guest users are only entitled to make changes to their own account. Either way, all user settings are dealt with in the User Accounts window, which can be opened by clicking the Start button, selecting **Control Panel** and choosing the **User Accounts** option. If you open the window as an Administrator, you'll see a list of all the current users. Limited or Guest users, however, will only see their own name and picture.

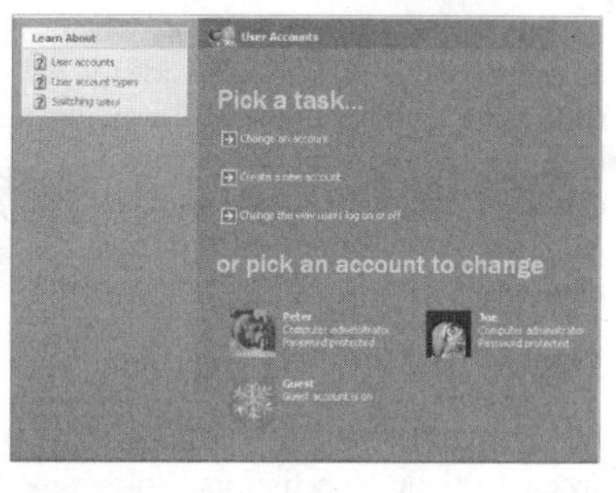

Most of the options and tasks in these windows are self-explanatory – "Change my picture", "Change my password" – but XP does offer a couple of further options that require a little clarification.

First, you can take the opportunity to create a **Password Reset Disk**, a special floppy disk that can be used to access your account and reset your password from the Windows Welcome page if you happen to forget it. Click the **Prevent a forgotten password** task, insert a blank floppy disk and launch the wizard, which will walk you through the process. This disk will not be specific to a single password, so you need only create the disk once, even if you change your password regularly.

Also on offer is the option of creating a **.NET Passport**, a special username (based on an email address) and password that lets you quickly log on to a family of Microsoft Websites and certain other participating sites. The idea is that it saves you having to remember loads of different usernames and passwords, but hard-bitten users might be forgiven for thinking that it's just another Microsoft attempt at world domination.

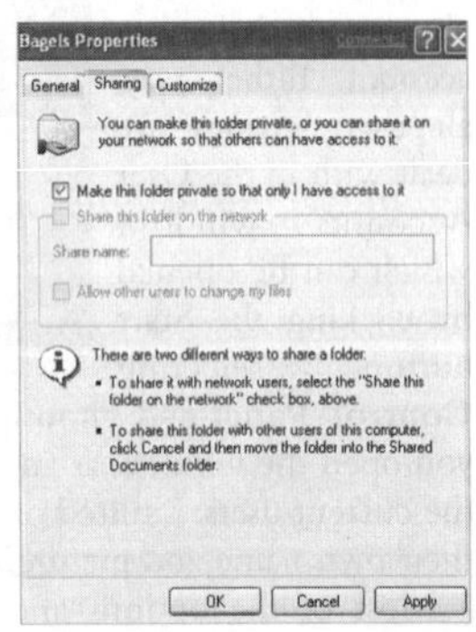

Shared and private folders

Limited and Guest Users only have access to their own files and folders, so if you want certain files to be accessible to all put the files in the **Shared Documents** folder, which you'll find in My Computer.

Administrators have a little more freedom than others to stroll around users' files and folders, though anyone can choose to make an individual file completely private – even from the prying eyes of Administrators – by right-clicking it, selecting **Sharing and Security** and then checking the box labelled **Make this folder private**.

Users in Windows Me and 98

In pre-XP versions of Windows you can set up user profiles via the Users icon in the Control Panel. To add someone to the list, click the **New User** button and follow the steps laid down by the Add User Wizard, clicking **Next** when you're happy with the options in each frame. However, security is pretty minimal on these older versions of Windows: passwords are not secure and every user has access to all files and folders on the system. You can restrict people on a network from viewing your private files (see p.229), but not other users of your PC. There's also only one type of user.

You can switch between users at any time by clicking the **Start** button and selecting **Log Off**. After you've confirmed your decision, a dialog box will appear so that another user can log on by entering their username and password (if they have one). In these older versions of Windows, though, switching between users takes quite a long time – the system essentially shuts down and restarts each time.

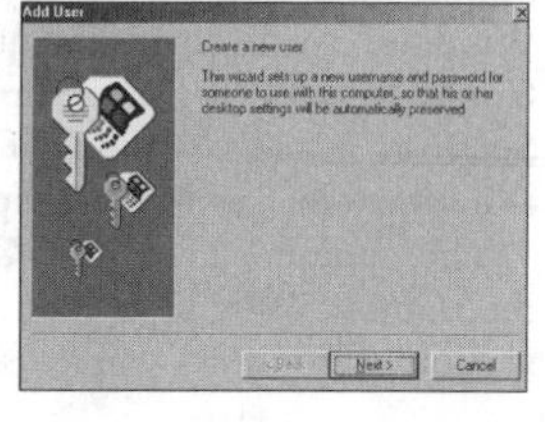

10

The Control Panel

tweaking the settings

The Control Panel is the place where you go within Windows to make all sorts of changes to your computer's settings. It houses everything from controls for pieces of hardware like your mouse and keyboard to utilities that change the appearance of your Windows work environment. You'll find the Control Panel in the **Start** menu (under **Settings** in older versions of Windows) and as a link or folder in **My Computer**.

The appearance of your Control Panel and the number of items it contains depends on two things: which version of Windows you're using and which programs you have

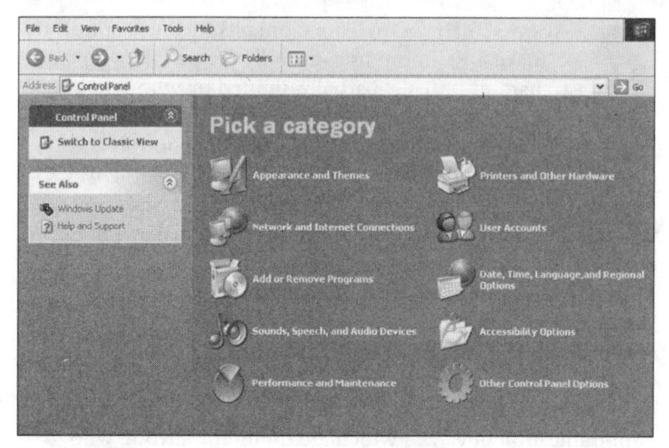

installed on your system. In Windows XP, the Control Panel items are arranged into categories – click on one and you'll be offered a list of **tasks** and **icons**. You'll also see a list of troubleshooting options on the left of the window, which launch wizards to help you sort out any problems you might be having. Older versions of Windows don't have the tasks or troubleshooters in their Control Panels – they just display the icons in a list (in Windows Me, you'll need to click the **View all** link to see them all).

You'll probably never need many of the Control Panel options, but having a browse is both informative and fun – as long as you **don't change any technical settings you're not absolutely sure about**. Next comes a run-through of the items you're likely to come across. You won't find all the ones listed here in your system, and you may well have additional icons – certain programs like virus scanners often add their own. Many of the options mentioned are covered in more depth in other chapters of this book, and some can be accessed from various different places in the Windows environment.

Accessibility Options Contains various controls to make a PC more user-friendly for people who are hard of hearing, partially-sighted or who find a standard mouse or keyboard difficult to use. By selecting the various tabs, adjusting the controls and clicking the **Apply** or **OK** button, you can: change the way your keyboard responds; set up SoundSentry and ShowSounds functions to warn you visually when your PC makes a noise; change the colour and contrast of your display to make it easier to read; adjust the speed of your mouse pointer; and enable your keyboard's number pad to move the mouse pointer. In the **General** tab you can set all these functions to switch off after the PC has sat idle for a period of time and enable **SerialKey devices** – special input gadgets, also known as "augmentative communication devices", which are useful for anyone who finds it difficult to operate a mouse or keyboard.

Add New Hardware When you install a modern Plug and Play device your PC should automatically recognize and configure it. If this fails, however, or if you're adding a non-Plug and Play device, run this wizard after installation to get everything going.

Add or Remove Programs These days, most programs are so easy to install that you're more likely to use these controls for removing programs than adding them (see p.250). This is also the place where you can add and remove elements from your Windows setup (and in Windows Me and earlier, create a Startup disk: see p.239).

Administrative Tools Opens a window offering all sorts of techie information and options, such as graphic representations of your processor usage and hard disk fragmentation. Not for the uninitiated.

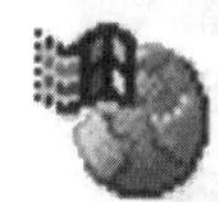

Automatic Updates Found only in Windows Me, this option allows Windows to automatically fetch and install any updates or missing device drivers from the Microsoft Website – assuming your PC is connected to a phone socket. Click here to turn this function on or off.

Date/Time (also accessible by double-clicking the clock on the Taskbar) This is where you go to set your clock and calendar. You can also select the time zone you are in from a dropdown list.

Desktop Themes Lets you select how everything in the Windows environment looks and sounds according to pre-installed themes such as "Nature" or "Science" (see p.139).

Dial-Up Networking (in **My Computer** in Windows 98) Displays a list of your Internet connections: double-click on an icon to connect, or right-click it and select Properties to view its settings.

Display Opens the Display Properties window, where you can make all sorts of tweaks to the appearance of the Windows environment. Its various options are covered in the Customizing Windows chapter (see p.136).

Folder Options (found in the **Start** menu under **Settings** in Windows 98) Lets you change how folders look and work (see p.200) and allows you to decide which programs your computer uses to open various types of file (see p.122).

Fonts Shows you all the fonts (text styles) installed on your system and allows you to install new ones.

Game Controllers For setting up joysticks and other gaming devices.

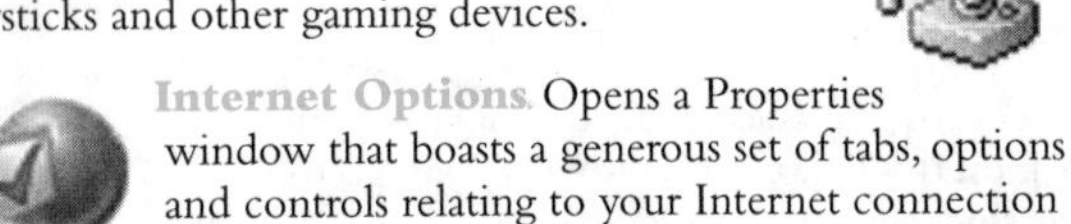

Internet Options Opens a Properties window that boasts a generous set of tabs, options and controls relating to your Internet connection and the way your Web browser behaves. It can also be opened from the Internet Explorer Tools menu. For more, see p.213.

Keyboard Lets you change the way in which your keyboard behaves – how quickly a letter is repeated when you hold down a key, for example.

Mail Displays and allows you to change the settings of your email accounts if you use certain email programs.

Modems Displays information about any modems currently installed and allows you to add new ones – though most modern modems don't require you to use this function during installation.

Mouse Lets you change your mouse settings: how the pointer looks on the screen, for example, and the speed needed for a double-click.

Network Connections Also accessible from the Windows XP Start menu, this opens an Explorer window listing all your Internet and Network connections. Double-click an Internet connection icon to connect, or right-click it and select

Properties to view its settings. You will also see an icon labelled **Make New Connection**, which launches a step-by-step wizard for adding a new connection.

Network Deals with all sorts of network settings (see p.244).

ODBC Data Source Techie stuff you don't need to know about.

Passwords For setting up or changing Windows passwords. Ties in with **Users** (see p.150).

PC Card Deals with PC card devices and connections (see p.18) – this option is generally only found in the Control Panel of notebooks.

Power Options (labelled **Power Management** in Windows 98) Lets you choose how long your system should sit doing nothing before slipping into its power-saving standby mode.

Printers Reveals details of any printers connected to your system. It also features the Add Printer Wizard, though thanks to Plug and Play technology (see p.62), you'll probably never need to use it.

Regional Settings Lets you tell Windows where you are in the world and choose a format for numbers, currencies, dates and times.

Scanners and Cameras For setting up digital cameras and scanners on your system – though most modern models will do this themselves.

Scheduled Tasks (in **My Computer** in Windows 98) Allows you to schedule Windows to carry out tasks or run programs at a certain time every day, week or month. This is only really useful if you leave your computer on all the time.

Sounds and Audio Devices This dialog box has various options for altering your Windows sounds (such as the noise the PC makes when it starts up), setting up your multimedia components and adjusting playback and recording settings.

Sounds and Multimedia This is the Windows Me's version of Sounds and Audio Devices option (see above). In Windows 98 Sounds and Multimedia are presented as two separate items.

Speech Lets you set your computer's default voice for reading text and dialog boxes aloud. In Windows XP you can select the kinds of information that you want to be read aloud by clicking Start and selecting Programs, Accessories, Accessibility, and then Narrator.

System (also accessible by right-clicking **My Computer** and selecting **Properties**) Brings up a dialog box showing which version of Windows you're running and displaying various information about your system such as the processor type and the amount of RAM. There are various other tabs that provide techie information such as a list of all your peripherals and ports. It's best not to change anything in here unless it's really necessary

Taskbar and Start Menu (in **Start/Settings** in Windows 98) For customizing the Taskbar and Start menu – see p.141.

Telephony Where Windows stores information about the country you're in and your telephone area code. Why not take a moment to make sure these settings are correct?

User Accounts (or **Users**) Lets you set up your computer so more than one user can have personalized settings. See p.150 for more.

Wireless Link (or **Infrared**) If your PC has an infrared port – usually only notebooks do – this is where you can alter its settings.

11

Built-in programs

Windows extras

Over the years, Windows has accumulated an extensive range of built-in utilities and programs, many of which can come in very handy. But unless you actually take the time to look, you might never discover just how many tools you have at your disposal – from little extras like a calculator to tools for tweaking

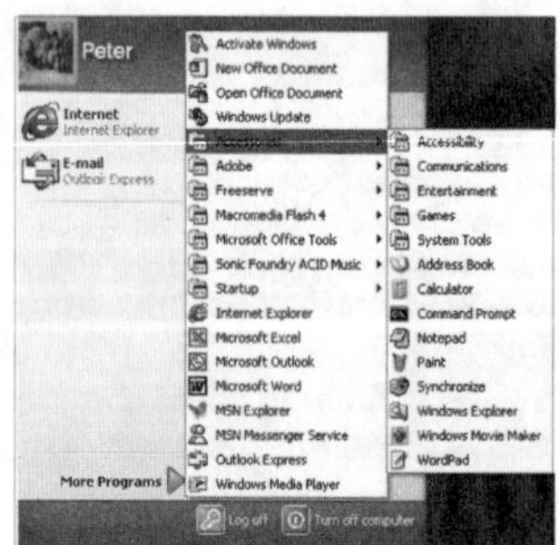

and checking up on your hardware to programs for dealing with music and video. This chapter gives you a guided tour of what's on offer.

Accessories

There's a wealth of goodies to be found within an area of the Start menu called **Accessories**. Click the **Start** button, select **Programs** then **Accessories**, and we'll begin. Try launching some of these:

Address Book This is pretty much what you'd expect: a computerized address book system with fields for various sorts of information and personal details. It's especially useful when used alongside an email program like Outlook Express (see p.218). Open it up and click **New** then **Contact** to make your first addition.

Calculator Select this item and you're presented with a standard and fairly boring calculator that you can operate either with your mouse pointer or keyboard. But don't fall asleep yet: from the **View** menu select **Scientific** – you've now got a powerful mathematics tool at your disposal.

Imaging Introduced with Windows Me, this is a photo previewing and editing tool. Though it's not especially intuitive to use and can seem rather limiting when compared to some other graphics packages (see p.259), it does cover all the basics: rotating, scaling, zooming and so on.

Command Prompt (or MS-DOS Prompt) This offers you a potentially scary glimpse of MS-DOS, the pre-Windows Microsoft operating system. If you click the icon you'll get a window housing a page which appears blank apart from a single line of coded text (such as **C:\WINDOWS>**), urging you to enter a command. This is only really for the initiated, so proceed with caution. In some versions of Windows you'll find this icon elsewhere.

Notepad Notepad is a very basic text program for writing and editing documents that don't require any formatting (special information about the font, spacing and so on). Anything you write in Notepad is saved in the ASCII, or "simple text", format and a single document can be no bigger than 64 kilobytes, which is around 15,000 words.

WordPad This program, which is covered in more detail on pages 182–186, is a step up from Notepad: it's a word processor that can handle various fonts, paragraph styles and even embedded pictures. It won't provide you with anything like the variety of tools found in a full-blown word processing package (see p.255), but it does handle all the basics and can save your work in various file formats, including simple text, rich text format (RTF) and Word.

Paint This is the Windows drawing and painting application, which is looked at in more depth on p.188–192. As with Imaging, it's a little clunky when viewed alongside specialist packages, but it's easy to use and gives you an introduction to the common tools. At the end of the day, it's what you do with it that counts.

Web Publishing Wizard This utility walks you through the process of getting your work onto the Web – from finding the files on your system to uploading files to a Web server. Though it doesn't offer all the utilities of a specialized FTP (File Transfer Protocol) program, it's a good basic tool. In XP, you'll find the Wizard in Windows Explorer: click a file and the Publish this file on the Web link will appear on the left. In Windows 98 right-click a file and select Web Publishing Wizard from the mouse menu.

System tools

If you click the **Start** button and select **Programs**, **Accessories** then **System Tools** you'll see a selection of utili-

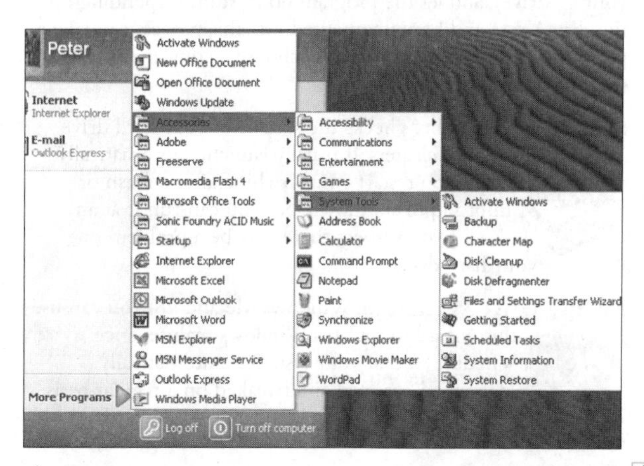

ties and programs that combine to make up your PC toolbox. Though several of the these tools are a little too techie to warrant much attention here, others are worth introducing – they will help you make sure your PC is an efficient, well-oiled and happy machine.

Disk Cleanup This is a handy little tool that helps you recover hard disk space by deleting **temporary files** and other redundant files from your system. It also prompts you to free up space by removing unused programs and emptying your **Recycle Bin** (see p.114).

Disk Defragmenter The Disk Defragmenter reorganizes the contents of your hard drive so that the read-write heads don't have to work so hard (see box). Once you've launched this item, select the drive that you want to defragment (this will most likely be your C: drive), and let the program do its stuff. Depending on the drive's size and how fragmented it is, this process can take a good few hours, so make sure you choose a convenient time to set the ball rolling.

ScanDisk This utility checks the surface of your hard drive for faulty clusters. It usually launches automatically when you restart your machine after a crash or impromptu shutdown, but you can run it at any time if you suspect there may be a problem on your hard drive.

Maintenance Wizard (in Windows Me and 98) You can use this wizard to set up a Windows maintenance schedule so that your system is automatically defragged, scanned and tweaked on a regular basis. You might, for example, create a schedule that

Tech Info | Tips & Tricks | Try This

Doctor, doctor – my hard disk's fragmented

Hard disks are made up of thousands of tiny little sections, called **clusters**, that hold individual portions of data. Whenever you delete a file, the relevant clusters become available, and then get refilled by more data when you save something new. The problem is that as time goes by, more and more deletions and additions can result in files being split between multiple locations on the disk, which means that when you come to retrieve a file your hard drive's read-write heads have to work ludicrously hard, darting back and forth collecting all the individual fragments of data that make up the file you're after. Though this will usually only result in things slowing down by a fraction of a second, it can make all the difference when carrying out real-time, or "streaming", tasks like recording live audio or playing back video. To get the best from your hard drive in terms of function and longevity, you should get into the habit of defragging every month or two, and in addition prior to saving any large audio or video files to your drive.

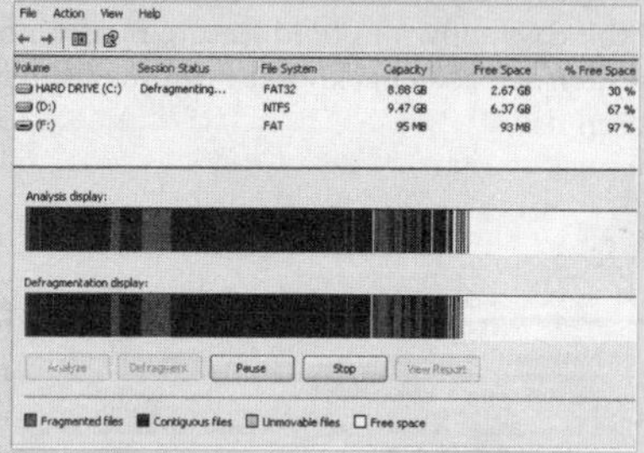

carries out these tasks every Sunday night when you're tucked up in bed. But you'll have to remember to leave your PC on before you go to sleep.

System Restore This feature, which you won't have if you're running Windows 98 or earlier, lets you turn back the clock and reinstate your Windows settings as they were at an earlier date and time: a very useful way to clear up problems relating to bad software installations or mischievous hardware drivers scrambling your setup. This function only relates to core system settings, so it won't affect your document files – and if it doesn't solve the problem, the restore can easily be undone. When you launch the System Restore program you enter a step-by-step process – much like a regular Windows wizard – that prompts you to either record the current settings as a **restore point** (also called a **system checkpoint**) or return your computer to a previous restore point. Once you have done this for the first time, you will also have the option to undo your last system restoration. If you do opt to choose an old checkpoint you will see a new frame with a calendar on it. All the days shown in bold feature restore points – click one, and then select a checkpoint from the list relating to your chosen day.

Select a Restore Point

The following calendar displays in bold all of the dates that have restore points available. The list displays the restore points that are available for the selected date.

Possible types of restore points are: system checkpoints (scheduled restore points created by your computer), manual restore points (restore points created by you), and installation restore points (automatic restore points created when certain programs are installed).

1. On this calendar, click a bold date. **2. On this list, click a restore point.**

July 2001

Mon	Tue	Wed	Thu	Fri	Sat	Sun
25	26	27	28	29	30	1
2	3	4	5	6	7	8
9	10	**11**	12	**13**	14	15
16	17	18	19	20	21	22
23	24	25	26	27	28	29
30	31	1	2	3	4	5

19 July 2001

There are no restore points created yet for this day. To restore immediately, pick another day and restore point, and then try again.

Tips & Tricks | Try This | Tech Info

Checkpoint Charlie

As well as restore points you create yourself, Windows automatically creates them at regular intervals. It stores a record of those created in the previous few weeks, but you can increase the amount of hard disk space available for old checkpoints by enlarging your checkpoint history. Right-click **My Computer** and select **Properties** to bring up the **System Properties** dialog box; click the **System Restore** or **Performance** tab and then the **Settings** or **File System** button. You'll see a slider that assigns disk space to System Restore.

Accessibility programs

In recent versions of Windows, if you click the **Start** button and select **Programs** then **Accessories** you'll find a folder called **Accessibility**. This contains a few little programs to make a PC easier to use for people with sight, hearing or mobility difficulties. **Magnifier** splits the screen into two parts; whatever your mouse is pointing at in the bottom of the screen is displayed much bigger in the top section. **Narrator** reads out on-screen messages and dialog boxes, and **On-Screen Keyboard** allows you to type with the mouse by clicking on a little virtual keyboard displayed on the screen. You'll also find **Accessibility Wizard**,

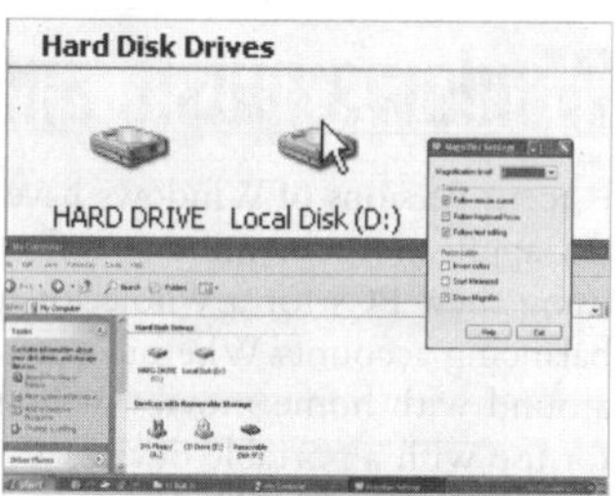

which will help you choose the best settings for your personal needs, and **Utility Manager**, with which you can quickly open and close the various programs. If you use Utility Manager a lot, you may find it more convenient to open and close it with a shortcut: hold down the **Windows key** and press **U**.

My Briefcase

This tool, which you may find on your Desktop, is a special document folder designed for people who use some files in two locations – at home and in the office, for example. If

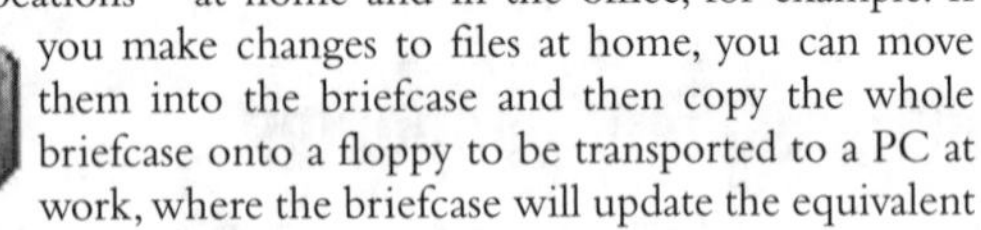

you make changes to files at home, you can move them into the briefcase and then copy the whole briefcase onto a floppy to be transported to a PC at work, where the briefcase will update the equivalent files. My Briefcase can also be used to synchronize files between two PCs linked by a direct cable connection (see p.227).

Windows music and video

Recent versions of Windows have been tailored with multimedia applications in mind – reflecting the fact that people are using their PCs for a whole lot more than writing letters and balancing accounts. Whether you're playing audio CDs, messing around with home movies or building a library of MP3 tracks for use with a portable device, Windows probably has a built-in tool to do the job. But before we take a look at these applications, let's take a quick tour of the Windows volume controls.

Volume controls

The Volume Control dialog box can be called up either by double-clicking the small speaker icon next to the clock on the Taskbar or by single-clicking the **Start** button and selecting **Programs**, **Accessories**, **Entertainment** then **Volume Control**. By tweaking the sliders with your mouse pointer you can change the volume of any device on your PC that generates sounds, such as an audio CD player or an integrated synthesizer. The first slider in the panel is the master control – if this is turned down you will hear nothing from any of the sound-generating devices of your PC – and the rest of the sliders refer to individual devices. They all give you the opportunity to adjust the balance (how a device splits its sound between a pair of stereo speakers) and if you want to silence a device altogether, click the **Mute** checkbox.

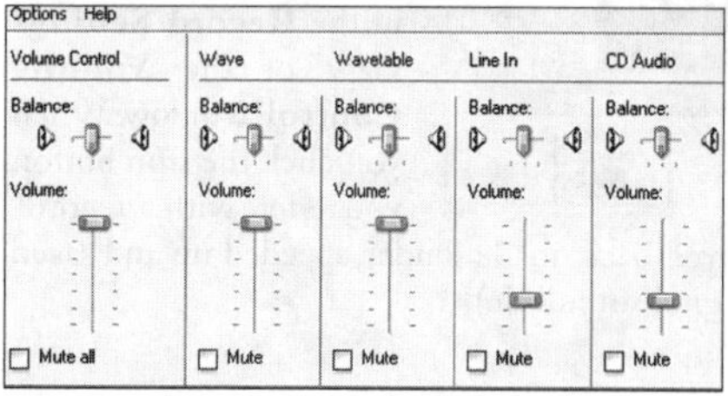

If you don't see the controls for a particular device, select **Properties** from the **Options** menu, look in the bottom half of the dialog box that appears and make sure the device's checkbox is selected. In this dialog box you can also choose to view the volume settings for **recording sounds** onto your computer from microphones, CD players and the like.

Sound Recorder

Though there are far more sophisticated programs available for recording sound using a PC (see p.263), several versions of

Windows do come with a natty little package called **Sound Recorder**, which can be found by travelling through **Start**, **Programs**, **Accessories** and then **Entertainment**. Basically, when you click the record button (the one with the red dot) the program begins to record sound from whichever source you have selected in the **Record Settings** view of the **Volume Control** window. When you click the stop button you're left with a recording that can be played back, made louder, speeded up and saved as a wave file (a digital sound file).

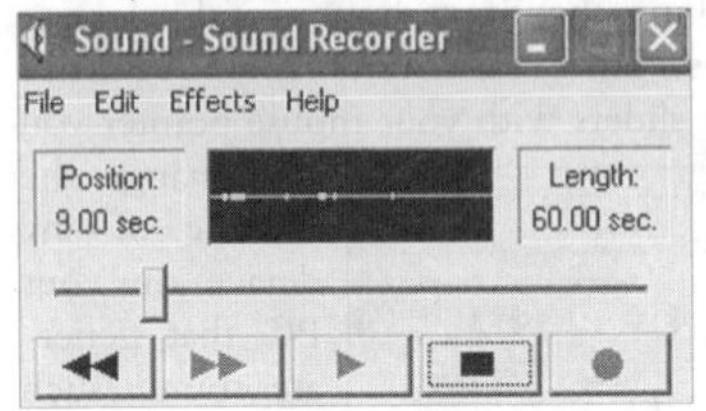

Windows media player

Recent versions of Windows come bundled with Windows Media Player. If you haven't already got a copy on your system or you're yearning for the very latest version, you can download it for free from http://www.microsoft.com/windows/windowsmedia.

More than just a CD player for your computer, Media Player can play back audio and video clips, help you organize an Internet-supported library of music files, encode tracks from CDs to your hard disk, tune into radio stations via the Internet and even – if you've got a CD burner – prepare selections from your files to make a compilation album.

When you open Media Player, on the lower edge of the window you'll see a selection of control buttons similar to those on a regular CD player: the big one is **Play/Pause**, the one with the square is **Stop**, the little slider is a volume control and the selection of triangles are for **Rewind/Fast Forward** and skipping between tracks. You'll also see a long slider that can be used to move to any point within the current track or video.

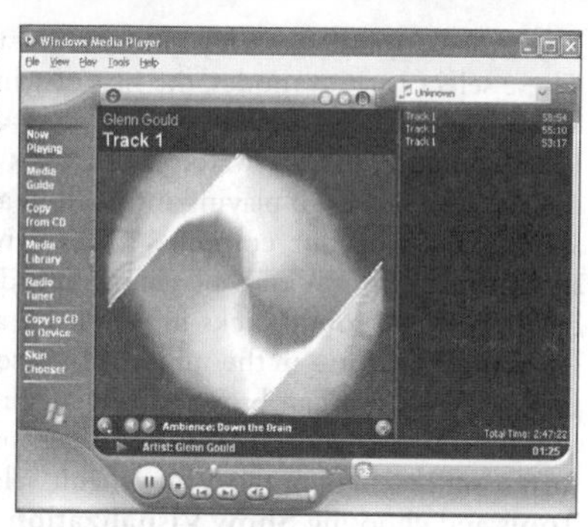

Try This | Tips & Tricks | Tech Info

Give Media Player a makeover

If you find the standard Media Player window a bit cumbersome, you can opt to view the **Compact Mode**. This makes the window a bit smaller but doesn't allow you to get at all the swanky tools. You can switch between the compact and normal modes by clicking the diagonal arrow icon in the bottom-right of the window (this icon sometimes appears in its own little **anchor window**). You can also change the style of the Media Player look by selecting the **Skin Chooser** button (on the left of the screen in the normal mode). Try it and preview some of the options: they're a little strange but you might find one that takes your fancy.

On the left of the screen you'll see several glossy-looking tabs. These select various modes, the first of which is **Now Playing**. When this is selected you'll be looking at the part of Media Player where you can watch video clips and find out which track you're on when playing music from a CD. Try inserting an audio CD into your computer's CD drive and Media Player should automatically start playing it (if it doesn't, click the **Play** button). As the sound kicks in, you'll see a psychedelic graphic – a **visualization** – in the middle of the screen, moving in time to the music. You can browse through various types of pattern using the little arrows underneath the visualization, or you can turn it off by clicking the **View** menu, selecting **Now Playing Tools** and choosing **Show Visualization**. In this section of the View menu, you can also select various tools such as a graphic equalizer (you have to select **Show Equalizer and Settings** first).

Copying music onto your hard drive

Instead of inserting a CD into your PC every time you want to listen to it, why not copy it onto your hard drive and start building a permanent library of all your favourite sounds? A hefty hard drive comes in very useful here – music files can be extremely large, and an audio library will quickly munch into your storage space. To view all the media files already on your PC, click the **Media Library** button on the left of the player. This brings up a split screen with a folder tree on the left which looks and works just like Explorer with the folder view open. The first time you click here, you may be asked whether you want to search your PC for media files – select **Yes** and all the sound and video files stored on your computer will appear in a list.

Before copying a new CD to your library you'll need to decide where you want to store all your music files: some versions of Windows come with a special **My Music** folder within My Documents that Media Player will use as a default location, but if you have other ideas you can choose a new location by selecting **Options** from the **Tools** menu, clicking the **Copy Music** (or **CD Audio**) tab and then selecting the **Change** button to choose a different folder.

To start the copying process, click the **CD Audio** or **Copy from CD** button on the left of the Media Player window – you'll see a list of the tracks on the CD currently in your drive and a red **Copy Music** button. Click this button and Media Player will start to encode your CD and save its contents to your hard drive. As this happens, the Copy Status of each song will change from "Pending" to "Copied To Library". If you don't want to copy all the tracks from a CD, you can deselect the checkbox for each track you don't want before you start copying.

Tech Info | Tips & Tricks | Try This

Compressed music files

When you encode music from a CD onto your hard drive, Media Player makes the files smaller by sacrificing the quality of the sound. You will always be faced by a trade-off between file size and sound quality, but, unless your speakers are high quality, some compression will not yield any noticeable difference in the sound. From the **Tools** menu select **Options**, and then click the **Copy Music** (or **CD Audio**) tab. Here you will see a slider that sets encoding quality, measured in **kilobits per second (Kbps)**. A setting of 128Kbps will barely alter CD sound quality, while 96Kbps is fine for most small PC speakers and personal stereo headphones. The most commonly used compressed music file is **MP3**, but Media Player uses its own **WMA** format as a default. However, in some versions of Media Player you can choose to copy in the MP3 format.

Naming the tracks

Once you've copied a CD to your hard drive, you can choose to enter the tracklist so that you'll be able to tell what's playing at any time very easily. Do this by right-clicking any track and selecting **Edit** to rename it. Alternatively, if your PC is connected to the Internet, you can press the **Get Names** button (at the top in the CD Audio section). Media Player then logs on to the Internet, finds its online database and prompts you for the name of the artist you are listening to. With any luck this should result in a full tracklist for your CD and also, if you click the **Album Details** button, the chance to read some blurb about the artist and recording.

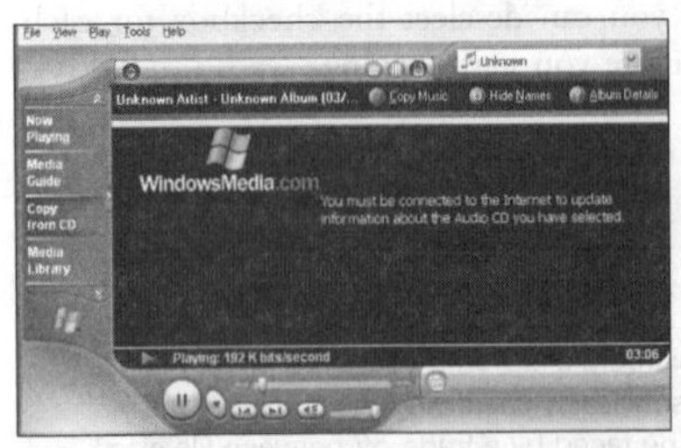

The first time you go online with Media Player you will also be prompted to download various **updates** and **plug-ins** (useful little extras) that have recently been made available. They are free, and easy to install once downloaded. You can check for updates whenever you like in the **Help** menu.

Creating playlists and burning CDs

A playlist is just what you'd expect – a list of tracks stored on your computer for Media Player to play back to you. Select **Media Library** and click the **New Playlist** button. You will be asked to give the new list a name – do this and click **OK** – and your new playlist will appear in the Media Library folder tree in the left-hand pane next to the **Sample Playlist**. Near the top of the folder tree will be an icon labelled **All Audio**: click it and a list of all the available audio files on your system – including MP3s and encoded CD selections – will appear in the right-hand pane. Selections from here can be moved to your new playlist in various ways: you can select a song and then click the **Add To Playlist** button to get a menu of available playlists; you can simply drag a track from one pane to the other; or you can right-click a track and select the **Add To Playlist** command from the mouse menu.

If you have a CD burner and a recent version of Media Player, you can create a playlist and write it straight onto a CD to make a compilation album. All you have to do is put a blank disc in your burner and select **Copy To CD** from the **File** menu. Media Player will ask you which playlist you want to put on the CD – select one and it should start writing the disc. If the Copy **to CD** function isn't available, try going to the Media Player download Website and downloading the most recent version or the Adaptec CD Burning Plug-In.

Windows Movie Maker

Another important member of the Windows multimedia family is **Windows Movie Maker**. This program first appeared in Windows Me, so if you're running 98 or earlier you won't have it. Windows Me and XP users will find it by clicking the Start button, selecting **Programs**, **Accessories** then **Windows Movie Maker**.

If you have the appropriate cable (and a port to plug it into), you can transfer footage from a video camera and then use Movie Maker to edit it. The footage is arranged into manageable chunks, called **clips**, that you can edit and move around on-screen to get your movie to look just right. You can also add a soundtrack or narration to your magnum opus and select individual frames to be saved as stills images.

A full description of how to use Movie Maker is beyond the scope of this book, but the basic principle is simple: you open individual clips on the left-hand side of the window and drag them down to the **Storyboard** at the bottom to turn them into a continuous movie. And you can view single clips or your whole film at any time on the screen on the right.

Movie Maker is pretty Web-friendly: when you've finished your movie you can export it – using the **Send** menu – to be part of an email or to be used as a Web page download. This function allows you to choose between various levels of image quality, based upon the expected times they will take to download – clever stuff.

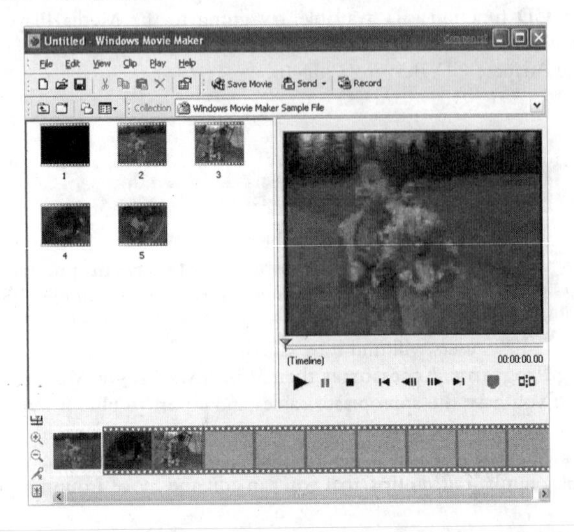

12

Document surgery

words and pictures

Now that you know your way around Windows, it's time to tackle some applications and get your head around creating and editing text and picture documents. In this chapter you'll learn about the kind of things you can get up to in word processing and graphics packages – using the Windows built-in programs as examples – but first let's look at some important editing tools that you're bound to run into again and again.

The big three: Cut, Copy and Paste

If you look at the **Menu bars** of several applications, you'll see that they all tend to offer a similar set of menus, starting with

File and followed by **Edit**, **View** and so on. Now take a closer look at the Edit menu, as it's the home of the three most important document editing tools at your disposal: **Cut**, **Copy** and **Paste**.

Let's try these tools out in WordPad, the Windows built-in word processor. Click the **Start** button and select **Programs**, then **Accessories**, then **WordPad**. WordPad will spring to life, complete with a pristine blank document all ready to go. Now click the **Edit** menu to locate our three heroes – **Cut**, **Copy** and **Paste**. When you first look at the options in the Edit menu they may well appear greyed-out. This is because there is no text, image or data selected for them to work with. So the first thing you need to do is click on the white page and write a few words. Try typing "Mary had a little lamb". Now highlight the text by holding down the left mouse button and dragging the pointer over the words. Then go to the **Edit** menu, select **Copy**, go back to the page and click to get a new **insertion point** (the flashing vertical line that shows you where you are), and then return to the Edit menu and select **Paste**. Your line of text will magically reappear at the insertion point.

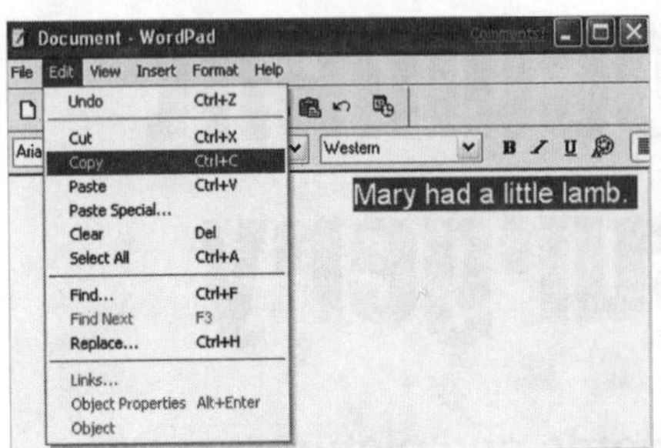

Now use your pointer to drag and select all the text on your page (alternatively, use the **Select All** command on the **Edit** menu or the keyboard shortcut **Control+A**). Then go back to the Edit menu and select **Cut** – everything will vanish. But

Where do the words go?

Whenever you select either **Cut** or **Copy**, the selected data is temporarily stored on what's called the **Clipboard.** In turn, whenever you select **Paste,** your PC looks to the clipboard for the data it is supposed to insert. If the Paste command is greyed-out in the Edit menu of a program, this means that the Clipboard is empty. In some Windows versions you can view the contents of the Clipboard at any time by clicking the **Start** button and selecting **Programs**, then **Accessories**, then **System Tools** and finally **Clipboard Viewer**. Generally the Clipboard can only hold one thing at a time. But some programs allow you to copy several selections to the Clipboard, which can then be pasted either separately or all together. This is sometimes called "spiking".

don't fret; if you select **Paste**, all the text you've just removed will be returned.

The really clever thing about Cut, Copy and Paste is that they can be used to move data between different documents in different applications. You could copy a selected image in a program like **Paint** (see p.188), for instance, and paste it into a **WordPad** document. This is all possible because the **Clipboard** exists independently of the individual programs you are using. As you become more confident with programs, you will doubtless find yourself using the Cut, Copy and Paste commands regularly. To save yourself the trek up to the Edit menu, though, you might find it easier to use either the toolbar buttons for these commands or their keyboard shortcuts.

Cut = Control+X

Copy = Control+C

Paste = Control+V

Stepping out with the big three

Cut, Copy and Paste also work on files and folders – even when no applications are running and there isn't a toolbar or Edit menu in sight. For example, try clicking on either a shortcut icon (one with a little arrow on its lower edge) or folder, so that it changes colour and becomes selected. Now try those keyboard commands: **Control+C** (Copy) followed by **Control+V** (Paste). You will have created a copy of the item and pasted it alongside the original. To delete the copy you made, simply drag it to the Recycle Bin. Also notice that Cut, Copy and Paste appear in the Edit menus and toolbars of Windows Explorer windows such as My Documents, allowing you to move and duplicate files and folders easily.

Undo and Redo

Another important function is **Undo**, which is also found in the **Edit** menus of most applications. Undo, unsurprisingly, "undoes" your last action, taking your text, illustration or whatever you're working with back to the state it was in before your last action. So if you accidentally delete a page of selected text, for example, use this command to turn the clock back. As with the other important editing tools discussed above, this invaluable utility has a keyboard shortcut – **Control+Z** – which is recognized by most applications. In some programs you can undo many actions, allowing you to go back as many stages as you like, while others only allow you to undo once. And in some applications, if you overdo the Undo you can undo the Undo with **Redo – Control+Y.**

Making words work

Whether you fancy yourself as a novelist or you just want to write the odd letter, it's time to scrap your rusty old typewriter and turn to your PC. Most word processing packages are pretty similar in appearance (when you open one up you'll see a Menu bar, various toolbars and a blank work area with a blinking insertion point eagerly standing by) and most allow you to do quite a lot of **formatting** – changing the size, style and positioning of the text.

Open WordPad again and type a few lines of text. Then select some words by dragging your mouse pointer over some of the letters – the selected text will be highlighted in blue – and you're ready to do pretty much anything you like. First try **bold**, *italic* and underline, which can easily be administered with the universal toolbar buttons displaying their initials. You can also change the colour of the text, though the toolbar button for this command changes from program to program.

Bold Italic Underline Text Colour

You'll also see dropdown menus for font style and size:

Then try changing the **alignment** of your text – whether it appears in the centre of the page, to the left or to the right. Most word processors (though not WordPad) also allow you to **justify** text: stretch it out so that each line fits perfectly to the width of the page. Again the toolbar buttons for these functions are universal:

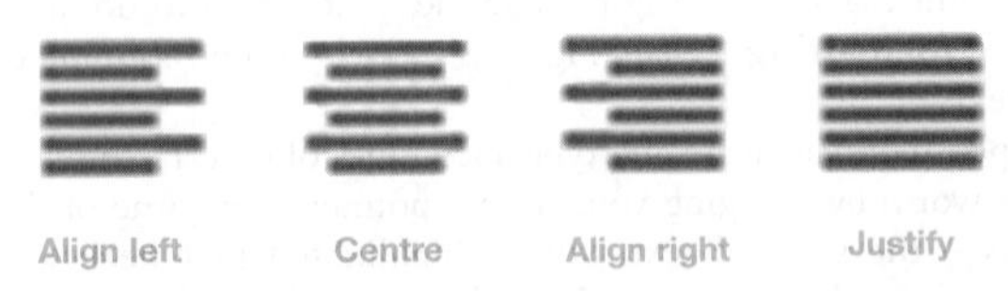

The **bullet** button allows you to insert bullet points whenever you hit the return key. You'll see similar buttons in most word processor packages.

All these changes can also be made in the dialog boxes for **Font**, **Paragraph** and **Bullets**, which can be opened from the **Format** menu. In WordPad these dialog boxes don't offer you many extra options (in Font, you can opt for ~~strikethrough~~ text, and in Paragraph you can edit the size of the margins for each paragraph). But the equivalent boxes in more comprehensive word processors offer literally hundreds of style and layout options. Full word processing packages (see p.256) also allow you to split the text into columns, add tables, headers and page numbers, check your spelling – the list is practically endless. DTP packages take things a step further (see p.256), offering a complete set of tools for producing layouts for magazines, leaflets and so on – though some basic desktop publishing is possible in many popular word processors.

Tips & Tricks | Tech Info | Try This

Macros

Some programs, such as Microsoft Word, allow you to record a series of commands – called a **macro** – which you can use to save the time and hassle of typing a string of commands in again and again. Let's say, for example, that you regularly take a list, turn it into a table and change the text to a particular font size, colour and style: with a macro you can do all this with one touch of a button or by using a customized key combination. To create a macro press **Record Macro** (sometimes found in the **Tools** menu under **Macros**) and make all your formatting changes (do it slowly and carefully, however, as everything will be recorded). The program will save the commands as a macro, and ask you to assign it a toolbar button or keyboard shortcut. Next time you come to do the same formatting, simply highlight the relevant text, press the button or keys that you assigned to the macro, and hey presto.

Making pictures work

Today's PCs are designed to do a lot more than just let you write letters and play Pac-Man. And one of the areas that has benefited the most from technological advances has been **imaging** – working with photos and pictures on-screen.

Whether you're messing with snaps downloaded from a digital camera, scanning and refreshing old photos or fashioning your own creations in a painting program, you'll find that many of the editing tools available to you are the same – whichever applications you're using. You'll even find that the icons in the toolbars will look very similar. This means that once you've grasped the basics of one graphics package you're in a good position to tackle another.

Chapter 12

Let's have a look at the Windows built-in graphics package, **Paint**, which you'll find by clicking **Start**, **Programs** and then **Accessories**. Though it's very limited compared to most graphics applications, Paint is fine for getting started.

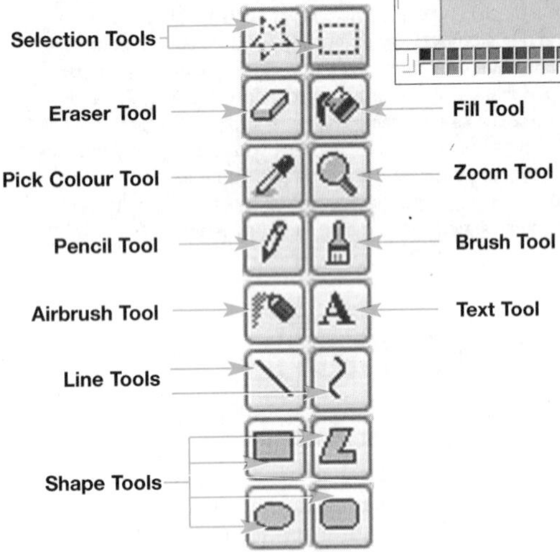

Selection Tools

Eraser Tool — Fill Tool

Pick Colour Tool — Zoom Tool

Pencil Tool — Brush Tool

Airbrush Tool — Text Tool

Line Tools

Shape Tools

Like an artist's toolbox, the toolbar on the left provides you with a selection of pencils, paintbrushes and so on. To select a tool, click it once and the button will become indented. Try out a few of these:

❐ **Pencil tool** Though not the first button in the panel, this is the best place to start. It allows you to draw freehand. Don't forget to choose a colour from the palette on the bottom of the screen before you start sketching.

❒ **Selection tools** Use these to select a part of your picture – either a "free-form" area with the left-hand button or a rectangular area with the right-hand button. Once selected, the area will appear within a dotted rectangular box, which you can then drag to a new location, or stretch by dragging the dots on the corners and edges of the dotted box. In more advanced programs, you can select an area of a picture and then do all sorts of clever things to it.

❒ **Eraser tool** As you'd expect, this allows you to delete unwanted bits of your picture. Click the tool, choose an eraser size from the options area under the toolbar and off you go.

❒ **Brush tool** This works in the same way as the pencil tool, but once you've clicked the button you can choose from a whole range of brush heads in the options area below the toolbar.

❒ **Airbrush tool** This creates an airbrush effect, which, used sparingly, can be very handy for touching up imperfections on photos. Once selected, you can choose from a number of spray options.

❒ **Pick colour tool** (or eyedropper tool) This valuable function allows you to select any colour within your image as the one to use with your next tool. Again, this comes into its own when you're touching up an image.

❒ **Text tool** Use this to insert text into an image with the keyboard.

❒ **Fill tool** This can be used to fill a section of your image with a selected colour. Be warned, however: you can get some

Oops!

Graphics packages seem sometimes to have a will of their own, and you'll often find yourself thinking: "Oh dear, I didn't want that to happen". In this situation go to the **Edit** menu and select **Undo**, or use the keyboard shortcut we mentioned earlier – **Control+Z**. This will back you out of whatever mess your last action got you into. Some packages will allow you several **levels of undo**, while others display the **History** of all your actions in a special window, making backtracking very easy indeed.

rather unpredictable results if a region you are trying to fill is not properly enclosed.

❒ **Zoom tool** This lets you zoom in on a particular area of your picture. The zoom on Paint is very simple; other packages invariably have two tools – one for zooming out and one for zooming in – and some let you drag a frame to select the rectangular area which you want to fill the screen.

❒ **Line tools** Again this is fairly simple: click the mouse in two places and a line will appear between them. The tool with the curvy line allows you to draw a line and then drag it in various directions to create a smooth arc between the two fixed points. This is very useful, but takes a bit of getting used to.

❒ **Shape tools** These allow you to draw rectangles, polygons, ellipses and rounded rectangles. When you select a shape tool, you can choose from three options below the toolbar. The top one provides an empty frame, the middle one a filled frame and the bottom one a filled shape with no frame whatsoever.

Once you feel confident with these tools, start to investigate some of the options available to you in the Menu bar. You will find that by selecting either all, or part, of an image you are

Tech Info | Tips & Tricks | Try This

TIFFs, GIFs and JPEGs

When you start working with images you'll soon discover that there are various different types of image file format, each with different strengths and uses, and some only compatible with specific programs. One of the most common non-Web image formata is the **TIFF** (short for **T**agged **I**mage **F**ile **F**ormats and recognizable by the **.tif** file extension). A TIFF is basically a bitmap (see p.76) that can support any size of image and any resolution. They can be black-and-white, greyscale or full colour. This format is favoured for images destined to be printed rather than used on the Internet.

When it comes to the Web there are only two formats commonly used: the **GIF** (**G**raphics **I**nterchange **F**ormat, with the **.gif** extension) and the **JPEG** (**J**oint **P**hotographic **E**xperts **G**roup format, with the **.jpg** extension). Both of these file types compress the information in an image so that the file is smaller and, in turn, faster to squeeze down a telephone line. The GIF uses what's known as a **lossless compression method**, which simply means that when it squishes an image to be used on the Web it's careful not to lose any of the original data. GIFs are especially good at compressing line-art and graphics with large areas of the same colour, but if you save complex photographic images as a GIF you'll be left with a big file. JPEGs, on the other hand, are much better for photos, though the compression process does discard some data, leaving you with an image inferior to the original. When you create JPEGs you get to specify the amount of compression you want, allowing you to trade image quality against file size. Experiment with various degrees of compression and see if you can tell the difference.

given various options that will **transform** it: flip it horizontally or vertically, invert the colours and so on. And if you like what you've created so much that you want to admire it all the time, you can set it as your Desktop Wallpaper by selecting the relevant option from the **File** menu.

Onwards and upwards

Windows Paint only scratches the surface of image creation and editing on the PC. In a serious graphics program (see p.259), the menus yield an unbelievable selection of tools, filters and options, allowing you to achieve remarkably professional results. So if you're at all serious about digital art, consider investing in something with a little more oomph.

13

Tips and tricks

clever keys and fancy clicks

It is possible to use a PC with very little coaching, but if you've got the time and the inclination you can greatly enhance your computing experience by learning a few clever mouse-clicks and keystrokes. In this chapter you'll find lots of hints and tips that'll help turn you into a quick and efficient user in no time at all.

Speeding up with shortcut keys

One of the best ways to slip into the fast lane is to start using shortcut keys. The mouse isn't very efficient for many tasks – why go through a series of menus with your mouse pointer to reach a dialog box that could be opened instantaneously with a key combination?

One of the most useful shortcuts is **Alt+Tab**, which allows you to move between open windows. Try it: open a few windows, press and hold **Alt**, and tap **Tab** (still holding down Alt). A little panel will pop up showing icons representing the windows currently open; keep pressing Tab and you'll move between them. When you get to the window you want, let go – the little panel will vanish and your selected window will move to the foreground. To move between your windows in the opposite direction hold down **Alt+Shift** whilst pressing Tab. Another useful Alt shortcut is **Alt+F4**, which closes the program you're currently working in.

Windows shortcut keys

If you have a **Windows key** (see p.102) on your keyboard, it can be used for all sorts of shortcuts, which will work in whatever program you're working with at the time. Try these out:

Windows	Launches the **Start menu**
Windows+E	Launches **Windows Explorer** with the folder tree showing
Windows+D	**Minimizes** and **restores** all windows for quick access to the Desktop
Windows+F	Launches a **Search** window
Windows+F1	Launches **Windows Help**
Windows+Pause Break	Opens **System Properties**
Windows+R	Launches the **Run** command dialog box
Windows+U	Launches the **Utility Manager**

Try This | Tips & Tricks | Tech Info

Why put mice on the menu?

Open **My Computer** and press the **Alt** key – the **File** menu on the Menu bar will become highlighted, showing that your menus are now active. Each menu title, and each item in the menus, has a single letter underlined: **File**, **Edit**, **Format**, etc. Instead of clicking a menu or item with your mouse, you can now simply press the relevant letter key on your keyboard. Alternatively, you can use the arrow keys to navigate left, right, up and down, and then press **Enter** to make a selection.

Document - WordPad
File Edit View Insert Format Help

This useful technique also works in Windows dialog boxes as well as in most programs (though sometimes you'll need to hold down Alt whilst you press the letter or arrow keys).

Seize control with Control

The Control key, often labelled **Ctrl** on keyboards, is the business when it comes to shortcuts – it can be combined with various other keys to carry out all manner of tasks. What each combination does depends on the program you're using, though the most useful shortcuts are near-universal:

Ctrl+A	Select all	Ctrl+S	Save
Ctrl+C	Copy	Ctrl+V	Paste
Ctrl+X	Cut	Ctrl+W	Close the current window
Ctrl+N	New window/ document	Ctrl+Y	Redo
Ctrl+P	Print	Ctrl+Z	Undo

When combined with non-letter keys, Control generally provides a more powerful version of whatever key it is used with. In Windows and most word processors, for example, the **left** and **right cursors** (the arrow keys) move your flashing insertion point along a line of text letter by letter. Hold down Control, though, and they move the insertion point a word at a time. Equally, where a tap of the **Enter** key takes you onto a new line, **Control+Enter** takes you to a new page. Likewise, the **Home** and **End** keys escort you to the beginning or end of a line; but combined with Control, they take you to the beginning or end of a whole document or Web page.

Take a look at the menus of your favourite programs and you'll probably find that next to each of the most important options a shortcut key is listed. This is a good way to find application-specific key combinations quickly.

Mouse magic

You can greatly add to the power of the mouse by using it in combination with the keyboard. Holding down Control, Shift or Alt whilst clicking can give you loads of different options – hold down Control, for example, to click and select multiple files in Windows. In many packages, even the scroll wheel has some hidden secrets: it can often be used to zoom in and out when combined with the Control key.

Accelerator keys

A little-known Windows trick is to assign special shortcut keys to each of your programs, allowing you to open them at any time without having to fiddle about with the mouse or the Start menu. Choose a program that you use a lot, go to its icon in the Start menu, right-click it and select **Properties**. Click the **Shortcut** tab (it will probably be open already) and you'll see the **Shortcut key** text box near the bottom, displaying **None**. Click in the box and simply hit the letter on the keyboard you'd like to use as the shortcut key for the

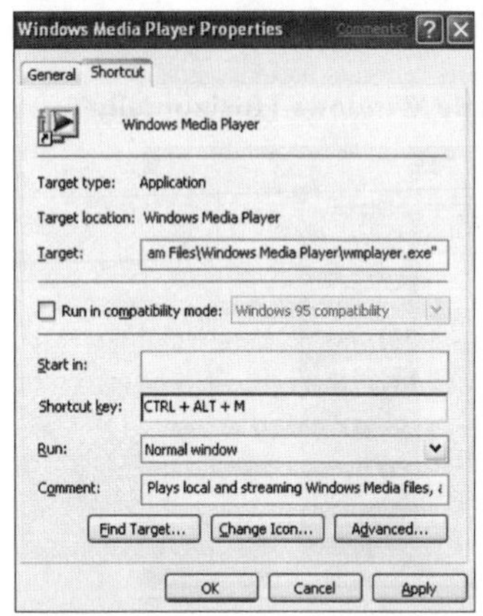

program – the first letter of the program's name makes sense, say **M** for Media Player. The box will then show **Ctrl+Alt+M** (or whichever letter you have entered). Click **OK** to close the dialog box. Now, whenever you hold down **Ctrl+Alt** and press the letter you selected, the program will spring into life.

Arranging windows

If you have lots of windows open at once, things can get messy. If you right-click any blank space in the Taskbar, including its bottom edge, you'll see a list of options including **Cascade**, which arranges all your windows into an orderly stack.

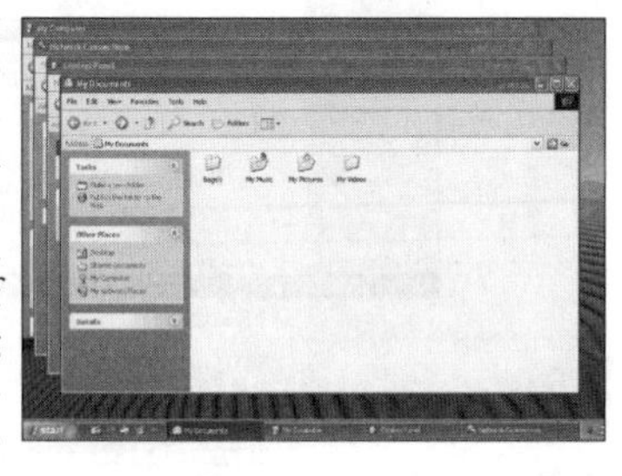

If you want to work in more than one program or document simultaneously, you can **Tile** the windows – divide the screen between them. Minimize or close any windows you don't want to see, right-click any blank area of the Taskbar and click **Tile Windows Vertically**.

You can also choose to **Tile Windows Horizontally**.

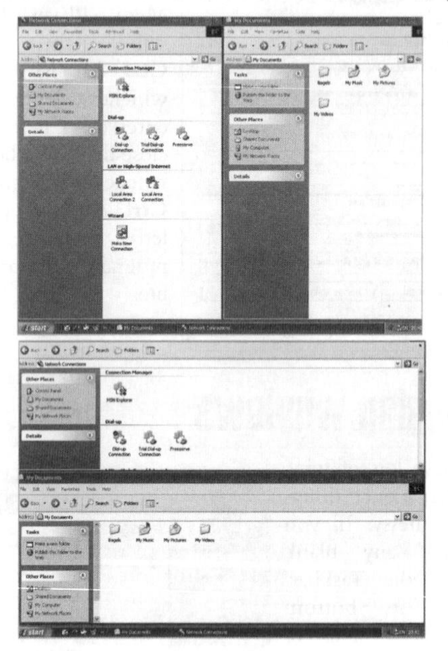

Other Windows tips

We could quite easily fill this whole book with additional Windows tips, cheats and hints, but we simply haven't got the space – so here's a selection of the most useful. If you want to find more, either search on the Web or just experiment.

Startup tips

❐ If you want **a program to start automatically** when you turn on your PC, find it in the Start menu, right-click it and select **Create shortcut**. Then drag the shortcut into the **Startup folder** (also in **Programs** in the Start menu). If you later decide that you don't want a program to start automatically, simply delete its shortcut from the Startup folder.

❐ To stop your Startup programs loading on a particular occasion, hold down the **Control** key while the Windows Startup screen is showing.

Tips for dragging files

❐ If you're **dragging a file** from one location to another and you see a little plus sign appear on the mouse pointer, the file will be copied rather than moved (the original will remain where it is). If you'd rather actually move it, simply hold down **Shift** while you drag.

❐ If you want to copy rather than move a file, press the **Control** key while you drag.

❐ If you see a little arrow appear on the pointer when you're dragging a file, you will **create a shortcut** rather than moving or copying the file. You can do this at any time by holding down the **Alt** key and performing the drag.

❐ If you want to drag a file into an Explorer window that is open but not visible, drag and hold it over the relevant window's button on the Taskbar. After a second or two the window will rise to the surface, allowing you to complete the drag.

❐ You can **abort a drag** by pressing the **Escape** key before releasing the mouse button.

Tips for browsing files

❐ Windows is set by default so that when you double-click a folder or drive icon in an Explorer window, the window changes to display the contents of the folder or drive. If you hold down **Control** when you double-click, though, a new window will open to display the contents.

❐ If you'd prefer this to happen all the time, it's easy to set up. Open **My Computer** and select **Folder Options** from the **Tools** menu (or the **View** menu in Windows 98). Under the **General** tab, check the **Open each folder in a new window** box and click **OK**.

❐ Selecting **Details** from the **View** menu of an Explorer window puts the items in a list and displays columns of information about them, telling you things like a file's size, its type and the date it was last modified. If you click the grey header of each column, the items will be sorted by whatever the heading relates to: click **Name** to sort alphabetically by name, **Size** to sort numerically by file size, and so on.

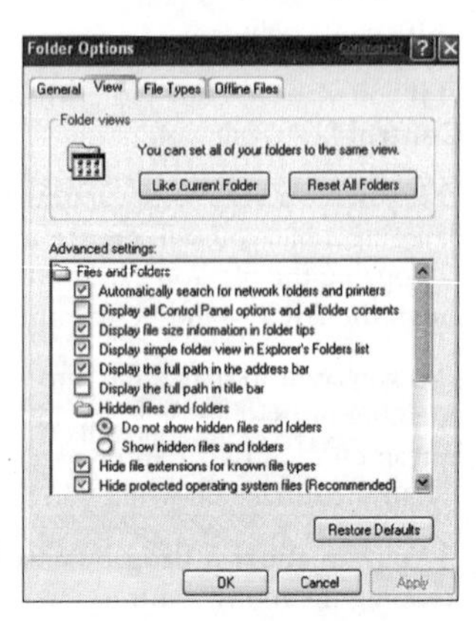

❐ To set a **default folder view**, open My Computer and choose your favourite view option from the **View** menu (such as **Details** or **Large Icons**). Then click **Folder Option** in the **Tools** menu (or the **View** menu in

Windows 98), select the **View** tab, and click the **Like Current Folder** button. From now on, whenever you open a folder its contents will be displayed with the view option you've chosen.

❒ You can **change the icon of a shortcut** by right-clicking it, selecting **Properties** and then clicking **Change icon**. You can either choose from a pre-installed selection or click **Browse** and select any bitmap file on your machine.

Tips for toolbars

❒ In Explorer windows such as My Documents – as well as in most application windows – you can customize the toolbars, removing buttons you rarely use and adding new ones for commands you frequently need. Often this is done by right-clicking the relevant toolbar and selecting **Customize** from its mouse menu. You will be presented with a dialog box packed full of options and button lists. You can also generally use this dialog box to hide the text labels attached to a button and make other alterations to its appearance.

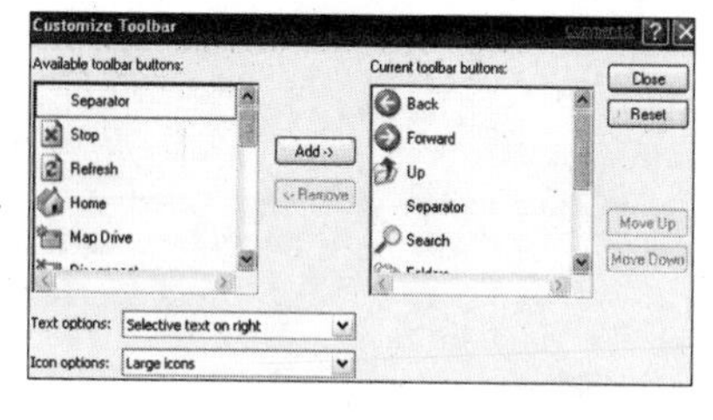

❒ Toolbars usually live up at the top of a window, but they can often be pulled around at will. Try left-clicking one, on either its edge or a blank section, and dragging it somewhere else. You'll probably discover that it can be repositioned anywhere, have its proportions changed or be anchored to any edge of the window.

part three

get yourself connected

14

The Internet

connecting, surfing, searching

For many computer users, an Internet connection is the main reason for buying a PC. This isn't surprising: from surfing to shopping to staying in touch, the Internet is an amazing tool, and it's one that is becoming ever more integral to the way in which we live. The following two chapters cover the basics: getting online, surfing, searching and using email. If you want to know more, check out this book's sister volumes, *The Rough Guide to the Internet* and *The Rough Guide Website Directory* – you could even buy them online.

Hooking up

The first thing you need to get online is a **modem**, a piece of hardware that lets your computer communicate with other computers via a phone line or some other type of connection. If you've bought a new PC recently, it will almost certainly have come with a modem built-in. But if you're without, fear not –

modems are inexpensive to buy (see p.57) and easy to add to your system (see p.314).

Once your modem is in place, you need to connect it to the outside world. Though there are various fast and fancy types of modem around, such as **cable** and **ADSL** (see p.58), most computers come with **56k** models that need to be plugged into a regular phone line. Your computer or modem should have come with a standard modem cable, with a phone plug on one end and a slightly smaller plug on the other which fits into a socket on the back of the computer. If the lead isn't long enough to reach from the PC to your phone socket, you can connect it with a standard phone extension lead.

Choose an ISP

Once you're plugged in you need to get yourself an account with an **Internet Service Provider** (**ISP**) – a company that will provide you with an Internet connection. Basically, the Internet is just a colossal network of computers – when you connect to the Web, you actually connect to a large computer belonging to your ISP, which in turn is connected to other machines spread around the globe. These computers collectively house the billions of Web pages available online.

There are two main factors to consider when choosing an ISP: **quality of service** and **cost**. When it comes to service, an inferior ISP may have too many customers for its facilities, so you might sometimes get a slow connection or the occasional line-busy signal when you try to connect, especially at peak times. Ask friends for recommendations and check Internet magazines for reviews. When it comes to cost, you'll be faced with a different set of options depending on which country you're in. In the US and Australia, most ISPs charge a monthly fee but you don't have to pay any extra for the time you spend online. In the UK, many ISPs are free, but you have to pay your telephone company for each minute that you're online – at the same rate the company charges for local phone calls. However, other British ISPs offer all-inclusive packages: you'll be charged a monthly fee but can make unlimited free calls either whenever you like or in the evenings and weekends, depending on the deal. Check Internet magazines for the latest offers.

Getting online

Once you've chosen which ISP to go with, there are various ways to proceed. The simplest is to get hold of one of their **free CDs**, which will provide you with the relevant software and take you through the process of connecting. ISP CDs are given out everywhere: on the front of magazines, in the mail, at computer shops. And they often include **free trials** – a week, month or number of hours online, with nothing to pay. If you can't find a CD for the ISP of your choice, phone the company: they should be happy to send you one. When it arrives, sim-

Welcome to the Internet Connection Wizard
This wizard helps you connect your computer to the Internet.
Sign up with a new ISP
Get my account information from my ISP
This is a good choice if you do not have all the information needed to set up a connection manually.
Set up a connection manually or through a local area network
To set up a connection manually, you need a user name, password, and other information from an Internet service provider (ISP).
If you are using a modem to connect to the Internet, make sure your telephone line is connected to the modem before you continue.
To continue, click Next.

ply put the CD in your drive and a wizard will guide you through the rest of the process. You'll be ready to start surfing in minutes. Alternatively, you could try to get connected using the built-in Windows **Connection Wizard**, which may well have its own icon on your Desktop. If you can't find it, the wizard can be summoned by opening Internet Explorer (the blue "**e**" on your Taskbar) or by opening the Control Panel, clicking **Internet Options** (under the **Network and Internet Connections** category in Windows XP) and clicking the **Setup** button under the **Connections** tab. The wizard will refer you to a list of your local ISP servers, and help you to create the new connection.

Surfing

A Web browser is the only piece of software you need to surf the Internet: it's the program through which you view Websites and navigate between them. Though there are other browsers around – see the box on p.209 – **Internet Explorer**, which comes pre-installed in Windows, is as good as any. It's very easy to use, and looks and works in a similar way to the Windows Explorer program that you employ to browse through your files and folders (see p.123). To open Internet Explorer, click its blue "**e**" icon, which you'll find on the Taskbar, in the Start menu or on the Desktop. When you do this, Windows will probably open the connection panel for your ISP and ask you to enter your password. Do this, and press **Connect**. (Usually there will be **Remember password** and **Connect automatically** checkboxes, which you can click if you want your machine to go online automatically every time you open Explorer.)

Once your PC has connected to the Internet, a Website – probably your ISP's – will appear in the main section of your browser. To visit a different site, simply enter its **address** or **URL** (such as www.roughguides.com) in the address bar and then either press the **Go** button to the right of the address bar or hit **Enter** on the keyboard. If you're using an old version of the Explorer program, you may have to put **http://** before each **www** address – but newer versions don't require you to do so. After a few seconds, the page should start to appear in the window. It's as easy as that.

The other browsers

Most people stick with Internet Explorer simply because it comes bundled with Windows, but other browsers are out there, and you may find one that you prefer. One popular option is **Netscape**, which ruled the roost before being overshadowed by Explorer. It's now resurfaced as an impressive open source product (see p.235). **Opera**, popular among Linux users, is very undemanding on system resources and claims to be "the fastest browser on earth". Then there's **MSN Explorer**, another Microsoft product that ships with XP; it may be easy to use, but its primary function is to make the Web a Microsoft-only experience. You're better sticking with Explorer or one of the others mentioned above. For more, see:

http://home.netscape.com/browsers
http://www.opera.com
http://explorer.msn.com/home.htm

N
Netscape

Move your mouse around over a Web page and you'll probably notice that at various times – when your pointer is hovering over some underlined text, for example – it turns into a little hand. This means you're pointing to a **link**, which can be clicked to trigger your browser either to download a new page or to take you to another part of the current one. Click with the mouse and you'll go to the new location. This is what surfing is all about: **browsing** from page to page by clicking links.

Inevitably you'll sometimes open a page you're not interested in or one that simply doesn't work (in which case you'll see an error message), and realize that you'd rather be at the page you were on before. Simply click the **back** button on the toolbar and back you'll go. Next to the back button you'll see a **forward** button, which will return you to a page that you've just backtracked from. These buttons come into their own when you're manoeuvring between pages that you've already visited, saving you the hassle of following links or typing in addresses again and again. Sometimes, the back and forward buttons will appear greyed-out (for example in a freshly opened Internet Explorer window) because the window hasn't yet displayed other Web pages for you to move between.

Try This | Tips & Tricks | Tech Info

There's no place like a home page

Once you're set up with an ISP, you'll probably find that every time you start Internet Explorer you'll be magically transported to their own Website – a cunning ploy to increase the value of their advertising space (which is calculated by the number of visitors, however unwilling). If this happens, it means that they set their site as your **home page**. But this isn't a permanent fixture, and you can make any site you like your home page – a **news provider**, perhaps, or your favourite **search engine** (see below). Or you could choose not to have a home page, so that you get a blank window waiting for instructions instantly when you open your browser. To set or delete your home page, open Internet Explorer and select **Internet Options** from the **Tools** menu. Enter the address of your desired home page, or click the **Use Blank** button, and click **OK**.

One surfing technique that can come in very useful is to hold down **Shift** on your keyboard while you click on a link. This will open the page that the link leads to **in a new window**. If you don't like what you see, you can simply close the window in the normal way (or with the keyboard shortcut **Control+W**) and the last page will still be sitting there in the background – you won't have to wait for it to reload, as you would have if you'd used **back**.

Searching

Surfing is all well and good for a leisurely exploration of the Web's endless content, but if you want to find something specific you'll need to search for it. This is where **search engines** come in: they are huge databases that index millions of Web pages, allowing you to search quickly and conveniently for the item you want. Using a search engine is easy: you go to its Website, type in a word or phrase and after a couple of seconds you'll be presented with a list of links to Websites that contain your text. There are loads of search engines out there – here are a few of the best:

Google http://www.google.com
All The Web http://www.alltheweb.com
AltaVista http://www.av.com
Northern Light http://www.nlsearch.com

There are also many search engines that only retrieve results from a particular country. Two examples are:

AltaVista UK http://uk.altavista.com (UK)
Yahoo http://www.yahoo.com.au (AUS)

Some search engines are better than others – faster and capable of retrieving a larger number of more relevant results. **Google**, for example, is lightning-quick, uses an ingenious way to find the best matches for your search and lets you read the line of text where the word or phrase that you searched for was found, to give you some idea of the context.

But before you start searching, bear two things in mind. First, **no search engine covers the whole Internet**, so if a search doesn't yield any results it doesn't mean the thing you're looking for isn't anywhere on the Web – it's probably worth trying other engines. Second, if you search for a common word or phrase you may end up with a **million results or more**. To avoid this, you need to make your search as **specific as possible**. There are various methods of telling your search engine exactly what to look for using inverted commas and plus and minus signs. To give you the idea, here are a few ways of searching for the same words:

Searching for:	Will bring up page containing:
my name	One or both words in any order
+my +name	Both words in any order
"my name"	The exact phrase
+my -name	The first word but not the second
"my name" -"name my"	The first phrase but not the second

These techniques will work on nearly all search engines, but they aren't universal, so it's worth reading the tips, found under "search tips" or "search help", on the home page of the engine you use.

Internet Options

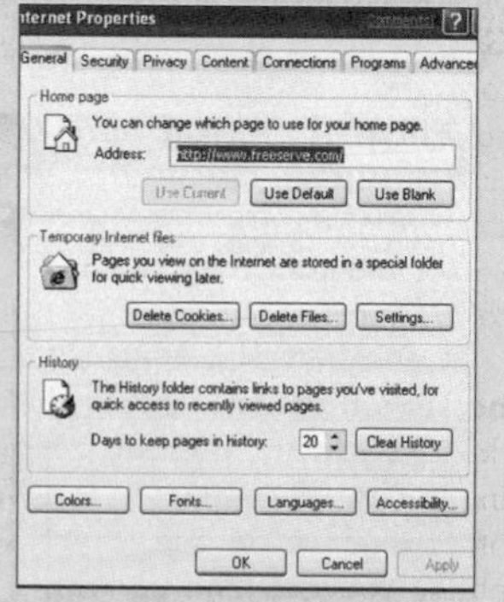

The Internet Options dialog box, which can be launched from the Tools menu of Internet Explorer (or from the Control Panel) contains a host of **Internet settings and options,** some of which are well worth getting to know. Under the **General** tab you can adjust your home page (see p.211) and the settings of your **History folder**, which keeps a record of all the Websites that you've visited recently. The **Connections** tab lets you adjust, set up and delete Internet connections, and under **Security** you can keep an eye on sites that you want to avoid because they may harbour viruses or other troublesome elements (see p.276).

Favorites

Look at the top of the Internet Explorer window and you'll see a **Favorites** menu. This is where you can store links to Websites you intend to come back to – whether they're sites that you visit frequently or pages that you've stumbled across and don't want to forget about.

To add a site to your Favorites list, simply go to the relevant site and click the **Add to Favorites** option in the Favorites menu of your browser's menu bar. A box will come up in which you can rename the link if you wish. Then click **OK** and the page will be added to the bottom of the Favorites menu. When you want to visit the site again, simply go to the menu and click the appropriate item – easy. If you use particular Favorites a lot, you can view them in a special frame on the left-hand side of the Internet Explorer window, which can be opened by clicking the **Favorites** button on the **Toolbar**.

Once you've been using your Favorites menu for a while,

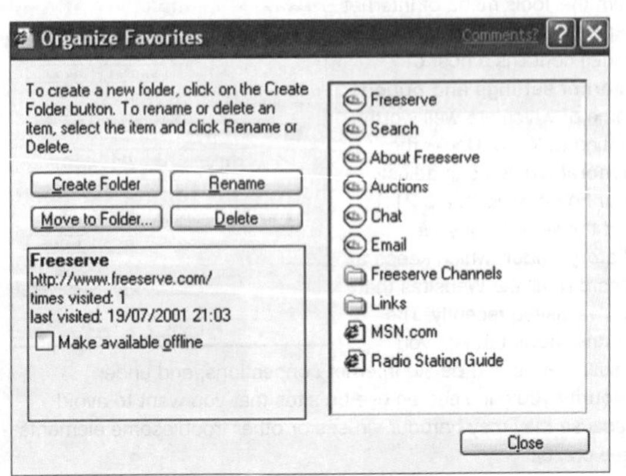

adding to it on a regular basis, the list can get rather messy. To smarten things up, click **Organize Favorites** at the top of the menu. In the dialog box that appears you can create folders for related links – books, news or whatever – and rename or delete individual items.

Disconnecting a dial-up connection

Though the Internet is addictive, at some point you have to disconnect – especially if you're paying by the minute for access. To do this, close all your Internet Explorer Windows and you'll probably be presented with a dialog box prompting you either to stay online or disconnect. Click the **Disconnect** button and your PC will sever its connection. If you don't receive this prompt, it probably means that your Internet Explorer **Auto Disconnect** feature has been disabled. To switch it back on, run Internet Explorer, open the **Tools** menu and select **Internet Options**. In the box that will pop up choose the **Connections** tab, select your dial-up connection from the list and click **Settings**. Another box will pop up, in which you should click the **Advanced** button (possibly under the Dial-up Settings tab). You'll now see a final dialog box in which you can check the **Disconnect when connection may no longer be needed** box.

Another way to disconnect is by right-clicking the **Connections icon** – generally a graphic of two connected PCs – that appears in the Notification area of your Taskbar when you're online. From the options that appear, click **Disconnect**. When you're disconnected, the icon will either vanish entirely or be obscured by a red cross.

15

Email

staying in touch

Email – short for **electronic mail** – has become the standard way by which businesses communicate, overseas friends and family stay in touch and office employees chat to their peers instead of doing any work. For the uninitiated, it may seem like a simple, perhaps even silly, concept: you type a message on one computer and send it to another instead of simply picking up the phone and talking in person. But as anyone who has tried email will tell you, it's not only a great deal of fun but brings about a whole different mode of communication – as informal and instantaneous as a phone call but with all the benefits of good old-fashioned letter writing. It also lets you do lots of clever stuff: send one message to lots of people, **forward** a message you received to someone else, **attach** documents and pictures to a message so that the recipient can open them on their machine – the list goes on.

Accounts and addresses

To receive email you need an email address, which, like a real address, is what the sender adds to their message to direct it to you. An email address always looks something like this: **myname@myISPorcompany.com**.

When you sign up with an ISP you'll automatically be given an email account and asked to choose one or more email addresses. Email accounts like these, which are called **POP3** (Post Office Protocol 3) accounts, require an **email program** – a piece of software for writing, sending, receiving, storing and managing your mail. Your ISP may provide you with an email program when you sign up, but a very good one, called **Outlook Express**, is built into Windows. A new email account may either set itself up for use with Outlook Express automatically, or by means of a self-explanatory wizard. If not, your ISP should provide instructions on making the settings.

Composing, sending and receiving

Using email is a breeze – there are only a few concepts to get used to and all of them are easy to grasp. The following paragraphs introduce **Outlook Express**, which you can open by clicking the little envelope icon in the Start menu or on the Quick Launch area of the Taskbar. There are many other email programs available, but they all work in pretty much the same way.

When you open Outlook Express you'll see this window:

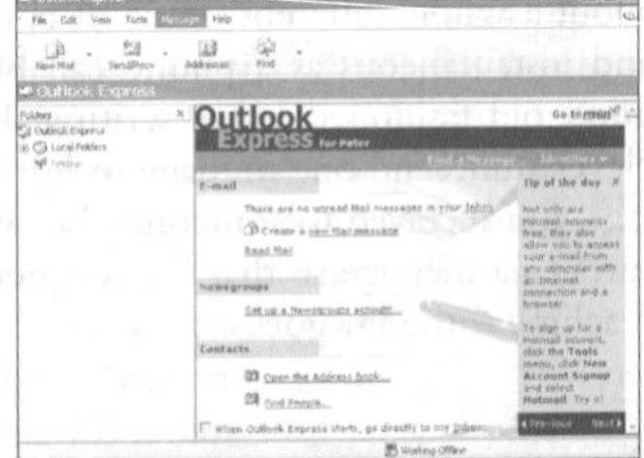

Web-based email

An alternative to using a POP3 account is to use a Web-based email account from one of the many free online providers such as **Yahoo** and **Hotmail**. With these accounts, you don't use an email program, but simply visit the Website of the provider (such as **http://www.yahoo.com** or **http://www.hotmail.com**), enter your username and password (which you'll be given when you open the account) then send, receive, store and manage your emails online. The advantage of Web-based accounts is that you can easily check your mail on any computer in the world that's connected to the Internet, and you can delete unwanted emails without having to wait for them to download. However, they do have their drawbacks: some have quite **bad security records**, you can only store a certain amount of mail at any one time, you can't view your mail without **going online**, and everything **takes longer** – especially if you have a slow connection. But why not open a Web-based account as well as your normal POP3 account? They don't cost anything and can come in very handy, especially if you travel a lot, because you can access them from anywhere that has a Web connection. You can even **synchronize** your two accounts, and set Outlook Express to download automatically from both your POP3 and Web-based accounts. (For more on setting up Outlook Express, see *The Rough Guide to the Internet*.)

Your emails are arranged into folders, which will appear listed down the left when you double-click **Local Folders**. The most important folders are the **Inbox**, where messages arrive; the **Outbox**, where messages you've written are held until you click **Send/Receive**; and **Sent Mail**, where copies of your outgoing messages are stored.

Click the **Inbox** and you'll see all the messages you've received so far in the top right-hand section of the screen – if you haven't given your address to anyone yet, there will probably just be a couple of nondescript welcome emails from your ISP and Outlook Express. To check if you have any new mail, simply click the **Send/Receive** button on the toolbar. Your computer will try to connect to the Internet and download any new messages.

Sending a message

Click **New Message** (**Create** or **Compose** in some programs) and you'll be presented with a blank message window.

Enter the email address of the person you want to send the message to in the **To** section. If you want to send the message to more than one person, simple write more addresses, separating them with semicolons. You can also **copy** the message to one or more people by entering their addresses in the **Cc** section (the term comes from "carbon copy"). They will receive the message but see that it was addressed primarily to someone else. Then enter a **subject** for the message – you don't have to, but it makes it easy for the recipient to see what the message is about and to find it if they need to refer to it later. If you have more than one email account set up in Outlook Express, use the **From** dropdown menu to choose your account, then simply write your message and click **Send**.

If you are replying to an email, it's even simpler. Click **Reply** on the toolbar and a new message window will appear with the To and Subject sections already filled in. If you've been sent a

Tips & Tricks | Try This | Tech Info

Organizing emails

Various columns of information tell you about each message in your Inbox or any other folder: who it's from, when it was received, its subject, whether there are any attachments (the paperclip column) and whether the sender has marked it as high priority (the ! column). You can **arrange the messages** by any one of these categories by clicking on the relevant column's grey header. To see all the messages you've received from one person, select a message from them and then click the grey header of the **From** column. All the messages they sent you that are stored in the folder will be displayed. When your Inbox starts getting full, you may want to **delete unwanted messages** or create various **folders** for the different types of message you've received (this can be done via the **File** menu). Then, as new mail arrives, you can drag items into these folders, keeping everything nice and tidy.

message that was addressed or copied to more than one person, you have the choice to click **Reply All**, which sends the new message to everyone who received the original.

Attachments

One of the beauties of email is that you can attach any file or files to a message – a photo, a document you'd like someone to look over, a form to be filled in and returned or anything else you fancy sending. All you do is click the **Attach** button when composing a message, select the files you want to add and click **OK**. Bear in mind, though, that large files can take a long time to **upload** (send) and **download** (receive), especially with a slow connection – so if you send all your friends a 50MB video file you may become unpopular very quickly. If you do have large files to send, consider **compressing** them to reduce their size (see p.134).

Address book

Try clicking the **Addresses** button on the Outlook toolbar to open your Windows address book (which can also be accessed via the **Accessories** section of the Start menu: see p.165). This is a very useful place to keep details of all the people you correspond with. If someone's name and email address is in your address book, you can simply type their name in the **To** section of a message and Outlook will immediately insert that person's email address for you.

Working offline

When you're writing a long email, bear in mind that you can choose to **Work Offline** via the command in Outlook's **File**

Windows Messenger

If you fancy chatting on the Internet using typed messages that are sent instantaneously, you may want to try out the **Windows Messenger**. Using this program you can check to see if your friends (fellow Messenger users) are online – and if they are, you can start communicating straight away. Up to four people can communicate with each other at once, which can be loads of fun. In Windows XP, set yourself up for the service by clicking the **Start** button, then **Programs** and selecting **Windows Messenger**. This will launch a wizard to walk you through the "sign in" process (if you haven't already, you will need to get a **.NET Passport** to complete the process: see p.154). If your Windows version doesn't feature Messenger, it can be downloaded for free from **http://messenger.msn.com**.

menu. This way you can disconnect from the Internet to free up your phone line – and save some money if you're paying for your connection by the minute. Then when you're ready, click **Send/Receive** and your PC will go online and send your mail. You can even set Outlook to automatically disconnect each time it finishes sending and receiving: from the **Tools** menu select **Options**, and then under the **Connection** tab, check the **Hang up after sending and receiving** box and click **Apply**.

16

Networking

hooking up the home

Though the term "**network**" is commonly associated with the complex computer systems of large companies, all it really refers to is a number of computers linked together so that their users can do neighbourly things like share files, an Internet connection and peripherals such as a printer. Whether you're using a notebook alongside a desktop system or you have an old PC lying idle in a cupboard, you might find that setting up a network is both useful and fun.

Networks are generally of two types: **local area networks** (LANs), where the PCs are all in the same building; or **wide area networks** (WANs), where the computers are in various distinct geographical locations, connected by telephone lines or radio waves. Obviously enough, home networks fall into the LAN category as all the PCs to be linked together will be within your home. And, as we shall see, the whole process is very easy to set up and maintain.

Tech Info | Tips & Tricks | Try This

Network-speak

Networking is a subject heavily polluted by jargon. If you explore the area in any depth, it won't be long before you're confronted with references to **topology** (the way a network is arranged; in a **star** or **ring** shape, for example). And you will also discover that networks use specific **protocols** – principles or rules – that define the way in which the computers talk to each other. This in turn describes the **architecture** of the network: whether the PCs are operating **peer-to-peer** (with all machines having equal responsibilities) or have a **client/server** relationship, with one machine acting as a **host**.

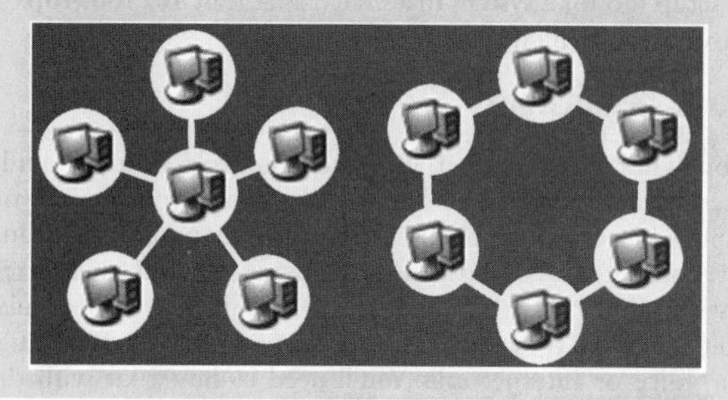

There are several different ways to set up a home network, each of which has advantages and disadvantages. The key things to consider are how easy it is to get the network up and running, and the **speed** of the connection you'll end up with. Here's a look at the main options.

Wired Ethernet network

This is the traditional method of networking, and it requires standardized lightweight cables (such as **10BaseT**) to be run between the PCs. Each machine will require a suitable **network interface card** (see p.59), and you'll also need a **network hub**, which acts like a junction box controlling the flow of data around the network. Notebooks can connect via special PC cards (see p.18) that you insert and remove as and when you want to connect them to the network. All this hardware can be purchased together as a kit; it's relatively inexpensive to set up, and gives you a very fast setup (go for a system that's rated as at least **10/100Mbps** if you want really high speed).

Telephone network

Though not as fast as Ethernet, a phone network is easy and tidy to set up: instead of running new cable around your house, you simply plug each computer into a different phone point and they communicate via the existing wires. Data is transferred between the PCs at a much higher frequency than regular phone calls, so your network will never interfere with either your voice or Internet calls. You'll need to buy a kit with the appropriate network cards.

Powerline network

This system works in the same way as a telephone network, but utilizes your home's electrical cabling, with the computers connecting directly to conventional power sockets. Though attractive in principle, this system gives a slow network connection, the wires tend to be very "noisy" (the signal may be unreliable), and there are also security issues to consider – it isn't difficult for people outside the home to intercept your data.

Tech Info | Tips & Tricks | Try This

Direct cable connections

An alternative to a full-blown network is a **direct cable connection**, which allows you to connect two PCs (one acting as the **host**, the other as a **guest**) with a cable running between their parallel, serial or USB ports. This saves you the hassle and expense of buying and installing network cards – all you need is the correct bi-directional cable. However, the data transfer rate is generally a bit sluggish, and the settings can be tricky to get right. Windows Help doesn't offer much in the way of support, but if you have a look on the Internet you'll find that there are many sites crammed with good advice. Take a look at:
http://www.wown.com/j_helmig/dccmain.htm

Wireless network (WLAN)

The coolest (but most expensive) option is a wireless network, which connects computers via radio waves or infrared, each PC using an adapter to receive and send the data transmissions. These systems are great if you use a notebook or handheld PC alongside a desktop system: as long as you're within range you can do everything from surfing the Net to printing documents without plugging in. When choosing a wireless system, look out for **Bluetooth** and **HomeRF** technologies.

Making it happen

Once you've decided which types of network to go for, bought the kit and installed the network cards (the same as installing any other PCI card: see p.314) and wired everything together, it's time to configure your PCs to recognize each other. This isn't too difficult – most network hardware kits come with decent software and instructions to guide you through the process. If you're running Windows 98 SE, you can use the Internet Connection Sharing Wizard; to get this utility running go to the Control Panel, select **Add/Remove Programs** then **Windows Setup**, click **Internet Tools**, select **Details** and check the **Internet Connection Sharing** box. For more on Windows 98 networks see: **http://creative.zdnet.com/adverts/micro/zdfuturehome/whitePapers/a_home_network.htm**

If you're running Windows XP or Me, it's even easier, as you can use the **Network Setup Wizard** or **Home Networking Wizard**.

Welcome to the Network Setup Wizard
This wizard will help you set up this computer to run on your network. With a network you can:
• Share an Internet connection
• Set up Internet Connection Firewall
• Share files and folders
• Share a printer

In XP go to **My Computer**, click **My Network Places** and click the blue **Set up a home network** link on the left; in Me, double-click **My Network Places** on the Desktop and select the **Home Networking Wizard** icon. The wizard will leap into action and ask you to enter various pieces of information; you'll need to name your PC so that it can be identified on the network, and define which files and features – such as printers – you want to share. In Me you will also be prompted to create a **network setup** floppy disk, which can be used to set up your other PCs for the network.

Don't worry too much about your initial network settings – you can always change them later in the Control Panel.

Using your network

Once your network is up and running, you can use any computer on the network as if it were simply an extension of your main machine. Assuming that the other PCs are switched on, you will be able to locate, browse, open or alter their "shared" files via the **My Network Places** icon on the Start menu, in My Computer, or on Desktop. This process also applies for shared printers: select **File** then **Print** and browse your way to the shared network printer. It's that easy.

Tech Info | Tips & Tricks | Try This

File sharing on a network

You can choose to make files and folders on one PC accessible to the others on the network. In Windows XP right-click a folder that you want to share, choose **Sharing and Security** from the mouse menu and check the **Share this folder on the network** box. You can also use this dialog box to assign the folder a network name, and to prevent others from editing the file's contents, by making it **read only**. In pre-XP versions of Windows right-click a file or folder, select **Sharing**, and you'll be presented with a dialog box with various options. You can choose between: **Read Only**, which allows others to look at a file but not change it; **Full**, which permits others to read and edit the file or folder; and **Depends on Password**, which allows you to give a different password for Read Only and Full access.

software

17

Operating systems

the software foundations

The one piece of software that you can't do without is an **operating system**, or **OS**. This is the underlying program that bridges the gap between the hardware of a computer and the application software running on it, and it also defines your user experience, determining what you see when you start up your machine and how you deal with files and programs.

Most modern operating systems have a **GUI** (graphic user interface), which allows you to communicate with your PC using icons, menus and a mouse pointer rather than having to type in encoded messages via the keyboard. But this user-friendly surface belies the complexity of these incredibly complicated multitasking programs, which do everything from helping a word processor save a document onto the hard drive to assigning RAM space and processor time to the various tasks the PC has been set.

Windows, Linux and other animals

The most commonly used operating systems are the members of Microsoft's **Windows** family – such as Windows 98, Windows 2000 and Windows XP – which between them are installed in around 90 percent of the world's PCs. This remarkable market position is largely the result of a situation that arose in the early 1980s (see p.346). To cut a long story short, Microsoft produced **MS-DOS**, the forerunner of Windows, for the first PCs, and as PCs boomed there were so many programs written to run on the operating system that before long no alternatives could really break into the market. Today, Microsoft's domination is such that most PCs come with the latest version of Windows pre-installed, and when people claim to know how to use a PC, what they really mean is that they know how to work Windows.

However, this isn't the end of the story. There are, and always have been, a number of alternatives to Microsoft's operating systems. One that has been rallying a great deal of support over the last few years is **Linux**, which is one of the many versions of the **UNIX** family of operating systems, traditionally used on non-personal computers. Identified by its cartoon penguin mascot, Linux is an **open source** product (see box opposite) that first gained popularity among amateur programmers, but recently it's become a realistic option for home and business use.

Linux started life in the early 1990s as the hobby of a young Finnish student called **Linus Torvalds**. He made the operating system and its source code available for free on the Internet

Open source software

Most software is distributed in a "compiled", execute-only form, meaning you can run the program but you can't actually see the **source code** – the code that the programmer wrote to make the software. Indeed, commercial source codes are preciously guarded corporate secrets. With open source packages like Linux, however, the source code is freely distributed, allowing experienced users to customize the programming as they require and catalyse the development of new software versions.

and when programmers around the world sent in suggestions and bits of code, he incorporated some into new versions. Today there are many versions of Linux available, most of which you can download for free, but there are also companies, such as **Red Hat**, that sell a commercial Linux package complete with technical support. For more information about Linux, see http://www.linux.org, and for lots of free Linux programs go to http://www.fokus.gmd.de/linux.

Windows versions

The Windows brand is now a household name – you'd have to have spent the last ten years on Mars not to have an inkling that it has something to do with computers. What many people are less familiar with are the various versions of this Microsoft operating system. Until 2001, Windows followed two distinct paths, one paved for domestic users and the other for businesses. For the last few years, the domestic realm has been dominated by **Windows 95** and **Windows 98** – collectively known as **Windows 9x** – and **Windows Me** (Millennium Edition). This branch of the Windows family was designed with multimedia applications in mind, and each new version had a few extra features and was a bit more stable (less

Partitions

A **partition** is a section of a hard drive that is treated as a discrete unit. A single drive can have many partitions, each of which will work as if it is a separate physical drive with its own letter (C, D, E, etc) and icon in My Computer. All hard drives have at least one partition, generally labelled as drive C, but the term is most commonly used in relation to extra partitions.

Some people use partitions simply to **organize their data** – document files on C and program files on D, for example. This is a particularly good idea if you work with video or music a lot, as the read-write heads of the drive will not have to dart around so much to retrieve files during playback. And if you fancy trying out an **alternative operating system**, partitions again come into their own: a drive with two or more partitions can hold more than one OS. Sometimes when you install a new operating system from disc, you'll actually be offered the chance to create a new partition as part of the installation process. You could even end up with two operating systems on one computer: this is known as **dual booting** and requires you to choose which operating system to boot each time you start up.

In Windows, you can create partitions with the **Fdisk** or **Diskpart** utility (see p.329) but it deletes all the information currently stored on the drive. If you don't want to lose the data on the drive you'll need to get hold of a program such as **PartitionMagic**, which lets you manage and alter the size and properties of your hard drive's partitions. (A free trial version of Partition Magic is available from **http://www.powerquest.com/partitionmagic**.)

Though it sounds simple in principle, partitioning can be quite a complicated process – so before you dive in, read a little deeper in magazines and on the Web.

likely to crash) than its predecessor. Business users, on the other hand, have been catered for by the various versions of **Windows NT** and **Windows 2000**. The strengths of these systems reflect business requirements: reliability, networking and security features are high priority, though they don't support many multimedia programs.

These two strands of Windows – 9x/Me and NT/2000 – are based on two different **kernels** (the underlying codes), though they look and feel very similar. It was a long-standing intention of Microsoft to integrate them, creating a Windows platform that could satisfy both home and business users. This became a reality with the advent of **Windows XP**, which is built on the Windows 2000 kernel – making it stable, secure and network-friendly – but which also features the multimedia power of Windows Me. Distinct versions of the platform are available for home and business use, but they all run the same underlying code.

Notebooks use the same Windows versions as desktops, but many handheld PCs come equipped with another member of the Microsoft family – **Windows CE** – which is a special slimmed-down version designed to run on these small devices.

Upgrading Windows

If you've just purchased a new PC, you'll probably have the latest version of Windows. But if your PC is running an older version, you might consider upgrading. Whether or not this is possible depends on the age and specifications of your hardware: the newer versions of Windows are bulky and fast – if you haven't got enough free hard disk space, plenty of RAM or a processor that's speedy enough, they either won't run or they'll seriously under-perform. For XP, Microsoft's stated minimum is a Pentium 233 MHz processor, 64MB of RAM and a 1.5GB of hard disk space. With this, however, your PC will be running by the skin of its teeth: a 300 MHz processor, 128MB of RAM and a few gigabytes of spare hard disk space are more realistic. If you haven't got all this you may well be able to upgrade your hardware (see Chapter 22) to make a newer operating system work smoothly, but unless your current Windows version is unreliable or doesn't possess the features you need, it may not be worth the time and money.

If you decide to go for it, upgrading between Windows 95, 98 or Me is very simple – though if you have the necessary hardware, you may as well **go straight to XP**. Doing this is just as easy, though you might have to reinstall some of your applications afterwards. XP is worth considering: it is much more stable than previous home versions and includes many new features. All the extras first introduced in Me are there – Movie Maker (see p.179), built-in file compression (see p.134), System Restore (see p.170) and others – as well as better security and networking features, remote management tools and more. Though you can choose to run it with the "classic" Windows appearance, XP also boasts a sharp new look, with different icons, a revamped Explorer and a better Start menu.

Installing Windows

There are two types of Windows installation. The first is an **upgrade installation**, which involves installing a new version over an old one. The second is a **clean** or **full** installation, which means putting Windows onto a blank system.

Upgrade installations

An upgrade installation is very simple – but be sure to back up all your documents, downloaded programs, emails and so on (see

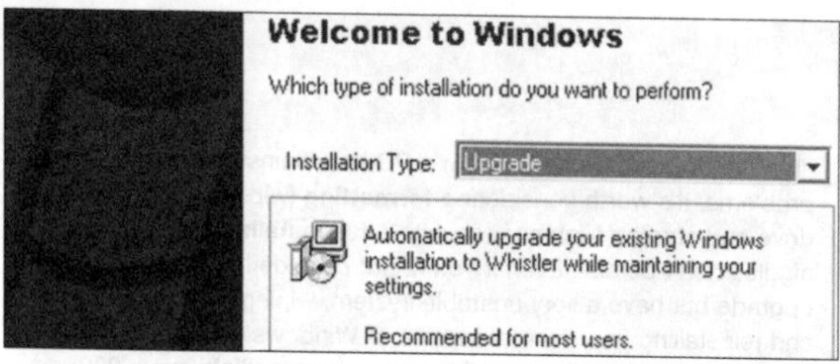

Welcome to Windows
Which type of installation do you want to perform?

Recommended for most users.

p.280) in case things go wrong. Once you've done this, insert the Windows CD into your CD drive and watch the **Setup Wizard** spring into action. This wizard will guide you through the process, asking for information along the way. When the wizard has finished doing its thing, the new version of Windows will boot for the first time – hopefully with all your old settings, files and applications intact.

Startup disks

A **Startup disk** or **boot disk** is a floppy disk containing enough information to allow a blank PC to navigate to the CD drive to get a Windows installation under way. They can also be very useful if things go wrong and your machine won't boot up normally. Your copy of Windows Me or an earlier version may have come with a Startup disk, but if not you can create one in the Windows Control Panel – use a friend's computer if necessary. Double-click the **Add/Remove Programs** icon, select the **Startup Disk** tab, insert a diskette into the floppy drive and click the

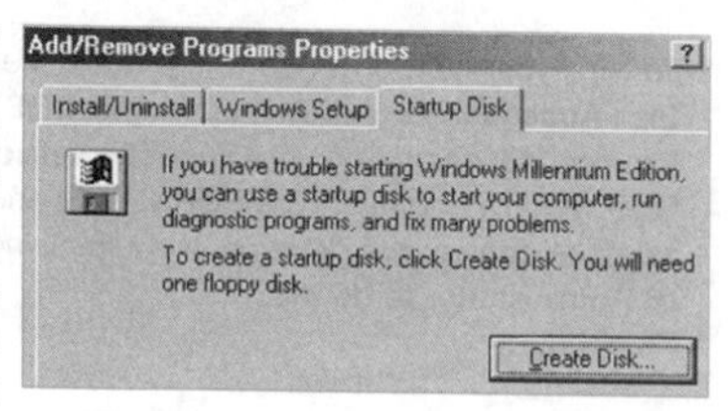

Add/Remove Programs Properties
Install/Uninstall
Windows Setup
Startup Disk
If you have trouble starting Windows Millennium Edition, you can use a startup disk to start your computer, run diagnostic programs, and fix many problems.
To create a startup disk, click Create Disk. You will need one floppy disk.
Create Disk...

Tech Info | Tips & Tricks | Try This

Making a fresh start

If you're upgrading Windows on a PC that is unstable or has other problems, it's worth considering **formatting** (wiping) your hard drive and starting from scratch with a **full installation** so that little niggles don't persist. Even if you're not considering a Windows upgrade but have a very unstable system, wiping your hard drive and reinstalling your current version of Windows could help. Either way, you'll need a **Windows CD** and a **Startup disk** (see p.239), and you'll have to **back up** all your data (see p.280) before formatting your hard drive and making the full installation. And once everything's up and running you'll have to reinstall all your programs and transfer your documents back onto the machine. Some PCs don't come with a Windows CD but a **Restore CD** instead, which will re-install Windows on your behalf. If you have one of these, try using it instead of formatting the drive – check your manual or contact the manufacturer to find out what to do.

WARNING: ONLY TAKE THE FOLLOWING STEP IF ALL YOUR DATA IS BACKED UP AND YOU HAVE A WORKING STARTUP DISK AND A FULL WINDOWS INSTALLATION CD!

To wipe your hard drive, go to the **Start** menu, select **Programs** then **Accessories** and click either **MS-DOS** or **Command Prompt** (depending on your Windows version). When a black DOS window appears, type **FORMAT C:** and hit **Enter**. You'll be asked to confirm the decision. If you're using XP, you'll need to be an Administrator to do this.

Create button. If you have a full version of Windows XP it will probably have come with the necessary floppy disk, but you should also be able to use a Startup disk created in Windows Me or 98.

Booting from CD

If you don't have a Startup disk but your machine is relatively new, you can try to get an operating system installation going by **booting from CD**. This requires you to go into your system **BIOS setup utility** (see p.331) and set the CD drive as the primary boot device. This is done in different ways in different BIOS utilities, but generally it's quite self-explanatory and just requires you to look through the menus until you find one named something like **boot devices** or **startup priorities**. Usually the machine will be set to boot from the floppy drive, then the hard drive. Change it so that the order is the CD drive followed by the hard drive (if this isn't possible your machine probably doesn't support CD booting). Exit the BIOS utility with the Windows CD in place and the installation should begin. You may want to return the BIOS boot settings to their previous order after the installation is complete.

Full installations

For a full installation you'll need a **Windows CD** – a full version, not an upgrade disc – as well as the product key number that came with it and a **Startup disk** (see p.239). If you're installing Windows 98 or Me on a brand-new drive you'll need to partition it using Fdisk and then format it before doing anything else (see p.330 to learn how to do this). Then restart the machine with the Startup disk in place.

Select **Start computer with CD-ROM support** from the menu that appears. You should be presented with a message (perhaps in the format **Drive E: = Driver MSCD001**) which shows you that your CD drive has been recognized. After a minute or two you may also be told that your CD drive has a new letter, probably E, and then you'll be presented with another A:\> prompt. Insert the Windows CD in the drive and type **e:\setup** then hit **Enter**. (If you were told that your CD drive was F: or some other letter, replace the "e:" in this command with the relevant letter.) If everything's OK, your blank hard drive will be checked by ScanDisk (see p.168) and then the **Windows Setup Wizard** will walk you through the rest of the install. If your CD drive doesn't seem to be recognized, it could be that the Startup disk doesn't contain the suitable drivers for it. Refer to your CD drive or system manual, or contact your computer's manufacturer for advice.

The final version of **Windows XP** isn't available at the time of writing, but it is intended that partitioning and formatting will all be part of the installation process. If you're using the setup disk that came with your copy of XP, follow the instructions provided. If you don't have a setup disk, you should be able to boot from CD (see p.241) or use a Windows 98 or Me Startup disk and follow the instructions provided in the above paragraph.

At some point you'll be asked for a **Product Key number** (which will be somewhere on the Windows packaging) and you'll have to decide where in your computer you want Windows to be installed (choose the default, **C:\WINDOWS**). You'll also probably have to choose between a **Typical** or a **Custom** install. A typical install is fine for practically all users, but if you're feeling brave and you have a knowledgeable friend to consult, a Custom install will give you more freedom to choose exactly what you do and don't want. You might also be asked if you want to visit the Microsoft Website and check for updates – if your modem is connected to a phone line, go for it, but if not, don't worry: it's not essential and can always be done later. Once the installation has finished it's worth checking that all your hardware is working. And if it's Windows XP that you've just installed, don't forget to "activate" it within fourteen days (see p.92).

For more on Windows versions and installations, visit: **www.winsupersite.com**

18

Program software

getting it, installing it

A piece of software – a **program** or **application** – is a special set of coded instructions that interacts with your operating system and hardware to enable you to carry out a particular set of tasks, such as editing a digital photograph or sending an email. Depending on the jobs that pieces of software are expected to do, they can either be tiny little things (often called **applets**) or hefty beasts that demand great chunks of your PC's resources.

Back in the 1980s, software would find its way onto your computer via **magnetic audio cassettes** or **floppy disks**. And because personal computers didn't come with a hard drive, you actually had to move a program onto your PC every time you wanted to use it, loading all the code from tape or disk into the PC's memory (RAM) before a single task could be performed. These days application programs will reach you either on **CD** or – ever more frequently – be downloaded straight from the **Internet**. You **install** them onto your hard drive, and from then on they are quickly unpacked to your RAM whenever you click the necessary icons.

Tech Info | Tips & Tricks | Try This

Parlez-vous Machine Code?

The fundamental language spoken by all PCs is **machine code**, which consists of binary numbers – 0s and 1s. Machine code is described as the **lowest-level** computer language. It's great for computer processors, but as you can imagine, it's not ideal for humans: it would be practically impossible for a computer programmer to sit down and write a program in 0s and 1s. Instead, programmers work with **higher-level** languages, which are then translated into machine code by special programs called **compilers**. The highest-level languages, such as **BASIC**, are the easiest to use: many of the instructions are very intuitive and contain standard English words such as "WRITE" and "CLOSE". Most programmers, however, use slightly less high-level languages – like **Java** and **C**, for example – which are better at producing faster, more compact code.

1010101010100101011100111000100010
1010111010101010111111100101001101
1111001110101011101010101011111110
0001000000101010110000101000011101
0011010000111010100001010101011000

Although installing software may seem incredibly easy to do, the stuff that goes on in the background is not as straightforward as you might think. It's not simply the case that you drag the program files onto your hard drive and plonk them wherever you fancy as you might with a document file. Nowadays applications come with their own special **installation programs** (or wizards) that need to be run in order for everything to be set up properly – so make sure you follow the instructions. Equally, when you remove a piece of software from your PC it needs to be properly **uninstalled** so that there are no loose ends left behind to confuse other applications (especially if several programs have been **sharing files**: see p.251).

This chapter covers all the issues relating to buying, downloading, installing and uninstalling software. If you're intending to splash out on some new programs, turn to the next chapter, where you'll find descriptions of many different types of applications and recommendations of some of the best around.

Shopping for software

If you thought the choices were tough when you were buying your PC hardware, just wait until you start shopping around for software. The number of applications is enormous, and that's before you even have to decide whether to purchase from a shop, a Website or a mail order company. Increasingly, though, you can also opt to **download programs straight from the Internet**: it's often cheaper, it saves you having to get to a shop or wait for delivery and it allows you to get the package of your choice 24 hours a day, 365 days a year. The only disadvantage of downloading software is that you don't get the big paper **manual** – though you can often have one sent by post, or you might even be able to download one as an **Acrobat document file** (see p.271) along with the software.

The really great thing about software, though, is that a lot of it is free. You might well find that when you buy a new peripheral it comes bundled with a couple of programs, and **PC magazine cover discs** are often worth checking out: either they'll contain complete versions of an application or, more frequently, they'll feature a trial version of a package that you can play around with before deciding whether to buy the full package. There are also lots of freebies available on the Internet, both **legal** and **illegal** (see box opposite). The legal stuff comes in two main forms, **freeware** and **shareware**. Though these terms are sometimes used interchangeably, freeware, technically speaking, is copyrighted software that the author distributes for free. Shareware can be downloaded for nothing as well, though you're encouraged to make a small voluntary contribution to the developers if you like and make use of their program.

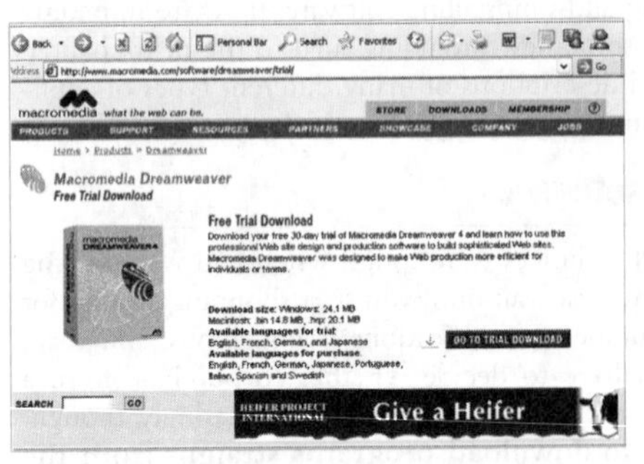

If you're interested in buying a particular package, before reaching for your wallet it's worth checking out the manufacturer's Website to see if they offer a downloadable **trial version** or a **free version**. The music hardware and software producers Digi Design, for example, offer a free, stripped-down version of their impressive Pro Tools system on their Website (http://www.digidesign.com). If you want to find out about a package but have no idea who the manufacturers are, try finding the software you want using a search engine (see p.211).

Pirates and their warez

When looking for software online, you should be aware that the Web is teeming with illegal, "pirated" or "cracked" versions of commercial software programs, collectively referred to as **warez**. The battle between software companies and crackers has been raging for years, but piracy has proved near-impossible to stop, especially with the level of anonymity offered by the Internet. Any measures designed to prevent the illegal movement of software are always quickly overcome by the pirates. For example, serial numbers and copyright protection keys are frequently published online, making it easy to activate an illegal piece of software. It's sometimes argued, however, that piracy is actually beneficial for the producers of industry-standard software, because their market position relies on people knowing how to use their programs – difficult if they are too expensive for educational use alone. Whatever your opinion, you should know that **downloading and installing such software remains very much against the law.**

Installing software from CD

Most of the applications you'll install will be from CD. Doing this is a very easy process: turn your PC on, insert the CD into the CD drive and sit back. With any luck you'll hear the drive start to spin and the first frame of an **installation wizard** (a little application that installs the main program for you) will appear on the screen. If nothing happens when you insert the disc, go to the **Control Panel**, select **Add/Remove Programs**, **Add New Programs** then **CD or Floppy** (or just click the **Install** button in earlier versions of Windows). Alternatively, go to the **Start** menu, select **Run**, type **d:\setup** (replace "d" with whatever letter represents the CD drive on your system) and hit **OK**.

Once the installation is underway, the wizard will do the rest. All you need do is read the contents of the various frames that appear, clicking **Next** to move through the various stages of the installation. You'll probably be asked questions about where you want the program to be installed and whether you want to do a **standard** or **custom** installation. In general, if you don't understand something, just click **Next**, as it's hard to go wrong with the default settings. You'll also need to enter some information, such as a **product key** (the security code that came with the CD, designed to stop people copying and selling software illegally), your name and, optionally, the company you work for. You may also be asked if you want to connect to the Internet to **register** your application with the manufacturer and search for any program updates. If you're connected and have a few spare minutes, by all means do so – you might find something worth having. But don't worry about this too much: if you decline now, the software will almost certainly hassle you to get online again sometime soon.

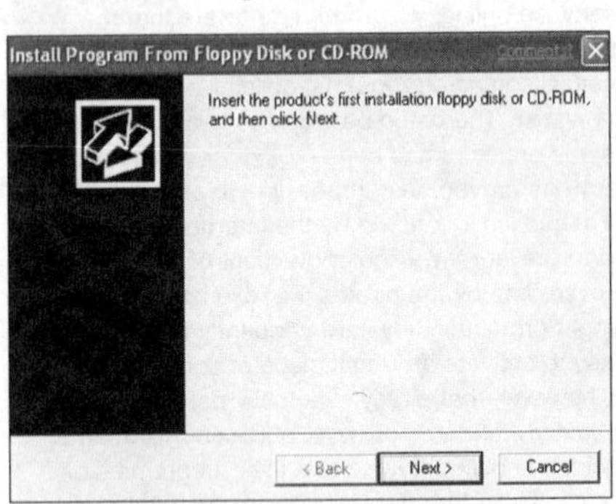

When the installation is complete you will see a final frame prompting you to click a **Finish** button. You may well be asked to **restart** your PC – which updates the various settings that have been altered by the presence of the new program – and you might be offered a peek at the **Readme** file that came with the software. Readmes are handy little documents that **usually open into**

readme

Notepad or WordPad (see p.166) and they are designed to bring you up to speed with various bits of information about the software. They tend to include an overview of the application, any last-minute tips that didn't make it into the manual and some hints on installation procedures – handy if you've encountered problems. If you want to check what's in a Readme prior to an installation, they can be found by browsing the folders on the software's CD using **My Computer**.

Floppy installations

Occasionally you might find yourself wanting to install some software from floppy disk. To do this, select **Add/Remove Programs** from the **Control Panel** and click the **Install** button. This launches an installation wizard that prompts you to insert your first disk. Alternatively, insert the disk into the floppy drive, head to the **Start** menu and select **Run**, type **a:\setup** and then hit your **Enter** key. If this doesn't work, try again, this time typing **a:\install**.

Downloading software

If you've found some software you want on the Internet, take a few moments to read through the manufacturer's guidelines and specifications – will the application do what you want it to do? Is it compatible with your system? If you're happy, hit the **Download** button on the site and Windows will display a special **Download dialog box**, which asks you whether you want to "open the file from its current location" or "download the file to disk". Click the latter, select where you want the file to go (you can put it anywhere, but perhaps create a folder called "downloads" on your Desktop) and press **OK**. The file will start to transfer itself to your system; you'll see a little graphic representation of files winging their way to a folder, and, more importantly, an indication of how much longer the download is likely to take – though this is not an exact science, as it all depends on the second-by-second speed of your connection.

If you lose your Internet connection halfway through the download process you'll probably have to start again from scratch, though Internet Explorer may try to continue where it left off.

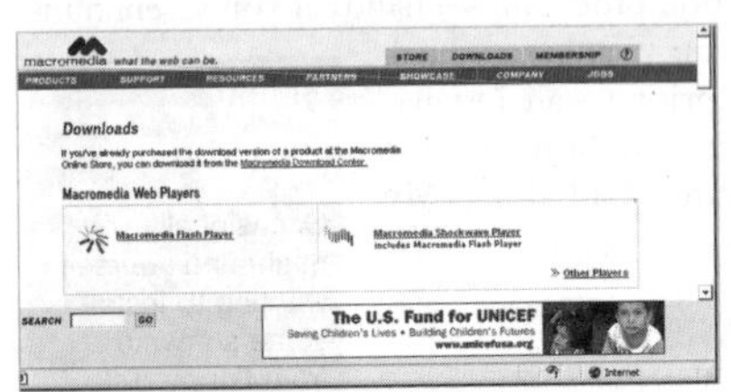

Given that applications are often rather large, most downloaded programs are **compressed** (see p.134) so that they can reach you faster. Some are **self-extracting**, meaning that once the file has downloaded you can simply double-click it to launch an installation wizard. But others are **zipped**, which requires you to extract them yourself. If you have Windows XP or Me this will simply involve double-clicking the zipped file; in older versions of Windows you'll need an extra program to "unzip" the file (such as **WinZip**: see p.134). Once unzipped, the downloaded file will either reveal a folder or a self-extracting program in the form of an icon that you double-click to get started. If you get a folder, it should contain a file called either **install** or **setup** (perhaps with a **.exe** file extension), which can be double-clicked to launch the installation.

Once the installation is complete, drag the downloaded file or folder to a safe place. It's also a good idea to make a backup of it (see p.280), so that you've always got the original files to hand if you need to reinstall the software at a later date.

Uninstalling software

To uninstall software – remove all traces of a program from your system – turn to the **Add/Remove Programs** dialog box in

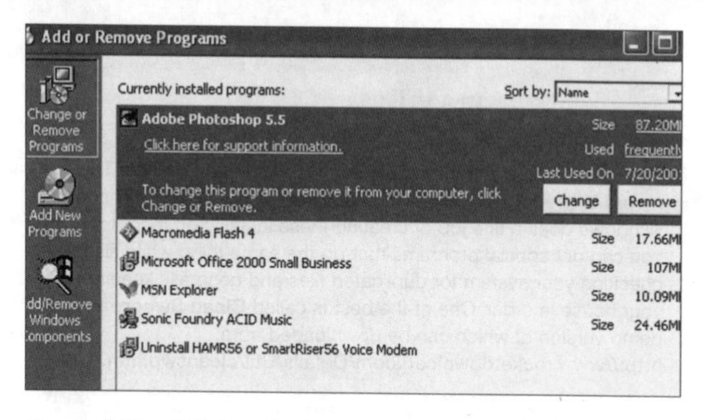

Control Panel. Select the program you want rid of from the list of installed applications and then click the **Remove** or **Remove/Change** button. Once you've confirmed that you wish to delete the program, Windows will remove all the relevant files from your computer (not including documents you created with the program). You might be told along the way that certain files are **shared files** – meaning that they are used, or potentially used, by other applications. It's best to play it safe and not delete these, as their removal could stop other programs from working properly.

If the program you want to remove is not in the Add/Remove Programs dialog box, see if you can find an **Uninstall** icon for it near its launch icon under Programs in the Start menu. If there isn't one, open **My Computer**, click the icon for your hard drive (most likely labelled **C**) and then open the **Program Files** folder, which should contain a folder for the program in question. See if this folder includes an **Uninstall** icon. If there isn't one, backtrack once and delete the unwanted program's folder by right-clicking it and selecting **Delete**. This will get rid of most of the relevant files.

Tech Info | Tips & Tricks | Try This

Installation logs

Whenever you install a new piece of software onto your system, Windows creates a record of all the files that were installed. This record is used if you uninstall the software at a later date. Though Windows does a fine job of creating these installation records, you can get special programs that do the same thing while also checking your system for duplicated files and generally keeping your house in order. One of the best is called **Clean Sweep**, a demo version of which can be downloaded from: **http://www.rocketdownload.com/Details/Util/cleanswp.htm**

19

Application roundup

reviews and recommendations

There is so much software on the market these days that the choice can be more than a little overwhelming. This chapter provides short descriptions of some of the best applications and downloadable freebies available – to help you turn your PC into the creative furnace that it should be.

Office software

Whether you're running a small business or just trying to manage your personal correspondence and accounts, you'll need some suitable software. As mentioned in Chapter 12, Windows comes bundled with WordPad (see p.182), but it doesn't take long to outgrow this very basic word processor. When it comes to extending your office tools you can either buy individual applications – such as a word processor, spreadsheet or high-end email program – or an **office suite**, which will include some or all of the standard office programs.

Office suites

When it comes to office suites, most businesses use one of the big three: **Microsoft Office**, **Corel WordPerfect Office** and **Lotus SmartSuite**. They're all very powerful packages, but Microsoft Office increasingly dominates the market and is the only one of these that's popular with home users. Depending on the version you buy – Standard, Professional, Small Business, and so on – you'll get a different selection of Microsoft's flagship office programs such as Word, Excel and PowerPoint. Because it's so popular, you'll rarely have a compatibility problem with Microsoft Office unless you happen to work somewhere that uses a different package. It's also very easy to use and packed full of features (especially **Office XP**, the most recent version), though you have to be a serious user to take advantage of them all. Microsoft Office doesn't come cheap, though if you're a school or college student, a parent or a teacher, you can pay substantially less – check out **http://www.microsoft.com/uk/education** (UK) or **http://www.microsoft.com/education** (US).

As well as the professional packages described above, there are various less expensive suites around designed for home use. One very popular package – often thrown in with new PCs – is **Microsoft Works**, a scaled-down version of Office. As far as features go, Works includes everything you're likely to need for most tasks, though its front end (which bombards you with task wizards) can be a bit annoying. Another budget option is **Ability Office**, which is unbelievably good value (it's sometimes even given out for free on PC magazine cover discs). With a word processor, database and spreadsheet, Ability includes more than enough features for the average home or small business user. Also check out **Sun StarOffice**, a completely free downloadable package that includes all the standard office applications, some image editing tools and more.

http://www.microsoft.com/office
http://www.lotus.com/smartsuite
http://www.corel.com
http://www.microsoft.com/works
http://www.ability.com
http://www.sun.com/staroffice

Word processors

Far more than all-singing-all-dancing digital typewriters, modern word processors include the tools you need to write, edit and lay out all sorts of documents. The most popular is **Microsoft Word**, which is available either separately or as part of Microsoft's Office suite. It's a great all-round player with loads of editing and layout tools, web publishing capabilities and options that let you customize the program to your specific needs. It also has the distinct advantage of being used by practically every business and college under the sun, so you're unlikely to experience compatibility problems. However, most people will only ever use a fraction of Word's many features, and for the same money you could get an inexpensive and all-inclusive office suite. Of Word's numerous competitors, the best of the batch is probably **Corel WordPerfect**, which offers loads of features at a decent price.

If you fancy yourself as a scriptwriter, **Final Draft** might be worth investigating. Specifically designed for use by writers, this package features various fancy script editing tools and it will even assign voices to individual characters and read your drafts back to you.

http://www.microsoft.com/word
http://www.corel.com
http://www.finaldraft.com

Desktop publishing

Desktop publishing (**DTP**) programs offer a broad range of tools for manipulating text, images and shapes to craft professional-looking page layouts, leaflets, posters and so on. Though you can print a document prepared with a DTP package on any printer, these programs are also designed for creating **PostScript files** to be submitted for professional printing. The industry-standard application is **Quark Xpress**, which is extremely powerful but prohibitively expensive for non-professional use. Among less expensive alternatives are packages such as **Microsoft Publisher**. Available alone or as part of Microsoft Office Professional, Publisher is usable enough and comes with various ready-to-go templates for cards, pamphlets and the like, but it's pretty limited overall. If you're simply producing documents to print at home, a

modern version of Word (see p.255) is, to be honest, just as good.

http://www.quark.com/products/xpress
http://www.microsoft.com/publisher

Databases

These programs are primarily used to store information about large numbers of people or things: employees at a company, books in a library and so on. Though they're not really designed for home use, if you have the time and inclination you could decide to build up a recipe database or catalogue your record collection. **Microsoft Access** is one of the most popular database programs, offering a complete and versatile array of tools and a work environment that's very similar to the other members of the Microsoft Office family. And with its split-screen setup, grabbing chunks of data is a breeze. Another popular choice is **FileMaker Pro**, which is especially good for database presentation and making your data available on the Internet. Again, though, for general use your money would be far better spent on a less complex package such as the one that comes in **Ability Office**.

http://www.microsoft.com/access
http://www.filemaker.com
http://www.ability.com

Spreadsheets

Specifically geared towards the manipulation and presentation of numeric data, these grid-like programs are mostly used for financial planning and budgeting, but can also, to a limited degree, be used as databases. **Microsoft Excel** is an easy-to-learn but hard-to-master program for sorting, summarizing and

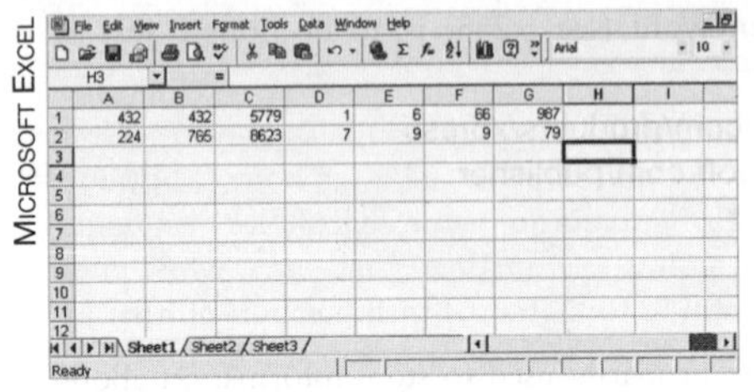

graphing data. It works well alongside the other members of the Microsoft Office suite, but it's very pricey and, unless you intend to get into the nitty-gritty of pivot tables and the like, you'll probably be served just as well by simpler programs such as the ones integrated into **Microsoft Works** or **Ability Office**.

http://www.microsoft.com/excel
http://www.ability.com

Presentation software

These packages are designed for producing slides, flowcharts and multimedia business presentations. **Microsoft PowerPoint** is by far the most popular and features an impressive array of tools – everything short of full-on pyrotechnics to help you impress your clients and boss. It's also very simple to use.

http://www.microsoft.com/powerpoint

And the rest . . .

Modern office suites may also include anything from a set of digital reference books to home-accounts software to route-planners to business proposal wizards. Though much of it will be little more than padding added to justify the "suite" tag, you may find something handy, so have a good rummage around once you've installed your new software.

Graphics software

There are two main types of graphics applications: those for illustrating or drawing, and those for editing photos. Illustration programs tend to offer **vector tools**, which let you define shapes in terms of points (or "anchors") and lines, while photo editing packages tend to focus on the manipulation of **bitmaps** (see p.18). Windows does come with one of each (**Paint** and **Imaging** respectively: see p.165), but they are fairly limiting – so if you want to spread your artistic wings you'll need to shop for some alternatives.

Packages vary greatly in price and performance: there are some amazingly powerful applications out there but they're expensive and complex, so if you only want to mess around with the occasional photo you'd probably do better finding something a bit simpler. The best way to find out which programs suit the work you want to do is, quite simply, to give them a whirl. You may be able to download a trial version from a manufacturer's Website; alternatively, look out for demos bundle with PC magazines – trial versions of the best programs can be found on cover discs month after month.

Photo and image editing

The industry-standard photo editing package is **Adobe PhotoShop**. With its incredibly powerful editing, effects and layer tools, PhotoShop is ideal for the serious photographer or computer artist, but it's expensive and takes quite a while to master. A more affordable and slightly easier-to-use option is **Jasc Paint Shop Pro**. It covers similar bases to PhotoShop, and recent versions also boast a healthy set of Web and animation tools. If you want a cheap and cheerful photo editor, check out **MGI Photo Suite**. This package is aimed at families, and it

helps you arrange your images into albums as well as actually edit them. Though it does come with some handy tools for removing red-eye and dust marks, don't expect anything too advanced.

http://www.adobe.com/photoshop
http://www.jasc.com
http://www.mgisoft.com/photo/photosuite

Illustration packages

One of the most popular vector illustration packages is **Adobe Illustrator**, a sister program to PhotoShop. Though it's a bit pricey and can take quite a lot of getting used to, it's a fully featured package, great for printing and Web publishing, and is capable of generating spectacular results. Other popular packages include **Corel Draw**, which can be bought as a complete but expensive graphics suite, and **Macromedia Freehand**.

http://www.adobe.com/illustrator
http://www.corel.com
http://www.macromedia.com/freehand

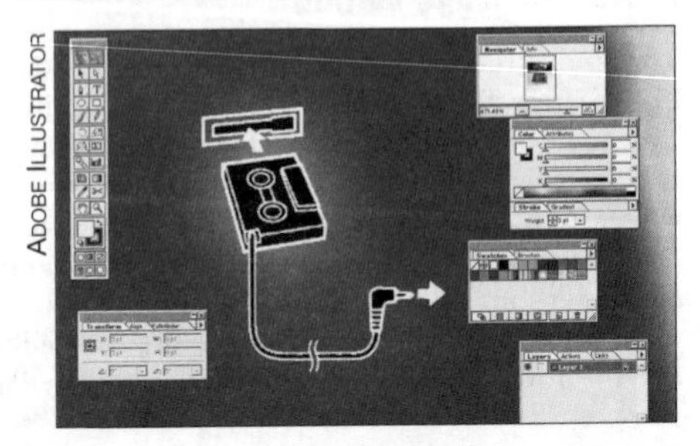

ADOBE ILLUSTRATOR

3D illustration

If you fancy branching out into the third dimension, you should consider **Ulead Cool 3D.** An inexpensive and user-friendly package, it's ideal for anyone who wants to learn the basics of generating and animating 3D shape, text and logos.

http://www.ulead.com/cool3d

Web design software

Once you've mastered the basics of processing images, you may want to try out your new-found skills by designing your own Website. This is not as hard as it sounds – the software available is intuitive to use, amazingly sophisticated and lets you construct pages without any knowledge of **HTML** (**H**yper**t**ext **M**ark-up **L**anguage, the code behind most Web pages). You can get away with building a site using a recent version of **Microsoft Word** (see p.255), which you may already have on your system. But for really good results you'll need some **dedicated Web design software**, perhaps even a couple of applications to cover the various different parts of the process. Creating simple pages is really very easy – in fact, probably the most difficult part about Web design is coming up with the initial idea that will make your site a stunner. Here's a look at some of the most popular packages.

Web design applications

These impressive packages include everything you require to build and maintain a Website. The industry standard, **Macromedia Dreamweaver**, is fully featured and easy to use, but it doesn't come cheap. A less expensive option is **Microsoft**

FrontPage; though it's a little less flexible than Dreamweaver, FrontPage is a delight to use, especially if you're already familiar with the Microsoft Office environment.

http://www.macromedia.com/dreamweaver
http://www.microsoft.com/frontpage

Web imaging and animation

If you get seriously into Web design you may want to add to your toolkit. **Macromedia Fireworks** offers a friendly environment for creating vector-based graphics and tweaking bitmaps for use on the Web, while **Macromedia Flash** can be used to create funky buttons, interactive animations and streaming audio to inject something a bit special into your site. If you fancy having a crack at animation without blowing loads of money, try **Swish**, a great value package that lets you produce Flash animations quickly and easily.

http://www.macromedia.com/fireworks
http://www.macromedia.com/flash
http://www.swishzone.com

Digital video editing software

Thanks to increasingly expansive hard drives, FireWire connections and a steady fall in the price of digital video hardware, creating and editing movies with your computer is becoming more and more practical as well as affordable. If you're just starting to experiment with video editing and you have

Windows XP or Me, you might as well learn some basic skills using the built-in **Windows Movie Maker** (see p.179). But if you want to transform your raw footage into slick, professional-looking work, you'll need some better software that offers advanced editing features (such as various ways to fade between shots) and the option to save your finished masterpiece in various different file formats, such as **Real**, **WindowsMedia** and **Quicktime**.

One of the best home packages around is the powerful and easy-to-use **Adobe Premiere**, but most users will get better value for money with **Sonic Foundry Vegas Video**. Vegas Video is cheaper, but still boasts an impressive set of editing features, various export options and an array of effects and filters.

http://www.adobe.com/premiere
http://www.sonicfoundry.com/vegasvideo

Music applications

Ten years ago the PC was not a music-friendly machine, but these days there are a wide range of programs available that are capable of turning your computer into a **fully-featured home recording studio** (as long as you have a decent machine with a suitable sound card: see p.54).

The most popular music-making programs are **multitrack** packages that allow you to assemble a piece of music layer by layer – instruments, sounds, vocals and so on. Most modern multitrackers can deal with both **audio** and **MIDI**. Audio describes "real" sounds that are recorded via a microphone or "sampled" from CD, tape and so on; MIDI, which stands for Musical Instrument Digital Interface, is a system that deals with synthesizer instructions, allowing your computer to communicate with electronic keyboards and other devices. MIDI enables you, for example, to record a synthesized string accompaniment or trigger pre-recorded audio samples. Working with regular audio, on the other hand, will allow you to replicate the processes of a regular recording studio.

The most popular multitrackers include everything you need to record and edit music: a virtual mixing desk, comprehensive recording facilities, a wave editor for dealing with audio, digital effects and even score production tools (which write whatever you play on virtual manuscript paper). But there are also music programs available that focus on single tasks, such as standalone **wave editors**, **soft synths** for generating sounds and dedicated **score production** programs.

Multitrack packages

There are three main contenders when it comes to all-in-one MIDI and audio multitrack recording programs. **Cakewalk Pro Audio**, the world's best-selling option, is a doddle to use and especially good for guitarists and singers requiring easy-to-produce accompaniments. **Steinberg Cubase VST**, the UK industry standard, is fully featured and user-friendly. **Emagic Logic Audio** is the most powerful package, but it's a little harder to get used to than Pro Audio or Cubase. These programs are all pretty expensive, but excellent scaled-down versions are also available for much less money – Cakewalk's **Home Studio**, Steinberg's **Cubasis** and Emagic's **MicroLogic**

- and they can all be upgraded if you find yourself needing more features.

A completely different type of multitracker is **Sonic Foundry Acid Music.** This program (which offers excellent value and is incredibly intuitive) takes any wave file thrown its way and fits it to a tempo of your choice, allowing you to make impressive sample-based songs in minutes. For non-MIDI multitracking, try **CoolEdit Pro** or **Sonic Foundry Vegas** (which also deals with video, making it ideal for soundtracks).

http://www.cakewalk.com
http://www.steinberg.com
http://www.emagic.com

Standalone wave editors

If you want professional-standard wave editing capability, go for a standalone wave editor such as **Sonic Foundry Sound Forge** or **Steinberg WaveLab**. These programs are very powerful, but they're pricey, difficult to master and contain many tools you're unlikely to need as an amateur.

http://www.steinberg.com
http://www.sonicfoundry.com

Score production

The two big-name score programs are **Sibelius** and **Finale**, both of which are excellent but expensive. Sibelius is great for composers – it's very user-friendly and with the right plug-in can even recognize

SIBELIUS

scanned-in scores – but Finale is favoured by many in the publishing industry. If you don't require professional results, various programs are available for a fraction of the cost: **Cakewalk ScoreWriter**, for instance, is an excellent buy.

http://www.sibelius.com
http://www.codamusic.com
http://www.cakewalk.com

Dance music programs

There are various programs designed specifically for making convincing dance music very easily. One of the best is **Steinberg Rebirth**, a virtual rack of classic analogue synths. It's an addictive package that makes generating techno ludicrously easy.

http://www.steinberg.com

Education and reference

With their high capacity and interactive multimedia potential, CDs and DVDs are an ideal medium for educational material. Courses in any language, school-subject, hobby or professional skill you can think of are available – so whether you want to master Thai cookery, become a virtuoso bagpiper or pass an exam, it shouldn't be hard to find a virtual teacher. Reference material, too, resides very contentedly on disc, and you can get hold of everything from the *Complete Works* of Shakespeare and global route-planners to interactive tours of the human body. And who wants a 20-volume paper encyclopedia when for a fraction of the cost and in 0.1 percent of the space you can access the same information on your PC, allowing you to search, cross-reference, email and print articles? There are so many tutors and works of reference available on CD and DVD that you can generally assume the thing you're after is out there somewhere, but if you're stuck for ideas here are a few examples to get your imagination going:

Mavis Beacon Teaches Typing

This incredibly popular program provides a virtual typing school. Mavis greets you on arrival and offers you lessons, tests and games.
http://www.mavisbeacon.com

National Geographic Complete Edition

Including 31 CDs, this remarkable box-set provides every article, illustration and photo printed in the **National Geographic** since the journal's 1888 first edition.
http://www.nationalgeographic.com

Encyclopædia Britannica

Updated annually, this virtual version of the world's most famous encyclopedia is undoubtedly one of the most comprehensive and well-presented reference works on the market. The Internet version is also excellent, and – what's more – most of its content is accessible for free.
http://store.britannica.com
http://www.britannica.com

CD burning software

If you have a CD writer – whether it came with your PC or was purchased separately – it will almost certainly have come with some software for creating and copying music and data CDs. And as we saw in Chapter 11, you can even use Windows Media

Player with the appropriate plug-in to burn audio disks (see p.178). However, many people find these utilities limiting or clumsy and go for sophisticated software offering more flexible tools, enabling you to fade in and out, alter the length of the gaps between tracks and even design CD jewel-case covers and labels.

When choosing CD burning software, check that it will do everything you want (some audio packages don't deal with data CDs, for example) and make sure it will work with your drive – especially if you have an old or external model. One very popular choice is **Adaptec Easy CD Creator**. Scaled-down versions of this package are often given away free with CD writers, but the high-end editions (which you can upgrade to without much hassle or expense if you already have a basic version) include many more tools and options. Or check out **Nero**: it's easy to use, and features everything from a built-in audio editor to a karaoke filter.

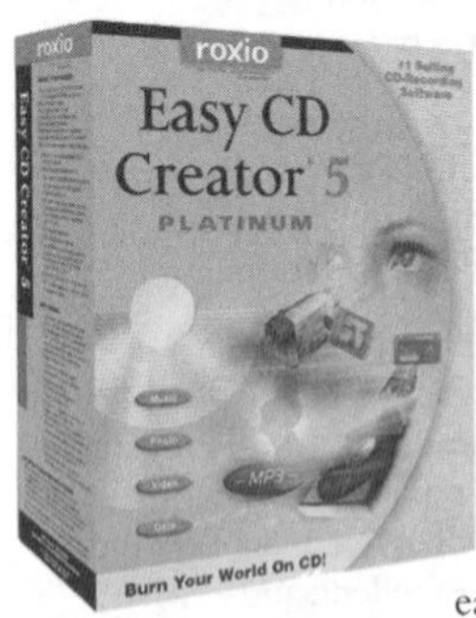

Another wise choice would be the slightly more advanced **Gear Pro**. It's fully featured and flexible, though not the easiest package to master.

http://www.adaptec.com
http://www.nero.com
http://www.gearsoftware.com

Games

There are thousands upon thousands of games available for the PC, many boasting staggeringly sharp graphics and packed with heart-stopping action. So whether you fancy fighting, driving, blasting or something a little more sedate – like the ever-popular **Sim City**, which lets you lord it over your very own metropolis – there's bound to be something out there for you. Though it's easy enough to find games in stores and read the blurb on the boxes, a far better way to cut through the hype is to check out *The Rough Guide to Videogaming*. You could also get hold of some PC gaming magazines or visit some of the countless gaming sites on the Web. To give you a head start, here are a few of the best:

SIM CITY

Game Dex

(**http://www.gamedex.com**)
One of the biggest and best PC gaming sites, with loads of reviews, tips, chat and links.

Download.Net

(**http://www.download.net**)
A general download site that boasts a healthy selection of vintage

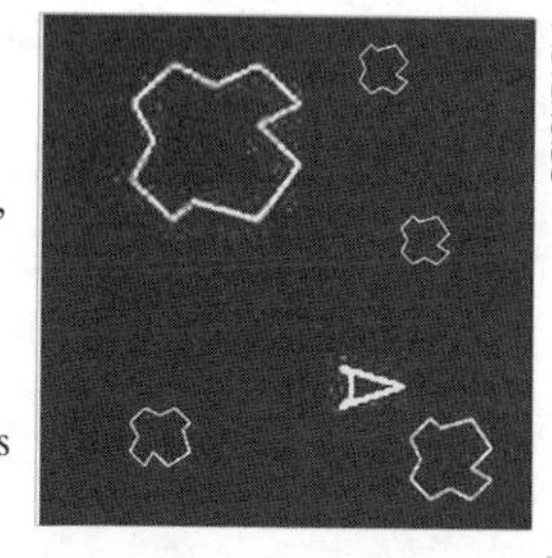
ASTEROIDS

games. Pick up free copies of classics like Super Galaxians, Asteroids and Jr. PacMan – these antiquated gems are so small that they download in seconds.

Grrl Gamer (http://www.grrlgamer.com)
This is a great site for girl gamers, with loads of useful info, comment and forums, all wrapped up in a load of snazzy graphics.

Handy extras

There are various little programs that are useful to have installed on your system, many of which can be downloaded for free from the Internet. At **http://www.zdnet.com/downloads**, for instance, you'll find a large selection of booty, including programs, demos, freebies and Windows utilities. (But remember that it's always worth running downloaded programs through a virus scanner: see p.278.) Other Windows-related download sites worth investigating include:

http://www.stuffall.com/software/winutils.shtml
http://www.cws.internet.com/menu.html

There are literally thousands of little programs out there that you can download and use, but there are a select few that it's worth making a special effort to get hold of, as you're likely to find them useful on a regular basis. The following are all free:

Adobe Acrobat Reader (http://www.acrobat.com)
This free program allows you to view Acrobat (.pdf) files, an increasingly common format for articles, manuals and forms downloaded from the Internet.

PowerArchiver (http://www.powerarchiver.com)
If you're running Windows 98 and earlier, you may find this program very useful for "unzipping" compressed files that you've downloaded from the Internet or been sent by email. It can compress files too – handy if you want to save room on your hard drive, or if you fancy emailing files as attachments. If you have Windows Me or XP you won't require a program like this, as both have compression tools built-in.

Shockwave and Flash Players
(http://www.macromedia.com)
These essential extras, downloadable for free, let you view and hear most Web animations and sound.

RealPlayer (http://www.real.com)
Lots of streaming audio and video on the Net (not to mention downloadable files) are stored in the "Real" format. This player lets you watch and listen to them.

QuickTime Player (http://www.quicktime.com)
Originally developed for the Mac, this program – the basic version of which is free – allows you to view pictures and play movie and sound clips in various file formats, including the special QuickTime format often used for compressed movie excerpts.

Copernic (http://www.copernic.com)
This nifty program (the basic version of which is free) is the super-detective of the Internet. You enter the word or phrase you want to search for and in a few seconds it retrieves results from around fifteen popular search engines.

Copernic® 2001 BASIC

[illegible]

[illegible]

[illegible]

[illegible]

of phrase you want to [illegible] effect [illegible]

[illegible]

part five

keeping it purring

20

Playing it safe

PC self-defence

Within just weeks of getting a PC, most people will have a lot of stuff saved on their hard drive. And after a year or two, a single drive can contain thousands of hours of work as well as huge library of downloads, pictures, music, contacts and Web links. The prospect of it all suddenly disappearing - or getting tampered with or spied on - is unpleasant to say the least, but unfortunately these things can happen. Though apparently lost data can sometimes be pulled back from the ether with suitable **recovery software** (see p.298), often when it's gone, it's gone. The first potential hazard is the hard drive itself: though pretty rare today, if a **drive crashes** you're up digital creek without a paddle. And that's not all. The risks may be frequently exaggerated, but it really is worth thinking about the possibility of **hackers** accessing your files through your Internet connection. Then there are **viruses**, destructive programs that can be transmitted via floppies and emails. For all these reasons, the most effective thing you can do is also the most obvious: **regularly back up your data** – either the stuff you can't exist without or everything on your system. Before we look at the backup process in more detail, though, let's unmask the villains that threaten your precious files. Read on.

Viruses and hackers

Despite their often-innocent names – "Melissa" and "I Love You" are two notorious examples – **viruses** can spread like wildfire from PC to PC, leaving a trail of data devastation in their wake.

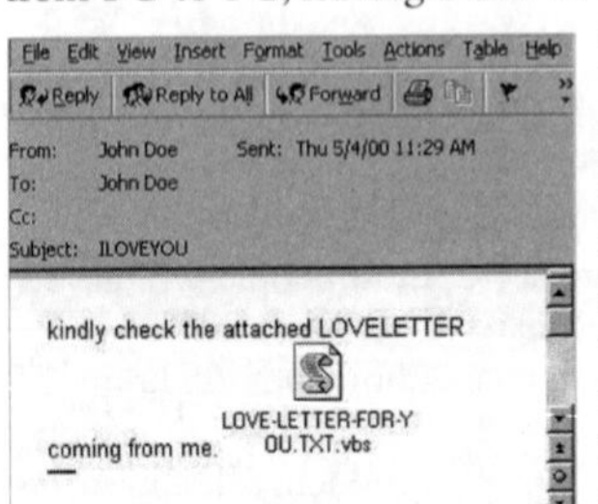

But what exactly are they? They're basically just small programs or bits of code that have been written just like regular applications. But these programs and codes have been designed to cause problems for computers, and generally for no reason other than the satisfaction of their creators.

There are **few things more annoying** than picking up a computer virus: they can wreak havoc with your system, destroy data, corrupt system files and generally make your computer pretty poorly. A virus is very much like a cold or the flu, sneakily finding its way into its victim before infecting them. With computer viruses this will most likely happen when you open an email attachment, try to install a piece of downloaded software (don't worry about CD installations) or insert a floppy disk that's been used in an infected machine. You can also pick them up when opening certain types of documents like spreadsheets or word processor files. These can conceal **macro viruses**, which are very common but, thankfully, often not that serious.

There are countless viruses out there looking for trouble: some nest in a computer and bide their time, while other types – called **worms** – spread by automatically forwarding themselves to everyone in your email address book. Still more, known as **Trojans**, find their way onto your system and then do a single piece of damage – perhaps disabling a specific system file or opening a gateway for **hackers** (individuals who try to access your data through your Internet connection) looking to invade your hard drive.

The Web also harbours a threat in the form of **ActiveX controls**, which are little pieces of Web programming code that are particularly good at transporting infection: your browser should warn you whenever one is going to download onto your machine. So, as you can see, you need to be especially careful when using the Internet; but don't despair, there are things you can do to protect your system.

Preventative medicine

First, think carefully about what you stick into your PC. Only download software from **reputable sites**, preferably the manufacturer's, and avoid duplicated software from friends – despite good intentions, they won't necessarily know their machine has a virus that's about to be sent your way. Equally, be suspicious of **email attachments** (see p.221) that you weren't expecting, especially if they're not regular document or media files. Always check with the person who sent it before opening any attached file with one of the following extensions: **.EXE**, **.REG**, **.COM**, **.VBS**, **.INF**, **.BAT**, or **.SHS**.

Internet Explorer zones

You can use Internet Explorer to restrict access to Websites that you may have had problems with in the past; and conversely, you can relax your system security when using a frequently visited and trusted site. From the Windows **Control Panel** select **Internet Options** (within the **Network and Internet Connections** category in Windows XP), and click the **Security** tab. You will see icons delineating four site zones – places where you can make lists of sites that you do or do not trust:

❒ **Internet** This zone refers to the Web as a whole and warrants a moderate level of security. This level is adjusted using the slider toward the bottom of the panel.

❒ **Local intranet** This zone allows you to prevent certain sites from being accessed by other users on your network, if you've got one.

❒ **Trusted sites** Use this list for sites where you feel confident about running all the content with minimal security.

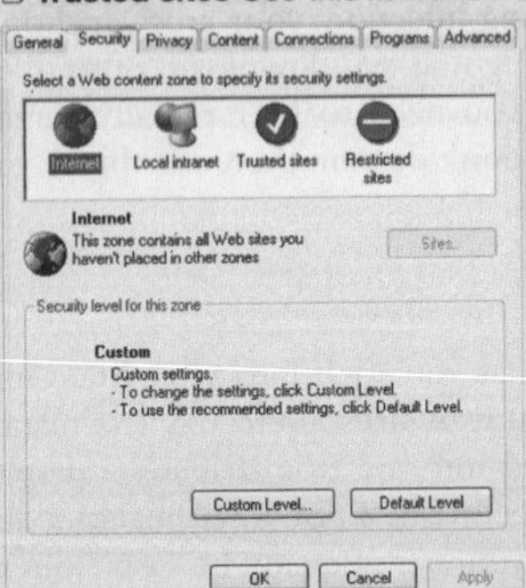

❒ **Restricted sites** This is the Web sin-bin: the place for sites you just don't trust not to damage your data. This zone needs a high security setting.

In addition you can use the **Custom Level** button to fine-tune specific elements of the security settings for a particular zone.

You may also find that your computer came with special antivirus software pre-installed – such as **McAfee VirusScan** (http://www.nai.com) or **Norton AntiVirus** (http://www.

symantec.com) – and if it did, one of their logos will appear in the Notification area of the Taskbar. Try clicking the icon to bring up a box of options and preferences for the utility. Make sure you keep this

software updated as new viruses are being discovered all the time. This can be done by visiting the company's Website; you may well be entitled to free updates, so it's worth checking this out.

You might also try employing the services of a Web-based utility like **HouseCall** (see p.298). This program can be downloaded for free and used to sweep your system for viruses.

Firewalls

If you're concerned about hackers trying to access the data on your PC, use a **firewall program** to protect your system; this will prevent anyone from even being able to detect your computer on the Internet, let alone invade it. Windows XP comes with its own built-in firewall program that can be enabled for your various network and Internet connections. In the **Control Panel** click the **Network and Internet Connections** category and then select **Network Connections**. Right-click the icon for the connection you wish to protect and select **Properties** from the mouse menu. Under the **Advanced** tab you'll see a box that can be checked to activate your firewall protection. If you're not running Windows XP, consider

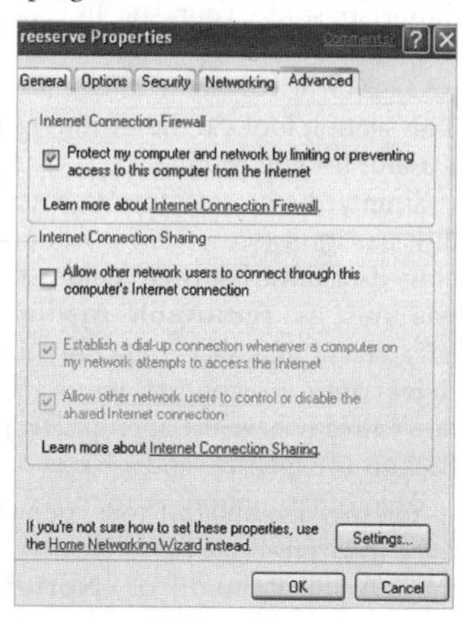

installing a branded firewall like **ZoneAlarm** (http://www.zonelabs.com).

For more about online threats, check out *The Rough Guide to the Internet*.

Backing up

In case you hadn't already noticed, the world is an imperfect place: things go wrong, break and get stolen. So if you want to stay one step ahead of Fate, get yourself into a routine of **backing up on a regular basis**. If you do it frequently it'll seem less of a grind, so start today.

The basic idea is to create **duplicate copies** of your important files and keep them in a secure place so that if your hardware ever fails or is stolen, you won't actually have lost the important stuff – your data. In Chapters 2 and 3 we talked about the kinds of hardware you can use to back up: tape drives (see p.53), Zip drives (see p.77), removable hard drives, and so on. This section looks at the various tactics you can deploy to set up a useful backup routine.

Simply duplicating files to a separate internal drive or hard disk partition (see p.236) is not good enough: it won't protect your data from hardware failure, fire or theft. To be really safe, you must use **removable media**. The ideal option is to regularly create an exact copy (an "image") of your **entire hard drive** onto a secondary removable hard drive or tape. If you don't already have the appropriate hardware, though, this kind of backup is expensive and a hassle to get going.

The other option is to carry out **partial backups** onto lower-capacity mediums such as a recordable **CD** or **Zip disk**. After all, much of your hard drive will be populated by programs which, as long as you have the original CDs, you could always reinstall later if necessary. Obviously you'll want to back up your **documents** – letters, spreadsheets, photos and so on – but some less obvious things are worth having a second copy of. Don't forget, for example:

❒ **Your emails** If you use Outlook Express you can use the **Export** function in the **File** menu to save your archive of emails as a folder of text files, which you can then back up like any other.

❒ **Your address book** If you use the address book, it can be a real pain to lose. Back it up by selecting **Export** from its **File** menu and then selecting **Address Book (WAB)** to save a copy in the Windows format, or select **Other Address Book** to save as a text document. You can then back up the copy like any other file.

❒ **Internet Favorites** A long and carefully cultivated Favorites list is a valuable asset, and it's easy to back up. If you Search for "favorites" on your C drive you will discover either one or several **Favorites folders** (there will be an individual folder for every user); these folders can be backed up like any other regular folder. Alternatively you can use the **Export** function in Internet Explorer's **File** menu.

❒ **Dial-up Networking** Back these up to save you the hassle of sorting out your various dial-up Internet connections should disaster strike. Create a folder on the Desktop or elsewhere. Then in XP open **Network and Internet Connections** from the Start menu (or **Dial-Up Networking** from the Control Panel or My Computer in older Windows versions) and drag the relevant connection icons into the folder to be backed up.

You can carry out a partial backup in various ways: with the program that came with your CD burner, for example, or just by dragging and dropping with a Zip disk. However, you could also use a special backup program, such as the one that comes bundled with Windows.

Windows Backup

Windows features a more-than-adequate backup tool that can be found in the **Start** menu by selecting **Programs**, **Accessories**, **System Tools** and then **Backup** – though you may find that in some versions of Windows this tool is not present (see box).

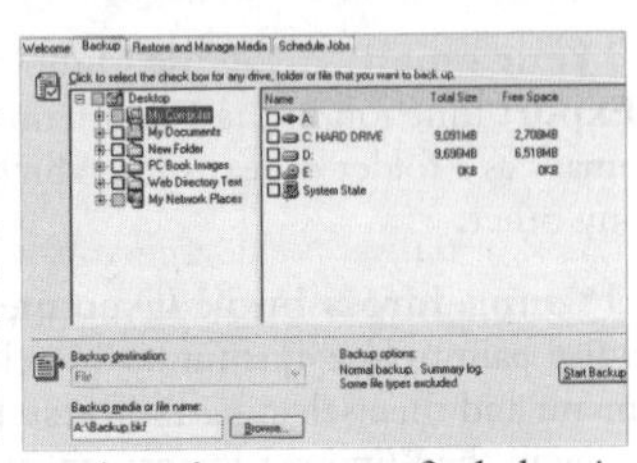

Where's Windows Backup?

If you can't find the Backup program in your version of Windows, dig out your Windows CD-ROM, pop it in the drive and select **Browse This CD** from the dialog box should appear on-screen. Select the add-ons folder and then the MSBackup folder. You should see a icon called msbexp – double-click it to install the utility.

In Windows XP, once the program is up and running you'll either be walked through various frames of the **Backup Utility Wizard** or presented with a dialog box where you can initiate the process manually under the **Backup** tab. In Windows 98 and Me the wizard is simply called the **Backup Wizard**, but it works in much the same way.

Whether you're using the wizard mode or regular mode to create your backup, decide which files you want to back up and select them by checking the boxes next to the files in the various layers of the folder tree. Then choose where you want the data to be backed up to – CD-R, Zip, whatever – and whether you want to use

Tips & Tricks | Tech Info | Try This

Wizardless backups

If your Backup program always launches as a wizard, uncheck the **Always start in wizard mode** box on the first frame of the wizard; you'll find that the next time you run the program many more options will be available to you.

compression to save space. You will also need to give the backup task a **name**. Next time you want to back up you can simply rerun your named backup process: the program compares your existing backup file with your current system and then resaves any files that have changed since the previous backup. There's no need to back up everything, every time – only the stuff that's altered.

The first time you perform such a backup, it's called a **full backup**, while subsequent backups are known as **incremental backups**. With Windows XP you are also given the option to

Welcome to the Backup Wizard
This wizard helps you create a backup copy of your data. In the event of a hardware failure or accidental erasure, you can use the backup copy to restore your data.
To continue, click Next.
< Back
Next >
Cancel

set up a backup schedule. As long as your machine is switched on at the specified time, your backup will be kept updated automatically – you could even set it to be made on a night when your machine is left on for other scheduled tasks.

If you ever want to retrieve either all or some of the files from a backup, again use the Windows Backup utility, but this time click the **Restore And Manage Media** tab (or just **Restore** in earlier Windows versions). Browse your backup media for the files you're after, select them by checking the relevant boxes on the folder tree and hit the **Start Restore** button.

Remember, backups aren't just there for epic disasters. You can also use them to retrieve a single file that you may have accidentally deleted, or even just to compare a piece of work with its earlier version.

21

PC trouble shooting

help is at hand

It may sound pessimistic, but PCs, like anything else, do occasionally go wrong; and even with endless technical refinements they probably always will. Though your first instincts may be to panic, cry or take a sledgehammer to your keyboard, there are a plethora of tools and techniques at your disposal for tackling both minor niggles and major hassles.

Hardware problems

Thanks to the advent of Plug and Play technology (see p.62), hardware connection problems are definitely rarer that they used to be. If you do encounter difficulties, they're most likely to be

Windows XP Troubleshooters

Though this book arms you against many of the problems you're likely to encounter, Windows XP users should also consider turning to the built-in **XP Troubleshooters.** They work like wizards, walking you through a series of diagnostic questions in an attempt to isolate your problem – and, with any luck, suggest a fix. You might have already seen buttons for specific tools in dialog boxes, simply labelled "Troubleshoot", but the best way to find them is by looking in the **Troubleshooter** menus on the left-hand side of the various **Control Panel** category views. For example, within the **Appearance and Themes** category, you will see troubleshooters for **Display** and **Sound.**

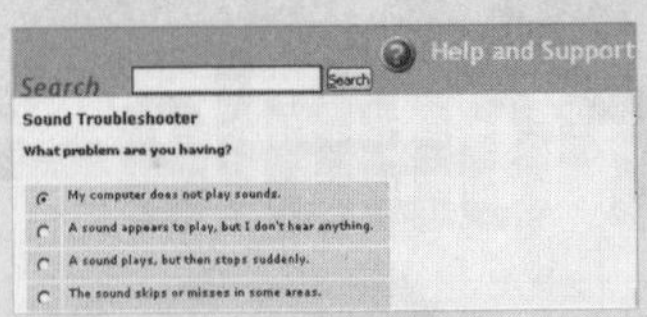

the result of something simple like a disconnected power cable or a plug that has become loose. But if you're still stuck after trying all the obvious possibilities, things can get frustrating. Here's a few of the most common problems and their solutions.

My mouse is sluggish and jumpy

If your mouse is unresponsive and tends to stick, it probably needs a good clean. First, unplug the mouse, turn it over, twist open the access panel and allow the heavy rubber ball to fall out. Now take a look inside and you'll see three little rollers that may well be clogged up with grease, hair or some unidentifiable gunk. Use a cotton bud or some tweezers to remove the sludge, then reassemble your mouse and plug it back in. If your pointer still isn't as perky as you'd like, try adjusting its "motion" and "acceleration" settings in the **Mouse**

Properties dialog box, which you'll find by clicking the **Mouse** icon in the **Control Panel** (within the **Printers and Other Hardware** category in Windows XP).

My monitor flickers

Depending on the limitations of your screen and graphics card, you could try resetting the monitor's refresh rate – anything less than 75Hz can look pretty strobe-like. From the **Control Panel** select **Appearance and Themes** and then **Display**. Click the **Settings** tab, and then the **Advanced** button. Then select the **Monitor** tab (the **Adapter** tab in some versions of Windows) and you'll find a list of available **refresh rate** settings. If several options are given, try a higher setting, but if possible check your manual to see what your screen can handle because too high a refresh rate can damage a monitor.

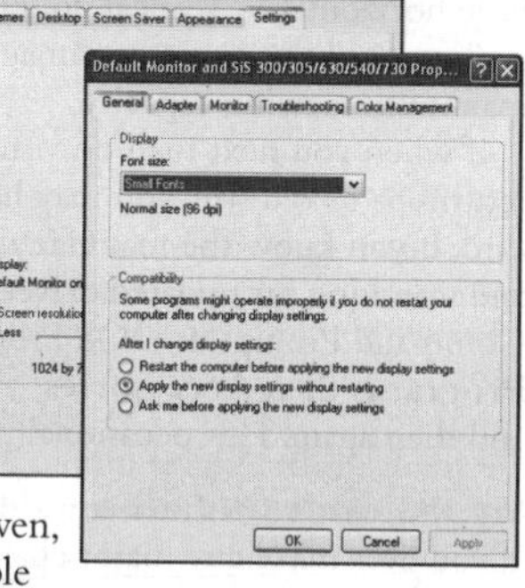

If you are only offered one option (60Hz), it could be that Windows can't find the monitor's Plug and Play configuration. To resolve this problem in XP, select the **Monitor** tab and click the **Properties** button: this will bring up a window that should tell you whether your monitor is working properly. It will also offer a button that launches the Windows **Video Display Troubleshooter**, which will help you to identify and correct any problems with your monitor and video card (or adapter). In older versions of Windows click the **Monitor** tab, check the **Automatically detect Plug & Play monitors** box and then restart your PC.

It may be the case that the monitor doesn't support any settings faster than 60Hz, in which case try experimenting with different screen resolutions (look under **Settings** in the **Display Properties** dialog box, see p.141).

The picture on my monitor doesn't fill the screen

To fix this you need to dig around in the controls on your monitor and find how to alter the two settings represented by little horizontal or vertical double-headed arrows. Tweak the settings until the on-screen image expands to fill the monitor's maximum viewing capacity.

If when you next turn on your computer the screen image returns to its old size, you may have a problem with your video card. If you know the manufacturer, try going to their Website and searching for updated drivers. Alternatively, try opening a Command Prompt or DOS Prompt (in the **Start** menu under **Programs** then **Accessories**) and hitting **Alt+Enter** once, and then again. This occasionally solves the problem.

My PC can't find all my devices

If you ever make any major changes to your system – upgrading your Windows version, for instance, or installing a new expansion card – you may find that certain pieces of hardware (modems, printers and the like) stop working completely or cease to be recognized by your system. This might be because you have a conflict of resources, or your hardware drivers might not be compatible with the changes you've made.

Though Windows should automatically detect the presence of devices connected to it, it's worth unplugging and reconnecting a problematic device to try and trigger the **Found New Hardware Wizard**. Alternatively, select **Add Hardware** from the Control Panel (in the "classic view" in XP) to launch the **Add Hardware Wizard**. Both these

Welcome to the Add Hardware Wizard
This wizard helps you:
• Install software to support the hardware you add to your computer.
• Troubleshoot problems you may be having with your hardware.

wizards will prompt you to insert the disk or disks that contain the device's software drivers. If you don't have these disks, or the software is not compatible with your fresh Windows upgrade, you can use the wizard to search online for a newer version of the driver to download and install. If you're running older versions of Windows you will need to get online and find your device's drivers yourself – have a look on the manufacturer's Website.

If your hardware problems persist, it's worth checking the port settings. Right-click **My Computer**, select **Properties**, and click the **Device Manager** tab (or the **Device Manager** button under the **Hardware** tab in Windows XP). Find and double-click the icon for the troublesome device. Select the **Resources** tab, and look in the **Conflicting device list** box to see if this is the source of the problem. If there is a conflict you could try disabling the device that is causing it, by right-clicking its icon in the **Device Manager** list, selecting **Properties**, clicking the **General** tab, and selecting **Do not use this device (disable)** or **Disable in this hardware profile**. However, you won't be able to use the conflicting device until you re-enable it.

Some of my USB connections won't work

The most common USB connection problems are with power. As well as actually connecting your PC to peripherals, USB ports sometimes send electricity to them. For many peripherals this isn't an issue because they have their own power supply; and, equally, USB ports on a PC's case or monitor base should have no difficulties delivering the juice when it's needed. But the USB ports found on some peripheral devices without power sources (like keyboards) shift far less power. Trying to use a USB device that needs a lot of energy – such as a scanner – with an unpowered port like this can be problematic. To solve the problem, either move the device to a self-powered port or invest in a **USB hub** with its own power supply.

My CD or DVD drive won't read a disc

If your drive will read some discs but not others, the likelihood is either that the lens is dirty or that some of your discs are scratched or unclean. Lenses can be cleaned using a kit that can be picked up relatively cheaply in most computer stores. When it comes to dirty or scratched discs, there are various things you could try. The easiest approach is to use a clean, lint-free cloth, but some people claim that putting a CD in the freezer for a couple of hours can do the trick, while others swear by the application of a polish. There are special disc polishes around, but certain metal polishes like Brasso can work surprisingly well (though these should be applied with caution to discs containing important data). If the problem disc contains a piece of software, try contacting the manufacturer: they might be willing to swap your old copy for a shiny new one.

I'm having problems saving files to a floppy disk, even though the disk appears to be empty

The first thing to check is that the little plastic write-protection tab on the corner of the diskette is closed: if you can see through the hole, slide the tab across to close it.

If you're still having trouble writing to the disk, try formatting it – but beware, as this will **IRRETRIEVABLY**

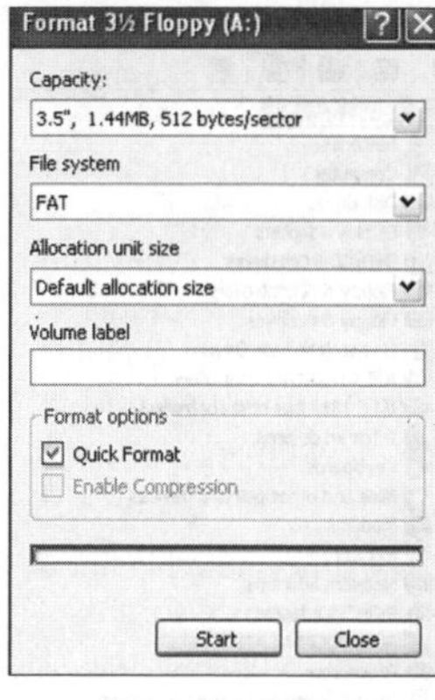

ERASE all the data on the disk. Insert the disk into the drive, and then in **My Computer** right-click the drive's icon (almost always labelled **A:**), and from the mouse menu select **Format**. In the dialog box that appears, uncheck the **Quick Format** box – you need to perform a **Full** format that will not only delete any files but also check the disk for errors and return it to a totally blank state. In this dialog box you can also choose to give the disk a **Label** (a name that will appear alongside its icon in an Explorer window). When you're ready, click **Start**; it will probably take a couple of minutes for the process to complete. If you continue to have difficulties writing to a particular disk it may well be physically damaged: the only option is to bin it and try a different one.

I keep being presented with printer error messages

Printers are notoriously difficult to keep happy, so this is a relatively common problem. First, check that the printer is plugged into its power supply, connected to your PC properly (with a decent cable), has paper in its tray and is online. If all this seems fine, try turning the printer off, waiting a few seconds and then turning it on again – this will clear its memory, which sometimes does the trick. If you've recently upgraded your operating system it may be that you need to download a newer **driver** from your printer manufacturer's Website. Equally, the driver you are using might be corrupted or suffering from a virus, so reinstalling drivers from the floppy or CD that came with the printer is always worth a try. To do this in Windows XP, open the **Control Panel**, click the **Printers and Other Hardware** category and select **Printers and Faxes**. In older versions of Windows open the **Printers** folder, which can be reached either from **My Computer** or the **Control Panel**. Now, right-click the icon for your current printer and click **Delete** in the mouse menu. Next click the **Add Printer** icon to launch the **Add Printer Wizard**, which will help you to reinstall your printer, either from the Windows built-in list or from the CD that came with the printer.

If you're still having problems, check the port settings. Right-click **My Computer** and select **Properties**. In Windows XP select the **Hardware** tab and click the **Device Manager** button; in earlier versions of Windows just click the **Device Manager** tab. You'll see a list of all the ports and devices on your system. Double-click either **Ports (COM & LPT)** or **Universal Serial Bus controllers** depending on the sort of connection your printer uses (parallel or USB respectively). Double-click the icon for your printer port, select the **Resources** tab and look in the **Conflicting device list** box for **IRQ** (Interrupt Request Line) or **DMA** (Direct Memory Access) conflicts. If there is a conflict you could disable the device that's causing it. Find the device in the Device Manager list, right-click it and select **Properties**. When

Diagnosing your hardware problems

There are various diagnostic programs available to help you with troubleshooting, such as the invaluable **SiSoft Sandra Standard**, which can be downloaded for free from **http://www.sisofware.demon .co.uk/Sandra**. This little program looks very much like a Windows Control Panel, but it's used for running tests on your system and creating reports. Whenever it finds something amiss in your system, it makes suggestions about how to fix it with step-by-step instructions.

a dialog box appears, click the **General** tab and select **Do not use this device (disable)** or **Disable in this hardware profile**. This may make the printer work, but you'll have to re-enable the device that you've turned off when you next need to use it.

Windows pains

Most of the problems you encounter on your PC will be related to your Windows operating system. Though these difficulties can seem perplexing and complicated, there are various built-in **System Tools** (see, p.167) and utilities at your disposal that can diagnose and fix many problems. As long as you keep a clear head and remember that most PC problems have occurred for a specific – and fixable – reason, Windows troubleshooting should be relatively straightforward and a valuable part of the overall learning process. Here are a few common problems that you might encounter:

Windows has displayed an alarming error message with loads of codes and file names I don't understand

Though they often seem bewildering and it's tempting to ignore them, error messages generally appear for a good reason,

Remote Assistance

If you're running Windows XP you can use the Remote Assistance utility to allow a trusted friend or technician to access your system from a remote location and try to deal with any problems you may be encountering. Equally, if you want to help someone else out with a problem, they could invite you to roll up your sleeves and rummage around in their system.

First, the party that needs aid (let's say Tom) has to issue an invitation to the individual that they think can help (how about Tom's cousin Lucy?). From the **Start** menu Tom selects **Help and Support**, then clicks the **Support** button, and then the **Ask a Friend to help** task. The invitation can be sent by either an email or Windows Messenger service. Once the invitation has been accepted by Lucy, control can be gained by her computer with a single click of the **Take Control** button that she sees on her screen.

While Lucy sorts out the problem, Tom can still use his mouse and keyboard – handy for recreating the conditions or actions that caused the problem in the first place – and with the additional connection of microphones and speakers to the two PCs, the pair can actually chat while the Remote Assistance is in operation.

To stop anyone using an email invitation to access your machine without permission, they come with an expiry date and can also be password-protected.

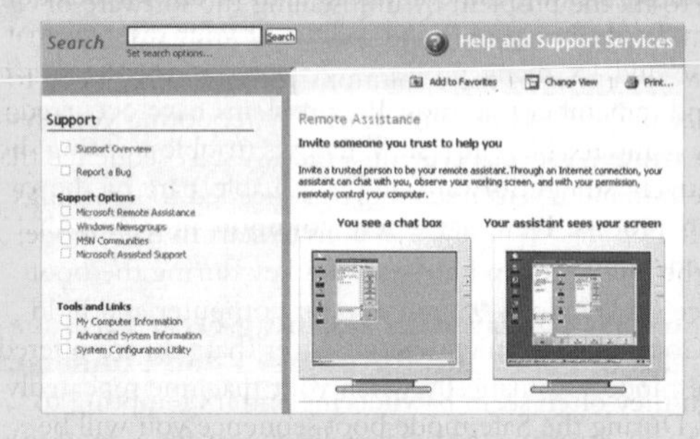

so they're worth investigating. Make a note of everything that the message says and then visit the **Knowledge Base** section of Microsoft's Website (**http://www.support.microsoft.com**). Here you should be able to find everything you need to know about your error message, as well as various tips about how to sort things out.

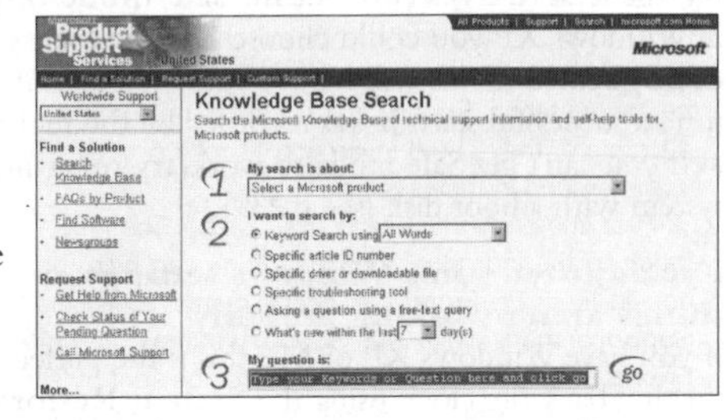

My machine is having problems starting Windows

This kind of predicament is most likely due to a problem with your Windows registry or settings, perhaps caused by a bad software or hardware installation. In Windows XP and Me, such problems are often easily solved with the **System Restore** tool (see p.170). If you're running Windows 98 or earlier, you may be able to fix the problem by uninstalling the software or device driver that was installed before the problem arose.

But to try either of these solutions you obviously need to get your machine up and running again. Try rebooting your system in **Safe mode**, a special type of Windows start sequence that uses the minimum settings and drivers needed to get things going. To get most Windows versions to start in Safe mode, restart the computer and press the **F8** key during the boot sequence (in Windows 98, restart your computer and hold down **Control**). You might also discover that you are offered the Safe mode automatically when your machine repeatedly crashes. During the Safe mode boot sequence you will be presented with a menu of Safe mode options, which will vary a little depending upon the version of Windows you are running. As a general rule, select the **basic Safe mode option**, though in Windows XP you could choose **Last known good configuration**. This will reboot your system as it was the last time a successful startup was recorded by the registry.

If you can't get Safe mode to work, try restarting your system with a boot disk (see p.239).

I've adjusted some Windows settings and now things aren't working properly

If you have Windows XP or Me, this is the perfect time to try turning back the clock using the **System Restore** function, found under **Performance and Maintenance** in the Windows XP **Control Panel**, and **System Tools** in Windows Me. See p.170 for more.

Certain programs start automatically when I boot Windows – how do I stop this happening?

You need to remove the programs from the Windows Startup folder (see p.199).

Some of my files seem to have disappeared, while other text documents look like they've been put through a mincer

First of all back up any important data (see p.280) in case anything else disappears. The problem could be caused by a virus, so it's worth scanning your system (see p.279), and also try uninstalling any software or device drivers that you installed just before the problem arose.

However, it could also be that your hard drive is on its last legs. Try opening **ScanDisk utility** (see p.168) and selecting the **Thorough** option to check the surface of your drive for bad or damaged sectors. You might well be prompted to delete detected **cross-linked** and **bad clusters**; this might be enough to solve the problem, but if files continue to vanish or be mangled, it could be that you'll soon need a new hard drive.

If something important seems to have permanently disappeared or if you can't find anything at all on your hard drive, you could try getting some data recovery software (see p.298). If things are desperate you may even consider employing the services of a data recovery company.

I'm having trouble with the setup of my Windows upgrade

In this situation, if you feel brave enough, the best thing to do is back up all your data, format your hard drive and make a **clean installation** (see p.241) of your new version of Windows.

I'm missing the volume control icon from my Taskbar

Open the **Control Panel**. In Windows XP select the **Sounds, Speech and Audio Devices** category and then click **Sounds and Audio Devices**; in earlier versions just click **Sounds** or **Sounds and Multimedia**. Click on the **Volume** or **Audio** tab of the dialog box that will appear, check the **Show volume control on taskbar** box and click **Apply**.

My machine is running very slowly, crashing frequently, and it keeps displaying "Low Memory" error messages

You might need to add some more RAM to your system (see p.307), but there are several other things you could try if you don't fancy getting your hands dirty. First, try creating a little extra room for your **virtual memory** (also known as the **pagefile** or **swapfile**) – the special file on your PC that stores any excess data that your RAM can't accommodate. This file adjusts its size as required, but it's limited by the available space on your hard drive. To give your virtual memory a little more elbowroom in Windows XP right-click **My Computer**, select

Advanced and then under **Performance** click the **Settings** button. In the next box, under **Advanced**, click the **Change** button under **Virtual Memory**: here you can adjust its size and location. In older Windows right-click **My Computer** and select **Properties**, go to the **Performance** tab and choose **Virtual Memory**. Select **Let me specify my own virtual memory settings** and try raising the maximum figure.

I think my PC might have a virus, but I'm not running an antivirus utility

FREE! HouseCall Online Virus Scanning Service

Though you should have an antivirus utility running at all times, don't worry too much: there is help to be found on the Internet. Try **HouseCall**, Trend Micro's free virus scanning utility (**http://www.housecall.antivirus.com**). After download, the program scans your computer's hard drive, finding and (hopefully) removing any viruses.

In some versions of Windows XP you also have the option of creating an **AVBoot floppy disk** – a special startup floppy disk utility that scans your computer's memory and all its local disk drives for viruses. If a virus is found, the AVBoot tool will try to get rid of it. To create an AVBoot disk, insert your Windows XP CD into your CD drive and click the **Browse this CD** option. Now double-click **VALUEADD** then open the **3RDPARTY** folder, then the **CA_ANTIV** folder, and double-click the **Makedisk** icon; insert a disk into your floppy drive and follow the on-screen instructions. To run the utility, insert the AVBoot startup disk into your floppy drive and restart your PC.

I've deleted a file that I actually need

The first thing to do is check the **Recycle Bin**. But if you've permanently erased the file, it won't be there and you'll need to get hold of some recovery software from the Internet. Try downloading a free version of Ontrack's **EasyRecovery** (http://www.ontrack.co.uk/easyrecovery). It will show you which files on your drives and disks are recoverable with the EasyRecovery program, letting you decide whether it's worth purchasing the full package. There are loads of other similar applications available – use a search engine (see p.211) to see what you can find – and try not to save anything to the disk or drive in question until you have recovered the file, as this could make recovery impossible.

I have forgotten my Windows password

In Windows XP you can create a new password for yourself by using the password reset disk that you hopefully created a while ago: for more on these disks, see p.154.

In older Windows versions you might find you can simply press **Cancel** when prompted to enter your password, though this may not open your account with all settings in place. If this doesn't work, or if you really want to sort out the forgotten password, you'll need to restart your computer using a Windows Startup disk (see p.239). When you're presented with a menu of options, hold down **Shift+F5** to get a command prompt – a black background displaying something like **A:\>**. Type **c:** and hit **Enter**. Then type **cd windows** and press **Enter** again. Next, type **dir *.pwl**, press **Enter** once more – a list of the password files on your computer will appear. Each password file will be named after the person who it relates to – if your username is "Elvis", for example, the password file will be named **ELVIS**. Though you won't be able to find the actual password this way, deleting the password file will allow you back in to the machine, and you can set a new password later. To delete the ELVIS file, for example, type **del ELVIS.pwl** and press **Enter**. You can check that it's been deleted by once again typing **dir *.pwl** and pressing **Enter** – the list should be displayed without the relevant password file.

Then remove the Startup disk and restart your machine (you

may be asked to choose from a menu once more – select **Start in normal mode**). When Windows loads, you may be asked to enter a new password – do so if you want to, but it's fine to leave it blank. If Windows still asks for a password, simply click **OK** without entering anything in the password field.

The sound from my PC sometimes clicks

This is quite a common problem, usually caused by misunderstandings between a graphics card and a sound card. Try right-clicking the Desktop and selecting **Properties** to open the Display Properties dialog Box. Click the **Settings** tab, then the **Advanced** button, and a new dialog box will appear. Select the tab labelled **Troubleshoot** or **Performance**, and reduce the **Hardware Acceleration** setting. If you can't get a satisfactory result this way, try going to the Website of your sound card manufacturer and downloading the latest drivers.

The clock on my Taskbar doesn't keep the right time

In Windows Me and earlier the clock is pretty unreliable – you may find that it gradually drifts out over a few days or weeks, or perhaps it's correct when the machine is switched on but loses time over the course of a session. There's no perfect cure, but there are various programs downloadable for free from the Internet that will set your clock automatically whenever you go online. Try **Atomic Clock** (http://www.philex.net/clock).

When I try to shut down, my PC stays on while the screen goes blank, leaving only a blinking cursor in the top corner

This is a common problem for people running the first edition of Windows 98. To solve it, select **Run** from the **Start menu**, type **msconfig** and hit **Enter**. The **System Configuration Utility** dialog box will pop up. Select the **Advanced** button and click the **Disable Fast Shutdown** checkbox.

Web problems

If you're having trouble accessing a particular Website, check that the addresses you are using are correct, and bear in mind that the site may be down or just very busy – meaning that you won't be able to connect. If this keeps happening, though, it's likely to be something more fundamental. Check the following troubleshooting tips, as well as those covered in *The Rough Guide to the Internet*.

My browser keeps crashing

Try clearing your browser of any old Web files and content that may be corrupted or troublesome. In Internet Explorer, select **Options** from the **Tools** menu to open the **Internet Options** dialog box. Under the **General** tab, in the **Temporary Internet Files** section, click **Delete Files**. Further down, click the **Clear History** button. While you're there, consider reducing your History's memory to only a few days; this will limit the likelihood of corrupt files causing trouble in the future but will mean that your PC won't keep track of all the pages you've visited for as long, making offline browsing less smooth.

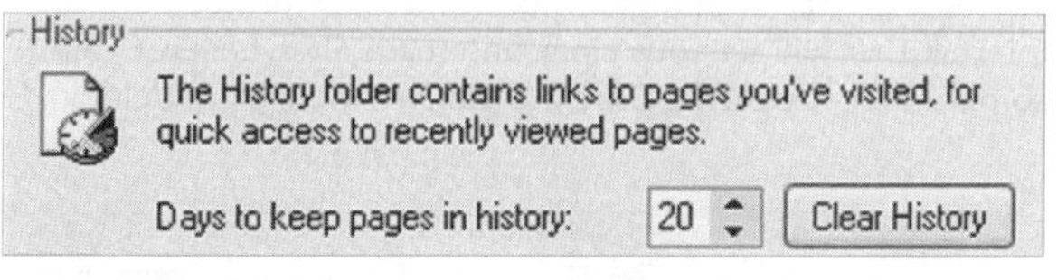

I'm having problems with my Internet connection

If you're constantly losing your Internet connection, especially at peak times, chances are that the fault is with your ISP rather than your machine. Try emailing your current provider to inform them of your difficulties or, if you don't get a satisfactory response, take your business elsewhere.

If the problem persists, or you find that your machine disconnects whenever you leave it for more than a couple of minutes, it might be that your PC is set to hang up after a certain amount of "idle" time. To see if this is so, open the **Control Panel**, select **Network and Internet connections** and click **Network Connections**. (In earlier versions of Windows, click **Dial-Up Networking** from the **Control Panel** or **My Computer**). Right-click the icon for the connection you're having trouble with and select **Properties** from the mouse menu. Under one of the tabs you'll find an option labelled something like **Idle time before hanging up**; increase the time to an hour or so.

I'm having trouble downloading a file – when I click the download link, nothing happens

This is a common problem, and one that's easy to solve. In Explorer, right-click the download link and select **Save Link As** or **Save Target As** from the mouse menu that pops up. You can then save the download to wherever you like.

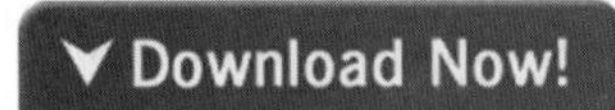

22

Upgrades and self-builds

doing it yourself

If your PC no longer cuts the mustard and troubleshooting hasn't helped, it may be time for an upgrade. First, you'll need to work out what your weary system actually needs. Then you'll have to make a decision: either to take the PC to a computer store and let them to do the rest or to be a bit more adventurous – buy a new component, find a screwdriver, get under the hood and make the upgrade yourself.

What can be achieved?

If you have a specific computer problem, a one-part upgrade is often enough to solve it completely. If you've run out of storage space, for example, a new hard drive will do the trick; if your machine is struggling to run large programs, a bit more RAM could be enough to sort it out; and if you have a reasonable processor but 3D games aren't up to speed then a new video card could make all the difference. But if your intention is to turn a very old PC into a high-end multimedia powerhouse, you may find that practically every bit of the computer needs replacing – you'll need a fast processor, which will almost certainly necessitate a new motherboard, which in turn will probably mean getting a new case. You'll also need new RAM (your old stuff will probably be of the wrong sort), and a better graphics card. And you'll probably want a bigger hard drive for storing programs, music, video, games, etc. Some components might be reusable – the monitor, modem, sound card, mouse and keyboard, perhaps – but you'll essentially be building a new PC. This isn't necessarily a problem, but if you're going to all this trouble you should at least consider going for an entirely new machine.

Can I do it myself?

If you're of a relatively technical disposition and patient enough to do the necessary research, most upgrades shouldn't be too difficult – especially simple operations such as adding more RAM. Things can get tricky, though, especially if you're adding components to an old motherboard, and there's always a small element of **risk** – you may even **invalidate the warranty** of your PC if you start tampering within the case, and you'll have no comeback if you **accidentally break something**. But for many users, the pros substantially outweigh the cons. Not only can you **save money**, but getting under the hood of a computer is the best way to demystify the machine and gain a real knowledge of its bits and pieces.

This chapter is only intended as a guide, not something to be followed step by step. It runs through some basics of PC

Upgrading notebooks

Upgrading notebook PCs used to be very difficult – usually the job could only really be done by a pro and often the options were very limited. But although they're still not as upgradeable as desktop systems, many modern notebooks feature easily accessible RAM slots, interchangeable CD, DVD and floppy drives, removable hard drives and other do-it-yourself possibilities. And much more often than with desktops, notebooks come with a manual specifying exactly what can be done in terms of upgrading and what types of components are required – and many even include detailed instructions about making the install. If your notebook didn't come with a manual, contact the manufacturer for information.

upgrading, and describes some commonly faced problems, but **each system is different** and yours may require alternative treatment. If a **manual** came with your system, read it – you may find it describes the exact upgrade potential of the PC and offers advice about buying components. And if your PC is a big-brand machine, it's worth visiting the manufacturer's **Website** to see if they have an upgrading section. If they do, it may even provide step-by-step instructions for various types of upgrade. Finally, always read the **instructions** provided with the device you're adding.

Getting under the hood

You shouldn't be intimidated by the prospect of opening up your PC and carrying out some basic surgery. As long as you're careful and methodical you will probably be fine, and if you get stuck you can always take the machine to a shop and get the staff to rescue you. But there are a few golden rules you need to be aware of before you open up a PC for the first time:

Safety first Most important of all, you need to protect yourself from electric shock. **Never take the case off a PC before turning it off and disconnecting the power lead**. And once the machine's open, don't touch anything unnecessarily: electrical components are easily damaged and some can carry a small charge even after the machine has been switched off.

Protect your components Computer components, especially RAM chips and CPUs, are incredibly sensitive to **static electricity**. A static shock from a finger so small that you wouldn't even feel it can be enough to fry a high-quality stick of RAM. Though this potential hazard is sometimes slightly exaggerated, before you unpack any new parts or touch anything inside, and at regular intervals when you're handling components, be sure to touch some grounded metal such as an unpainted gas or water pipe. Or even better, buy an anti-static wristband – they're inexpensive and are available from many electronic and computer stores.

Work in a sensible place Before you begin, unplug everything from the computer and move it to a flat, stable and well-lit surface such as a table, with some small containers to hand for storing any screws you remove. If you don't have an anti-static wristband, avoid working on the PC whilst sitting or standing on a carpet, as this will increase the risk of picking up static electricity.

Equipment There are some excellent PC toolkits available which include everything you could conceivably require for repairing a computer, but for a simple upgrade these aren't really necessary. Probably all you'll need is a small crosshead screwdriver – though some other tools may be required depending on the situation and the type of screws used on the case. A pair of pincer-nosed pliers can come in handy for removing power leads and other stubborn connections, though they should be used with care.

Opening the case Opening up a PC is usually very simple. The top section of the case is normally secured by a few small screws or clips at the back of the machine. Remove these and the top section should simply slide off.

While you're in there . . . When you open up the case to carry out an upgrade, you may be surprised at just how dusty everything is inside. This is largely due to the cooling fan or fans, which pull a lot of air through the case. If you have the hood off you may be tempted to give everything a quick clean. This is a good idea, but circuitry should only really be cleaned by carefully spraying with compressed air, which is available in cans from electronic stores. Make sure you blow the dust out of the machine rather than simply rearranging it, and never hold the can too near to the components.

Adding more RAM

This is the commonest upgrade of all, and it usually gives the most notable performance increase for the amount of money you spend. The easiest way to proceed is to take your machine to a shop and ask them to install the new RAM chips for you, but it's much cheaper – and usually surprisingly simple – to do it yourself. But first you need to choose the correct type of RAM.

Choosing the right RAM

There are many variables when selecting RAM: there are several different types, and each one comes in various speeds and with various different specs. The easiest way to find out what type of RAM your PC will take is to look at the manual that came with the system or motherboard. If you don't have a manual, ask the person you bought the PC from, check the manufacturer's Website or use an online retailer's system identifier (such as the one on the Crucial Memory Website at **http://www.crucial.com**), which will guide you to the correct type for your PC and give the option of purchasing directly. If none of these options work, have a look inside your system to see what's currently installed (see p.305) and buy more of the same type. If you still can't work out what sort it is, remove the RAM that's there and take it to a computer shop. As a general rule, if you're not sure what you're buying, purchase from somewhere

that will let you return it if it won't work with your system.

Here's an explanation of some of the jargon and variables you'll come across when buying RAM:

Type of RAM Most machines made before around 1998 take FPM and/or EDO RAM, which comes on modules called 72-pin SIMMs (the pins are the little teeth which stick into the motherboard). FPM and EDO RAM shouldn't be mixed. Most machines made more recently take SDRAM, which comes on two types of modules: 168-pin DIMMs for standard computers and 144-pin SODIMMs for small PCs and notebooks. Some machines can take DIMMs and SIMMs, but you shouldn't mix them. Recent high-end PCs may take DDR SDRAM, which comes in 184-pin DIMMs, or RDRAM, which comes in 184-pin RIMMs (or SORIMMs for small and mobile PCs).

PC number This refers to the speed at which a DIMM module can transfer data. SDRAM is available in PC66, PC100 or PC133 (transferring data at 66, 100, 133 megahertz respectively). Ideally the RAM that you fit should match the speed of your motherboard chipset – PC100 for a 100MHz motherboard, for example. Most, but not all, motherboards can happily run a mixture or PC66, PC100 and PC133 RAM. However, the overall speed will be limited by the slowest component, be it a RAM module or the motherboard. Because the speed doesn't affect the price much (faster is often cheaper, in fact) most people buy PC133 RAM even if they have a 66 or 100 MHz motherboard – the computer won't run any faster but a PC133 strip is likely to be more useful in the future. DDR SDRAM comes in PC1600 and PC2100 modules (operating at 200 and 266 MHz respectively). On most DDR motherboards you can mix PC1600 and PC2100, though the system will run at the speed of the slowest module or the motherboard, whichever is slower. RDRAM comes in PC600,

PC700 and PC800 – the numbers refer to the maximum data transfer rate in megahertz. On most RDRAM motherboards, these three speeds can be mixed, but again, the slowest module will limit the speed. Some motherboards don't take PC700.

Non-parity, Parity and ECC (Error Checking and Correction) Parity and ECC are error-correcting technologies, which are only really useful for servers and some other "mission critical" systems. Always get non-parity RAM unless you already have some Parity or ECC RAM (you can check your current RAM by counting the rectangular chips on the memory module – if the total isn't divisible by three, you have non-parity RAM).

NS speed This techie specification, which you don't really need to worry about, is an internal speed thing, measured in nanoseconds. A lower number means a very slightly faster speed. Different speeds can be mixed, though the whole lot will run at the speed of the slowest chip.

Buffered or unbuffered? Buffers help RAM chips to deal with very large flows of data and are generally only used by servers, so most PC RAM you will come across will be unbuffered.

CL number Another techie specification: this relates to latency, the amount of time the memory wastes when starting to send data. A lower number is better – CL2 being very slightly faster than CL3, for example. Usually you can ignore this spec, though some systems do require a particular CL number.

Before you buy

First you need to see how many spare slots you have in your system. Unplug your PC, open up the case and have a look at your

RAM slots and chips to see what's currently installed. The slots are easy to spot: they're plastic, about ten centimetres long, lined up in parallel, and generally there are between two and four of them. At least one will have a strip of RAM in it. If the RAM slots are obscured by lots of cables, expansion cards or drives, these obstacles may have to be temporarily removed. If you find this idea intimidating, you may decide at this point to take the machine to a shop; if not, remove each problematic item in turn, making sure you carefully note down where and which way round each cable or item went.

DIMM slots are black with plastic catches on the ends. If you're adding SDRAM, you'll probably want to simply add a single DIMM into a spare slot. If you don't have a spare slot, you'll have to remove your smallest current DIMM to make room for a bigger one – don't throw the old one away as it may come in handy in the future. SIMMs work the same way except that their slots are white, and they have to be installed in identical pairs – **you can't add a single SIMM.**

If your PC takes RDRAM RIMMs, you'll find that all the slots are already full. But they won't necessarily be full with actual RAM modules, as RIMM slots not currently in use have to be filled with dummy modules called **continuity RIMMs** (CRIMMS). You can tell the difference between a real and a continuity module simply by looking – real RIMMs have metal covers, continuity RIMMs don't. As with SIMMs, RIMMs have to be installed in identical pairs in most motherboards.

If you want to add RAM to your notebook PC, refer to the manual to see how easily it can be done. Often a little screw panel on the bottom of the machine reveals the RAM slots, but in some machines (especially older ones) they are difficult to get at. If your notebook's slots are full or inaccessible, you could consider buying RAM in the form of an easily insertable PC card (see p.18).

How much do you need?

All motherboards have a limit to the amount of RAM they can handle, so make sure you check your manual or a Web-based system identifier if you're planning on adding a serious amount. Currently, 128MB is sensible for most tasks, though 256MB – or even more – is useful for serious multimedia activities such as video, music editing and high-end gaming. If you're buying a DIMM, you may as well go for at least a 64MB strip – anything less will be almost the same price. Large SIMMs are much more expensive, so if you want to add a lot of RAM to an old PC, it would probably make more sense to get a new motherboard that can take DIMMs (though this may also require a new case) rather than blowing large sums on old-style SIMMs.

Making the install

Make sure you're free of static electricity before touching a RAM module (see p.306). And never touch the metal teeth – while installing or removing modules try to touch the edges only.

Your **DIMM** slots will be numbered – usually 0, 1, 2, etc – on the motherboard, and the lowest numbered slots should be filled first. Also, the biggest module in terms of megabytes should be inserted in the lowest-numbered slot, so if you're adding a new DIMM that's bigger than those already installed you'll have to rearrange the modules to allow this. To remove a DIMM, simply open the little clips holding it in place (pull them away from the centre of the slot) and it will pop out. To install a DIMM, make sure you have the module the correct way around (align the two notches in the module with the ridges in the slot) and press it into place with your thumbs until the clips snap shut. You might need to apply quite a lot of pressure – to make this easier, lay the case on the table in such a way that the motherboard is flat – but don't press too hard.

SIMM slots are numbered 0, 1 and so on in pairs called "banks", each of which has to be filled with a pair of identical SIMMs. As with DIMMs, SIMMs needs to be inserted in the lowest available bank of slots, and your best bet is to stick the largest pair in terms of megabytes in the lowest numbered bank, which will probably require you to move your old modules. To remove a SIMM you have to prise open the metal clips that are holding it in place. This can be quite tricky and is sometimes easier with the help of a pointed non-metal object. Once the clips are open, gently rotate the SIMM until it's at a 45-degree angle to the motherboard, and then pull it out. To add a SIMM, make sure the clips aren't in the way, align it correctly with the slot (it will only fit in one way round because one corner is snipped off), and gently put it into the slot at a 45-degree angle. Then pull it to an upright position and the metal clips should close around it.

RIMMs slot into place in the same way as DIMMS, but depending on your motherboard they may have to be installed in identical pairs like SIMMs. And you'll have to remove the CRIMMs that will be occupying any spare slots.

Switching on

Once your new RAM is in place, replace the case, plug everything in and switch on. You should see your memory being counted on the initial startup screen, and then Windows should load as normal. Right-click **My Computer** and select **Properties** to open the **System Properties** dialog box, which displays information about your computer. At the bottom of the box you'll see how much RAM is recognized – hopefully the correct new total. If there is less than you expected it could be because your graphics card uses "shared" memory. If you have 128MB of RAM installed, for example, and your motherboard has in-built graphics with 8MB of shared memory, only 120MB will be recognized.

It doesn't work!

If after a RAM installation your PC won't start up, don't panic. Open up the case, make sure that the RAM is in the lowest numbered slots and that any SIMMs are installed in identical pairs. Check that the modules are securely held in place – if they wobble, take them out and put them in again. Also make sure that anything you moved or unplugged is back as it should be. And if you're mixing RAM speeds – PC100 and PC133, for example – try swapping them around so that the slowest strip is in the lowest-numbered slot. If the machine still won't work, remove your original RAM and try your machine with the new RAM on its own to rule out a conflict between the various modules. If it still doesn't work, it could be that your new RAM is incompatible with your motherboard – or possibly damaged. Hopefully you bought it from someone that guaranteed it would work with your motherboard, in which case you should be able to return it.

If your system has recognized the extra RAM but is actually running slower than it was before, it could be that your motherboard can't handle the new amount. This is very rare if you followed the maximums suggested in your manual, but it can happen. Remove the new RAM and think about investing in a new motherboard or system.

Adding expansion cards

Many PC upgrades take the form of adding an expansion card. The most common expansion cards are **graphics cards**, **sound cards**, **modems**, **TV cards** and **network cards**. But there are many other types, including **SCSI**, **USB** and **IEEE 1394** interface cards, which add extra ports to your machine. Adding an expansion card is pretty simple, and in most cases should be relatively trouble-free. But before you attempt an operation there are a few things you should know. First, don't buy a card until you've checked that you have the necessary slot. Second, if you're adding a video or sound card to replace the graphics or sound functions that are "integrated" (built into your motherboard), you'll probably need to disable these in-built capabilities. This can be a bit of a pain – for details check your manual, contact the PC's manufacturer or search for information on the Internet. Third, if you're replacing a video card, you'll probably be in for a smoother ride if you reset the system to a standard Windows display setting first. Right-click the Desktop and choose **Properties**, then select the **Settings** tab, click the **Advanced** button and another dialog box will open. Click the **Adapter** tab, hit the **Change** button and a wizard will appear. When offered, choose **Show all devices**, select **Standard Display Adapter (VGA)** and click **OK**. Windows will prompt you to reboot – you're now ready to switch off your machine and swap the old card for the new one.

Locating the slots

Unplug the PC and open up the case (see p.305). Along the rear of the case you'll see a number of removable panels which will match up to plastic slots on the motherboard. Some – but hopefully not all – of these slots may already be occupied with expansion cards, which look like rectangular pieces of circuit board with a metal panel on the back. There are three types of

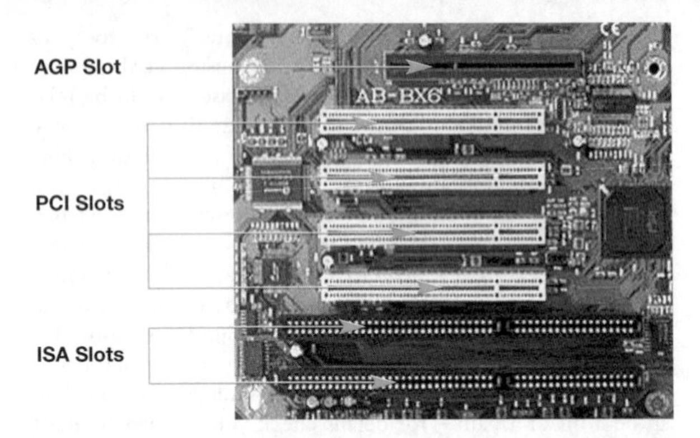

slot: AGP, PCI and ISA. If you have a newish motherboard, you'll probably have one AGP slot (for graphics cards), a number of PCI slots (for all sorts of devices) and maybe one ISA slot (for old devices). Each slot should be labelled on the motherboard – and in the motherboard's manual – to show you what type it is, but they're easy to tell apart just by looking: AGP slots are brown, PCI slots are white and slightly shorter and ISA slots are big and black. If the appropriate slot is available, you can go ahead and buy the expansion card of your choice. If not, you'll have to remove one of your current cards or get a new motherboard.

Installing the card

Before unpacking a new expansion card or touching an old one, be sure to rid yourself of static electricity (see p.306). Try to hold the cards only by their edges, and never touch the metal teeth that slot into the motherboard.

Choose a slot of the correct type – it shouldn't matter which if there is more than one of that type, so choose the one that will give you the most room – and remove the relevant panel from the rear of the case. This usually entails taking out the little screw holding it in place, though some old cases may have panels that need to be levered out with a screwdriver (be extremely careful not to touch any components with the screwdriver tip).

Once the panel is removed, press the card into the slot. Sometimes it's easier to insert one end first and then push the other end into place, but make sure you always keep the card at the correct angle, perpendicular to the motherboard. You should feel when it slots properly into place. You may have to apply quite a lot of pressure, but **don't force it** – pull the card out, check everything's aligned and try again.

Turning on

With the card in place, close up the case, plug everything in and switch on. If all goes well, Windows will start up, display a **New Hardware Found** message and open a wizard to guide you through the installation of the driver. When prompted, insert the CD or floppy that came with the expansion card – click the **Have disk** button if there is one – and guide Windows to the appropriate drive.

Problems

If you switch on but there's no sign that the new hardware has been recognized, open the **Control Panel** and select the **Add New Hardware icon** (select the classic view in Windows XP). This will prompt Windows to search for the new device.

If your system gives you trouble after you've added the card – it won't start up, keeps crashing and generally does weird stuff – it may be worth removing the new card and trying it in a different slot. If it still plays up, try swapping your cards around. This shouldn't really be necessary, but motherboards do sometimes accept cards in one order and not in another (a network card in a PCI slot next to the AGP slot can sometimes cause problems). If that hasn't helped, try downloading an up-to-date driver from the card manufacturer's Website.

If you've added a new graphics card and when you switch on you don't see anything on the monitor at all, make sure that the card is properly "seated" in the slot – try taking it out and pushing it in again. And make sure the monitor is properly attached to the port on the back of the card.

Adding CD and DVD drives

Adding a CD or DVD drive to a system is generally fairly simple. If at any point you get stuck you can always call in someone a little more experienced for help, and in a worst-case scenario you can always take the machine to a computer store and have them finish the job – though this is rarely necessary.

This section assumes you'll be adding a standard ATAPI or IDE drive – one that will connect to an IDE port on the motherboard. Though there are other types of drives available – SCSI models, for example (see p.46) – they're more expensive, less convenient and not as widely available.

Before you buy

If you plan to add a DVD drive to a machine that is 450MHz or slower, your PC may struggle to keep up, so you'll need to add an MPEG decoder card or a new graphics card with DVD support. The card will slot into an AGP or PCI slot and do some of the work. Many DVD upgrade packs are available, which include a drive, a card, installation instructions and playback software.

For CD drives there are no such problems, though if you're buying a CD burner for an old, sluggish machine, try to get one with BurnProofing. This will greatly reduce the chance of a CD being ruined halfway through the burning process because the machine got confused.

Drive bays

CD and DVD drives fit into 5.25" drive bays at the front of a PC. You can tell if you have any spare just by looking – each bay will be occupied either by a drive or a removable plastic panel the same colour as the rest of the case. If you don't have a spare bay, you'll have to replace your existing CD drive (CD burners and DVD drives function perfectly well for reading CD-ROMs) or get a new case.

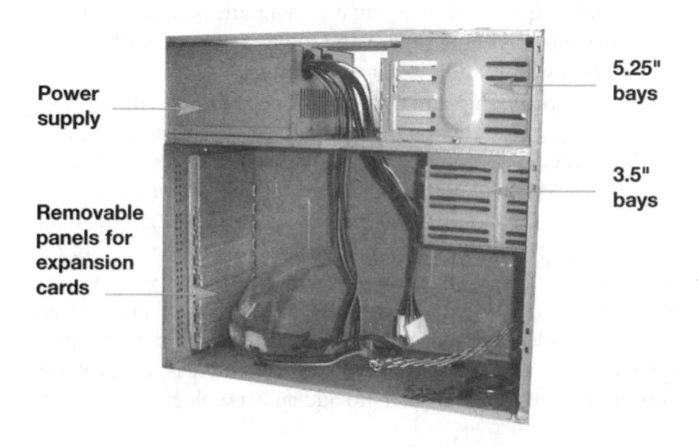

Making the install

THE BACK OF A CD DRIVE

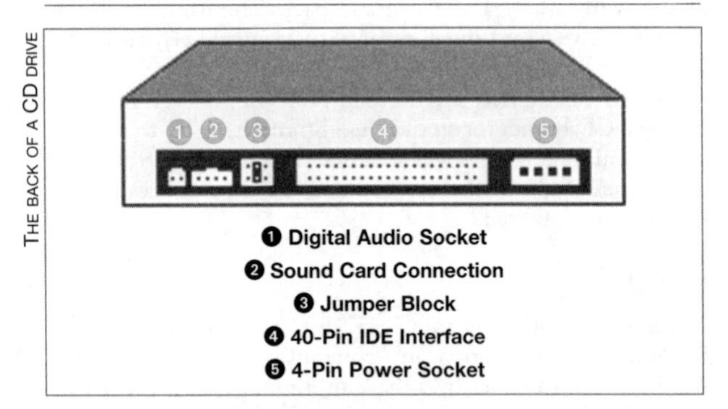

The first thing to do is open up a 5.25" bay to put the new drive into. Unplug the PC, make sure you're free of static electricity and open the case (see p.306). If you're replacing an old drive, carefully pull the various leads from its back and take out the screws holding it in place – usually there are two on each side of the drive bay – while supporting the drive underneath if necessary. Then simply slide it out of the front.

If you're opening up a new bay, you'll need to pop out the front panel using the little clips on the inside. To get to the panel, you may need to lever out an interior metal drive cover with a screwdriver – if so, be very careful not to touch the motherboard or other components with the tip. If you have a choice of bays, consider the length of the IDE cable that you'll be attaching to the back of the drive (see p.322) – if you're using it for two devices you may not have much slack. Also check you have a spare **power connector**: these flat-headed four-pin plugs come off the main power supply, connected by coloured wires. If you don't have a spare one, you can buy an inexpensive "Y-adapter" to add an extra plug.

Before inserting the new drive, you need to decide whether to put it as a slave on the same channel as the hard drive or as the master or slave on the other IDE channel. And then you need to **set the jumpers** accordingly – this is all explained in the box on p.322-323. If attaching a DVD drive, it's generally best to put it as the master on the secondary IDE channel. If you're installing a CD drive it doesn't matter so much, though if you're adding a CD burner and intend to do a lot of copying from CD-ROMs to recordable CDs, your best bet is probably to put the CD burner as the secondary master and the CD-ROM as the primary slave. Some drives may come with instructions that suggest installing them in a particular position.

If you're installing a drive on an unused channel, you'll need to attach the IDE lead to the socket on the motherboard. The socket should be easy to spot – it's rectangular and about two inches long, usually dark in colour, and will be next to another similar slot with a cable already connected. When attaching the cable, be sure to line up the red edge with the **pin 1** mark on the motherboard.

You're now ready to slide the new drive carefully into the bay from the front, giving it support from underneath if necessary. Line up the holes in the side of the bay with the holes in the side of the drive. Before securing the drive with screws, look to see whether there will be sufficient room to connect the cables in this position – if not, you may have to connect the cables with the drive half in and half out of the bay and then slide it into place and put the screws in. Assuming there is enough room, secure the drive with the screws that came with the drive, putting two on each side. Screw them down firmly, but **don't over-tighten** them.

Then attach the IDE cable to the back of the drive – being careful to line up the red edge with the **pin 1** mark on the drive – and insert the power supply plug. If you're going to be using the drive for playing music, you'll also need to plug the audio

IDE basics

IDE, also called **ATA**, is the standard way of connecting internal PC drives. Most modern motherboards have two IDE ports, or "channels", and they're referred to as **primary** and **secondary**. Each port takes an IDE cable, similar to the one pictured, to which you can attach either one or two devices, making a total of four. If you require more than four IDE devices you can get special expansion cards to provide more ports.

There are various types of IDE connection. As well as the old-school standard IDE, there's the newer **EIDE** and the high-speed **Ultra ATA** variety. Also known as **Ultra DMA**, Ultra ATA comes in three standard speeds, transferring data at up to 33, 66 or 100 megabytes per second. And to add to the confusion, CD and DVD drives that attach via IDE are usually known as **ATAPI** devices. Despite all these different types and terms, all IDE devices can be attached to a standard motherboard IDE port. But to achieve the full speed of a fast device like an Ultra ATA/100 hard drive, you'll need a suitable motherboard. And Ultra ATA devices need an appropriate (80-connector) cable.

There are three plugs on an IDE cable: the one on the end furthest from the central one plugs into the motherboard; the other two are for the drives. One edge of an IDE cable is usually coloured red. When you insert the cable into the motherboard or drive you need to make sure that the red edge lines up with the **pin 1** mark on the port. This is very important, because inserting it the wrong way round can damage a drive – though today most sockets and cables are keyed (shaped asymmetrically) so that they will only fit the correct way round.

cable to the sound card, or to the motherboard if it has integrated sound. For this you'll probably be able to use the digital cable that ships with most drives – check your sound card,

Each drive on an IDE cable must be set up as either a **master** or a **slave**. If there is just one device on the cable it should be set as the master; if there are two, one must be set as the master and the other as the slave. The primary hard drive – the one that Windows boots from – is attached as the master on the primary IDE channel. Apart from that, there are no strict rules about what should go where. Generally, a device on its own cable will work slightly more efficiently, as two drives sharing a cable have to take turns to send or receive data.

CSM
SLA

Drives are set as masters or slaves with jumpers – tiny plastic and metal connectors that connect two pins to complete an electrical circuit. Nearly all IDE drives have one or two jumpers on their back or bottom, and all you have to do is position the jumper(s) according to the option you want. In addition to master and slave there is usually a third option called **cable select**, though this isn't relevant for most users (you need a special cable and suitable motherboard). Often there is just one jumper and six pins, labelled CS, SL and MA as shown in the diagram. In this case, the jumper should be placed vertically below SL for slave or MA for master. But often it's not as obvious as this, so always read the instructions that came with the device, or try the manufacturer's Website if you don't have any. Hard drives usually come pre-jumpered to the master position.

Ultra ATA cables are colour-coded: blue on one end for the motherboard, and black on the other end for the master device. If there's also a slave device it uses the grey plug in the middle of the cable. With a standard old-fashioned IDE cable, the slave device can attach with the plug on the end or in the middle.

system or motherboard manual to find out where it needs to be attached. You can often only correct one drive this way, so you may have to remove the cable from your old CD drive.

If you're also adding an MPEG decoder card, you'll need to insert it into a spare slot of the correct type – follow the instructions that came with the card.

Turning on

Make sure all the connections are secure, replace the case cover, plug in the monitor, mouse and keyboard if you removed them, then switch on. With any luck, Windows will load as normal, detect the new drive and prompt you to install the drivers for it – if so insert the disc that came with the drive and direct Windows to it. From now on when you open **My Computer** you'll see an icon for the new drive, and you may find that the old drives are now relabelled – D may have become E, for example. If the drive isn't detected, try running the **Add New Hardware** wizard, which you'll find in the **Control Panel** (select the classic view to find it in Windows XP). If that doesn't work, open up the case and make sure everything is attached properly. And when you switch on again look at the initial screen – the white type on a black background – which will temporarily display a list of your various IDE devices. If the new drive isn't included in the list, you could try entering the BIOS setup program (see p.331) and setting it there. All you'll have to do is find the relevant IDE channel and set it accordingly. If this seems too techie, or if you can't sort it out in the BIOS, it's probably time to call an experienced friend or a professional.

Adding a hard drive

If you're short of storage space there's no better solution than to add a new hard drive, and adding one that's faster can make a difference to performance too – especially for certain tasks such as working with video and recording music. Adding a hard drive and setting it up for use isn't impossible for the uninitiated, but it is more complex than the other upgrades covered in this chapter. You have to physically install the drive, check that it's recognized in the BIOS setup (see p.331), and then go through the slightly frightening process of preparing it for use by partitioning and formatting it. If you don't fancy all this, you'll have to get a friend or pro to do it for you.

Before you buy

If you do decide to go ahead with a hard drive upgrade, there are a few things to consider before buying a drive:

- If you have an old PC it may not be capable of handling the modern-sized drive. This could be because of the BIOS or the operating system. Early editions of Windows 95, for example, can only handle drives of up to 2GB (you can use a bigger drive but you'll have to partition it into separate drives of 2GB or less). These complications are beyond the scope of this chapter – check your system manual for information about what your system will take, or contact the manufacturer. Alternatively, search for information on the Web.

- If you're choosing a drive for increased speed, be aware that an older system may not be equipped to exploit all the speed of the new drive. If you want to achieve the best possible data transfer rate from an ATA/100 drive, for example, you may need to get an expansion card with an appropriate IDE socket on it.

- Ultra ATA hard drives require a suitable Ultra ATA cable, though this may come with the drive.

- Some drives come with clear instructions and special software for preparing the drive for use. You don't need this software but it may make everything a bit easier.

- When buying a hard drive, be sure to get some suitable screws to attach it to the case – using the wrong sort can cause damage.

- It's always worth backing up all your important files (see p.280) before moving or replacing your existing drive.

- A quick guide to partitioning and formatting a new drive is provided below; for more, including information about Windows 95 systems and instructions on creating multiple partitions on a single drive, visit **http://support.microsoft.com/support/kb/articles/Q255/8/67.ASP**. You could even print it out before attempting the upgrade.

Add or replace?

If you're adding a new hard drive you have two options. The easiest thing to do is to keep your current hard drive in as the primary one – the one the operating system boots from – and use the new drive as storage space for programs and files. The other option is to set up the new drive as the primary drive and either remove the old drive or use it just for file storage or back-up. This will usually result in the best performance, but it will require you to install Windows on the new drive (or copy the content of the old drive onto the new drive using special software).

Bays and brackets

If you're planning on keeping your current drive and simply adding a new drive, you'll need to check you have a spare drive bay for it to live in. Standard hard drives live in 3.5" bays hidden away inside the PC (see illustration on p.319). Unplug your machine, open up the case (see p.305) and look inside. In standard tower cases, the 3.5" bays are located at the front of the case below the other bays used for CD, DVD and floppy drives. But in flat desktop cases and other types of design, the drive bays will be elsewhere.

If you don't have a spare 3.5" bay, you can get special brackets to allow you to insert a hard drive in a 5.25" bay, like those used for CD and DVD drives. Many drives come with such brackets.

Master or slave?

A hard drive has to be correctly **set with jumpers** as either a master or a slave before being attached to an IDE cable, as explained on p.323. If you're keeping your old drive as the primary drive you can either install the new one as the slave on the same cable as the old drive, or as the master or slave on the secondary channel. Any position is fine, though if your new drive is faster than your old one its speed may be limited if installed as a slave on the primary cable. If you want to get the best out of your new, faster drive, put it as the **master** on the secondary IDE channel (though if you have a DVD drive this position may already be occupied) or consider making the new drive the primary master and installing the operating system on it.

Physical installation

Before installing a hard drive, check that you have a working Startup disk (see p.239). Unplug your PC, remove the case and make sure you're free of static electricity (see p.306). If you plan to attach the drive to a currently unused IDE channel, you'll need to attach the IDE cable to the motherboard, being sure to line up the red edge of the cable with the **pin 1** mark on the motherboard's port. Then you're ready to insert the drive.

If you have a choice of empty bays and you plan to install the drive on an IDE cable with another device, go for a bay near to the other device so the cable will reach. Gently slide the new drive, with its jumpers set correctly, into the bay, supporting it underneath if necessary. Line up the holes on the side of the drive with those in the bay and secure the drive with two screws on each side. Tighten the screws enough to hold the drive firmly in place (drives have been known to vibrate themselves loose) but **don't over-tighten them** – you don't want to damage anything.

Connect the IDE lead to the drive, being careful to line up the red edge of the cable with the **pin 1** mark on the drive's socket. If it's too awkward you may have to unscrew the drive, move it, connect the cable and then screw the drive back in. Next, attach the power cable: you'll probably find a spare plug on the multicoloured power lead coming from the main power supply and connecting to all your other drives. If you don't have a spare you can buy an inexpensive adapter to provide one.

BIOS settings

Check everything's secure and in the right place, put the cover on the computer and plug everything in. Switch on and read the white text that will briefly appear on the screen. You should see the machine counting its memory and also a list of all the IDE devices, labelled as primary master, secondary slave and so on. If the new drive appears correctly in the list, you're fine. Otherwise you'll have to enter the BIOS setup program (see p.331). Navigate through the various menus until you find the one that deals with the system's IDE connections – checking your system manual could be helpful here. When you find it, look at the setting of the appropriate position (primary slave, secondary master or whatever). If nothing is listed there, try setting it to **Auto** – this should help the motherboard to find it – and exit the BIOS program. If Auto isn't listed as an option, you may be able to input the information about the drive (number of sectors, etc) manually. This information may be written on the drive or the paperwork that came with it. If you feel out of your depth at this point, you may want to put the cover on the machine and take it to a professional.

Preparing a new secondary drive

If you left your old hard drive where it was, Windows should boot as normal. You're now ready to partition and format the new drive to get it ready for use. If the drive came with special software, your best bet is probably to use it. If not, and you don't happen to have a friendly third-party program like Partition Magic, you'll have to use the Windows built-in drive utility. In Windows 98 or ME, open the **Start** menu, click **Run**, type **Fdisk** and you'll be presented with a black DOS window. If you're asked whether you want to **enable large disk support**, type **y** followed by **Enter**. You have to **tread extremely carefully** in this program as it has the power to completely blank any hard drive on your system. If you're not confident at any point, it's worth getting the help of an expert.

At the top of the window should be written **Current fixed disk drive: 1**, and underneath this there will be a list of options. Hit **5** to select **Change current fixed disk drive**, and you'll be offered a list of the drives on your system. (If 5 isn't listed as an option, your computer hasn't recognized the new drive properly.) Assuming that the new drive is the only hard drive in the PC other than the primary drive you'll then see **Current fixed**

disk drive: 2 written at the top, showing that you're now dealing with the new drive. Choose the first option, **Create DOS Partition or Logical DOS Drive**, and then choose **Create Primary DOS Partition**. Fdisk will examine the drive, then ask if you want to use its maximum available size. Choose **Yes** and Fdisk will verify the full drive integrity – this takes a while. When it's finished, exit Fdisk by pressing **Escape** as many times as necessary. Restart your machine and when Windows loads, open **My Computer**. You should see the new drive – it will probably be designated as drive **D**, with the CD and any other drives pushed one letter up the alphabet. Right-click the drive's icon and click **Format** to prepare it for action (choose **FAT32** if you're asked what format you require).

Though the final version of **Windows XP** wasn't available as this book went to press, Fdisk is due to be replaced by a utility called **Diskpart**, which will be opened by selecting **Run** from the Start menu, typing **diskpart** and clicking **OK**. For information about using Diskpart, search Windows Help. Alternatively, you could try using a Startup disk from Windows Me or 98, as described above.

Partitioning and formatting a new primary drive

If you're planning on installing Windows 98 or Me, insert a working Startup disk and select **Start Computer without CD support** when presented with a list of options. At the **A:>** prompt, type **Fdisk** and press **Enter**. If asked whether you want to **Enable large disk support**, choose **yes** and you should be presented with a screen saying **Current fixed disk drive: 1** at the top. Choose the first option, **Create DOS Partition or Logical DOS Drive**, and then choose **Create Primary DOS Partition**. When asked if you want to make use of all the disk space, answer **yes** and Fdisk will start to do its thing. Exit Fdisk by pressing **Escape** as many times as necessary, and restart the

BIOS Setup

Pronounced "bye-oss" or "bye-ose" depending where you're from, **BIOS** (Basic Input/Output System) is essential software stored on a PC's motherboard. It enables the machine to boot up, and acts as the bridge between the operating system and the hardware – but you'll probably hear the term most commonly in relation to the **BIOS setup utility**, a program that allows you to make various changes to your PC's settings. This program is essential when performing certain upgrades or building a PC, but it should otherwise be left alone – it contains some very techie options that can cause all sorts of serious problems if set up incorrectly.

Also sometimes referred to as **CMOS setup** (after the special memory chip that the configurations are stored in) or just "setup", the BIOS setup program is accessed differently on different systems. When you turn on your PC, some text will appear on the screen – the memory will be counted and the disk drives listed. Usually you'll then see a message towards the bottom of the screen inviting you to press a certain key or key combination to "enter setup" – most commonly **Delete** or some combination including **Escape**. If you don't get such a message, check any manuals that came with your system to find out the necessary key or do some research on the Web. BIOS setup programs are all different but they work in a very similar way: you browse through various menu options and make changes using the keyboard. Usually it's pretty clear which keys you have to press to select and change each option.

machine, still with the Startup disk in place. When the menu appears, select **Start Computer without CD support**; at the **A:>** prompt type **format C:/s** and press **Enter**. (If you're told you've entered a bad command or file name, type **extract ebd.cab format.com** followed by **Enter**, and then try again.) After you've confirmed your decision by pressing **y**, the drive will be formatted and you'll be offered the option of naming the volume – do so if you wish, or just press Enter to skip this step. You're then ready to perform a full Windows installation as described on p.241.

The final version of **Windows XP** wasn't available as this book went to press, but installing a copy of the new operating system onto a blank hard drive should be very straightforward. Check the documentation that came with your copy, but probably all you'll need to do is insert the XP CD and floppy disk that came with it and switch on. Everything should be pretty self-explanatory from there. Alternatively, you could try using a Windows Me or 98 Startup disk as described in the above paragraph, or entering your system's BIOS setup program and setting the CD drive as the primary boot device (see p.241).

Other upgrades

As well as the common upgrades described above, there are various other things you may want to do to bring your system up to scratch – inserting a better processor or motherboard, for instance, or getting a new case. We don't have the space to cover everything here – not because it's too complicated, but because there are many variables depending on your exact setup. Still, the following information should at least point you in the right direction.

Processors

Inserting a new processor can be a little fiddly but it's otherwise very easy. However, your motherboard defines the type and speed of processor you can use, so always refer to your system or motherboard manual before buying a new processor. As well as the brand and speed, you need to get a processor of the right

slot or **socket** format (socket 7, slot 1, etc). And remember to buy a suitable heat sink and fan for the processor you're adding – your old one may work, but faster processors generally run hotter so it's worth getting something suitable.

If you have a look in some magazines and e-stores you'll almost certainly come across various **processor upgrade kits**. These can include anything from a new processor and a tool to help you remove the old one to a special expansion card to improve your PC's computational power.

Motherboards

There are various reasons why you might consider getting a new motherboard: the old one may be damaged, for example, or you may want to add a faster processor and better RAM. Replacing a motherboard isn't really that difficult. First you have to unplug everything from the old one and remove it from the case (many cases have a motherboard panel that can be removed to allow easy unscrewing of the board). Then you attach the new board with a number of screws and spacers that should have come with it. The final stage is plugging everything in before going into your system BIOS to set the processor speed and ensure that the drives are recognized properly. Before buying a new motherboard, make sure it will be compatible with your processor and case – an old **AT** case won't take a new motherboard such as an **ATX** model.

Cases

Replacing the case can be a bit of a pain – if only because the motherboard, expansion cards and all the drives will need to be moved (you leave the processor and RAM on the motherboard). However, it's not usually very difficult.

Building a PC

If the upgrades described in this chapter don't strike you as too intimidating, building your own PC is unlikely to be a problem. A complete step-by-step guide to doing this is beyond the scope of this book, but the following paragraphs provide a rough outline.

The first thing you'll need to do, obviously enough, is buy all the **components**. The absolute essentials are: case; motherboard; CPU with fan and heat sink; RAM; hard drive; video card (unless the motherboard has in-built graphics); monitor; CD/CD-R drive; keyboard; floppy drive; and mouse. But you'll probably also want a modem and sound card. These components are discussed individually in Chapters 2 and 3, but for detailed information on the latest products and prices you may want to try the hardware review sites listed in the Web Directory (see p.390). When selecting the body parts for your PC-to-be, you have to make sure they're all **compatible**. These days some items, such as CD drives, are pretty much compatible with any system, though with certain components you have to be careful – you'll need the correct motherboard for the processor, and the correct RAM for the motherboard, for example. If you buy all the bits from one supplier, you can ask about compatibility – and you may well also get a discount. Try and get a motherboard that comes with a good, clear **manual** that will guide you through the building process.

Putting it all together

Though different people have different views on the best way to put a PC together, basically it involves fixing the motherboard to the case – including attaching the connectors for the case's power supply, lights and buttons – and adding the RAM and CPU (with heat sink and fan, which will attach to the motherboard). Then you'll need to fix the hard drive, floppy and CD or DVD drives into the case's bays, and attach them to the motherboard with the necessary cables. Fit any expansion cards to the motherboard and run the audio cable (if there is one) from the CD or DVD drive to the sound card. (Most of these processes are described individually earlier in this chapter.) When all this is done you can switch on, enter the BIOS setup program to tell the motherboard which processor you have installed and check that the IDE drives are recognized. Then finally you're ready to partition and format the drive and install your operating system.

part six

contexts

23

Brief history of the PC

The modern personal computer is not the brainchild of any one person – no single cry of "Eureka!" heralded the beginning of its development. Instead its history is a tale of leaps, bounds and hold-ups stretching back five thousand years to the invention of the **abacus** in Mesopotamia. This brief history outlines some of the important people and events in the evolution-

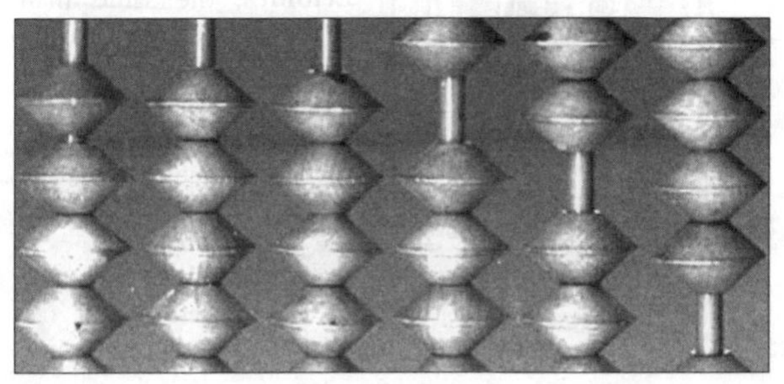

ary passage from wooden bead-counter to multimedia workstation.

The mechanical era

In this age of microelectronics, computer components are not only powerful but also incomprehensibly small – it's atoms, not inches, that count. But the forerunners of today's computers were mechanical: they were made of cogs, shafts and sliders large enough to put together by hand, and were operated not by a keyboard and mouse but with dials and handles.

The earliest breakthroughs were made by the likes of **Leonardo da Vinci**, who designed a simple **mechanical calculator** in 1500, and **William Oughtred**, who in the early 1600s came up with the **slide rule**, a handheld tool for speeding up arithmetic which was still being used in schools three-and-a-half centuries later. By the 1640s, the French mathematician **Blaise Pascal** had invented a machine capable of multiplication and division which was later improved by **Gottfried Leibnitz**, the same man who is credited with having laid down the principles of **binary** – the number system using only 0s and 1s that is the fundamental language spoken by all modern computers.

Babbage's Difference Engine

The greatest achievements of the mechanical era, though, came courtesy of the eccentric British mathematician and inventor **Charles Babbage**, whose inventions included the **Difference Engine** (pictured) and the **Analytical Engine** of 1833. Though he died before it could be constructed, the Analytical Engine could not only cope with complex mathematics, but it could be **programmed** to deal with various types of problem and make decisions based upon its own results – thus heralding the leap from calculator to "real" computer. Babbage's partner in crime was none other than **Ada Byron** – aka Lady Lovelace, the daughter of the poet Lord Byron – who is now sometimes described as the first ever computer programmer.

Punch cards and vacuum tubes

It wasn't until the end of the nineteenth century that computers actually started to prove themselves useful. Just before the 1890 census the US government held a design contest to find an efficient way of counting the records of its exploding population. It was won by a German immigrant named **Herman Hollerith**, whose electric tabulating machine read data from paper punch cards, saving many years of manual counting and marking a significant point at which computing became as much to do with data management as performing calculations. Hollerith's Computing-Tabulating-Recording Company went from strength to strength, and in 1924 it merged with a rival to form International Business Machines – **IBM** – which grew into one of the most significant forces in computer design.

In the meantime the **vacuum tube** was being developed, from which a new generation of computers was to grow. The tubes did the same job as mechanical or electrical switches, but they were capable of switching on and off thousands of times faster, facilitating a whole new level of computing speed. This technology reached its zenith in machines designed on both sides of the Atlantic during World War II. The British utilized it in their powerful code-breaking machine, **Colossus**, but more significant was the American **ENIAC** (Electronic Numerical Integrator and Computer), developed between 1943 and 1945 to calculate missile trajectories. Containing nearly 17,500 vacuum tubes, ENIAC was the first multitasking computer, and it could add 5,000 numbers or carry out fourteen ten-digit multiplications per second – making it about a hundred times faster that its closest rival.

While ENIAC was still being built, its designers **J. Presper Eckert** and **John V. Mauchly** joined forces with another key figure, mathematician **John von Neumann**, to work on a new machine. What they came up with was **EDVAC**, the first computer to have a **stored program**. This was a real breakthrough: instead of spending hours or even days turning knobs and pressing buttons to instruct a computer to carry out a particular task, the commands could be written as numerical code and stored inside the machine. This made everything much faster, but more significantly it paved the way for the programming languages of the 1950s – which in turn led to the development of modern software.

Transistors and microchips

For all its speed, ENIAC highlighted the shortcomings of vacuum-tube technology: it was 150 feet wide, weighed 30 tons, produced so much heat that it regularly burnt out and guzzled electricity in such quantities that the lights in the neighbouring towns dimmed each time it was switched on. These problems were soon to be overcome with the advent of the silicon transistor, which was better than the vacuum tube at controlling the flow of electricity while being much smaller and generating considerably less heat. Transistors were invented back in the 1920s, but it wasn't until 1954 that reliable silicon models were manufactured commercially, bringing small, reliable and affordable computers a significant step closer.

The ensuing years saw the birth of the **microchip** or **chip** – a single piece of board containing many transistors. As time went by, chips became increasingly powerful and ever more tiny, until in 1971 a company called **Intel** (**Int**egrated **El**ectronics) released their **4004** chip, the first **microprocessor**. The 4004 combined 2300 transistors and all the essential elements of a computer on a single chip, and in the space of a few square inches provided roughly the same computational power as the

17,500 vacuum tubes of ENIAC. These developments, combined with great advances in programming languages and other breakthroughs such as the invention of the **floppy disk**, made it possible to produce smaller and faster computers which were more flexible and less difficult to use.

Computers get personal

Despite all these advances, computers remained in the realm of academics, governments and big business, and it wasn't until 1975 that a vaguely personal computer – something that individuals could actually afford to buy – came onto the market. It arrived in the form of the **MITS Altair 8800**, which shipped with an Intel processor and 256 bytes of memory, around one millionth of the amount found in a decent modern PC. And it wasn't just in the memory department that the Altair was lacking: it had neither a keyboard nor a monitor. Instructions were fed in by small switches and results displayed by a pattern of little red lights – great for discos, but not a lot else.

THE ALTAIR 8800

But this was soon to change. In 1977, **Stephen Jobs** and **Steve Wozniak** produced the **Apple II**, which, with its neat plastic case and video-out socket (allowing you to use your TV as a monitor), was an instant success. While the Altair was primarily of interest to hobbyists and enthusiasts,

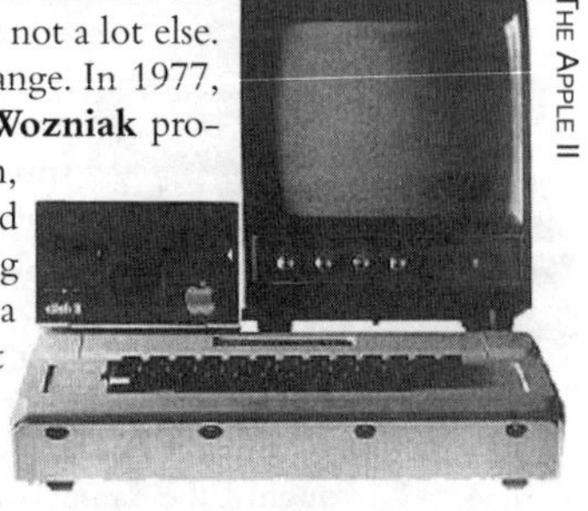

THE APPLE II

the Apple II was actually useful for businesses, and programs began to appear which could save hours of manual number-crunching – such as **VisiCalc**, the first ever **spreadsheet** program.

During this time the price of components plummeted, and various bargain computers started appearing on the market. By the end of the 1970s, a variety of machines were available for a few hundred dollars – like the **Radio Shack TRS-80,** which became incredibly popular in homes and schools.

The PC is born

The next big turning point came in 1981, when IBM released their **Personal Computer** – the **IBM PC** – which was the blueprint of the modern PC. Though the design was strong, it was not just the computer that made IBM's new machine so popular: it was the company's decision to tell the world, in near-complete detail, how the PC worked and how it was built. IBM did this in the hope that other developers would produce extra pieces of hardware that would be compatible with the PC – which they did, by the truckload. However, it soon occurred to these developers that they weren't limited to manufacturing add-ons; they could produce their own versions of the whole machine and sell them cheaper. This was possible because IBM only held a patent for the **BIOS** (basic input/output system: see p.331), and because most of the internal components of the PC had been bought off-the-shelf from other manufacturers. Very soon computer companies everywhere were manufacturing their own copies of the IBM design; they could run all the same programs and data could easily be moved from one machine to the next. These computers were collectively known as **IBM-compatible PCs**, but it wasn't long before PC became a generic term used to describe any computer based on IBM's original.

Chapter 23

The rise of Microsoft

When IBM designed the PC they commissioned the young Micro-Soft company (later **Microsoft**) to provide the all-important **operating system** or OS: the underlying software that bridges the gap between a computer and the application software running on it (see p.233). It was called the Micro-Soft Disk Operating System – **MS-DOS** – and though it had been developed for IBM, Microsoft shrewdly retained the copyright. As PC clones began to spring up everywhere, nearly all were installed with MS-DOS, and though Microsoft's founder **Bill Gates** didn't know it at the time, this was soon to make him the world's richest man.

As time went by, it became increasingly difficult for new types of computer to get a decent foothold in the market. Inexpensive machines like the **Commodore 64** were very popular among home users, but any new system that set out to compete with the PC was faced with the problem of not being able to run all the software that had already been written for use with MS-DOS. Other PC operating systems were proposed by IBM and others, but they never really got off the ground or failed to gain the popularity of the Microsoft option. The MS-DOS PC still faced serious competition from established manufacturers such as Apple, however, who introduced the **LISA** and the **Macintosh** (the **Mac**) in 1983 and 1984 respectively. These were the first personal computers to use an operating system with a **Graphic User Interface** (GUI), meaning that the user, instead of typing encrypted instructions into the machine, could run programs and organise files by using a **mouse** to click on windows, icons and dropdown menus.

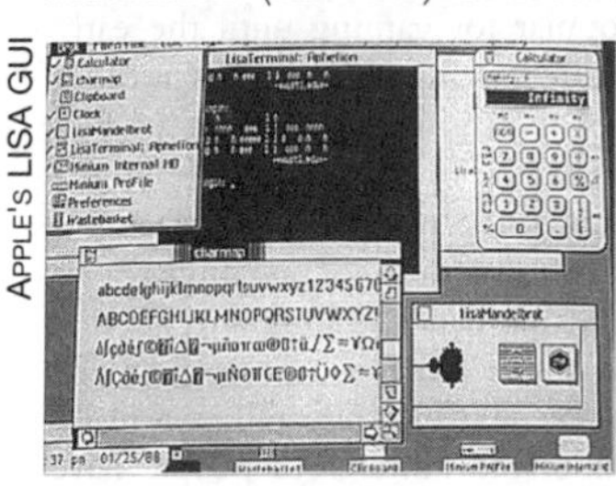

APPLE'S LISA GUI

Soon afterwards, Microsoft released their own GUI operating system: a reworking of MS-DOS called **Windows**. Many of the features were very similar to those of the Apple system, and Apple promptly threatened to take Microsoft to court, claiming they had ripped off their design. In the end, Microsoft agreed to license certain elements of the Apple design to avoid court proceedings, and they managed to arrange it so that the features could be used in all future Microsoft programs. But when **Windows 2.0** came out in 1987, Apple thought Microsoft had overstepped the mark and this time actually took them to court for breach of copyright. Microsoft won the case, in part because of the previous licensing deal and in part because many of the original ideas for the Apple system had originally been developed by **Xerox** for non-personal computers. This made it easy for Gates and Co to say, "Well, we may not have invented it, but neither did you . . .".

And the rest is history

As time went by, PCs and Macs held their ground as the most popular systems, and Windows – after the release of version 3.0 in 1990 – became the dominant PC operating system. Machines designed for things that PCs and Macs didn't do very well continued to enjoyed success: the **Atari ST** and **Commodore Amiga**, for example, were popular for gaming until the early 1990s. But with the rise of specific gaming stations such as those made by **Nintendo** and the ever-increasing versatility of the PC, computers such as these started falling by the wayside, leaving a two-horse contest between Windows-driven PCs and Macs.

And for the time being this situation seems unlikely to change. Once a company or user has data and programs for one platform, switching to another can be a major – and potentially expensive – upheaval. Perhaps the next big shift will be a move towards free software. A considerable number of people have already turned to **Linux**: they can get an operating system and an ever-growing selection of high-quality applications that are both free and legal.

As for the future of hardware, the tendency for ever-faster machines in ever-smaller boxes seems unlikely to lose pace. Who knows – a few years down the line the latest edition of this book may be sold as a thumbnail-size data chip to slip into your watch-cum-computer. We'll just have to wait and see . . .

24

Glossary

A

A The letter normally assigned to the primary floppy drive of a PC.

Access time Measurement of how long it takes a device, like a disk drive, to find a piece of data; measured in milliseconds (ms).

Active partition Part of a hard drive used to load the operating system at startup.

Active window The window that is currently being worked in, and which appears "in front" of any other open windows. See also *Foreground task*.

ActiveX Concept developed by Microsoft, allowing a program to run inside a Web page.

Adapter See *Expansion card*.

Add/Remove Programs Feature of the Windows Control Panel, primarily useful today for uninstalling programs.

Address bar The strip near the top of a Windows or Internet Explorer window where you can enter either a Web address or the path to a file on your computer.

Administrator A type of User account in Windows XP that allows full control of the computer.

ADSL (Asynchronous Digital Subscriber Line) System for high-speed transmission of digital data over standard phone lines, used for Internet connections. Faster than ISDN. See also *DSL*.

AGP (Accelerated Graphics Port) Motherboard slot, designed for video cards, that can handle a much heavier data flow than PCI slots.

Alt (Alternative key) Standard keyboard key that can be used in combination with other keys to create characters or commands outside the normal keyboard range.

Analogue A signal that can be smoothly varied in strength or quantity, or a device that produces, records or stores such a signal. Contrast with *Digital*.

Antivirus software Program that detects, and sometimes removes, computer viruses.

Applet A small application program.

Application See *Program*.

Apply A dialog box button that enforces changes without closing the box.

Archive File that bundles a set of other files together under a single name for transfer or backup. Often compressed to reduce size, or encrypted for privacy.

ASCII (American Standard Code for Information Interchange) Text format readable by all computers. Also called "plain text".

Aspect ratio An image's height divided by its width.

@ (At) This symbol separates the user's name from the domain name in an email address, eg **peter@roughguides.co.uk**.

AT See *ATX*.

ATA (AT Attachment) See *IDE*.

ATA-2 See *EIDE*.

ATA/33 ATA/66 ATA/100 See *Ultra ATA*.

ATAPI (**AT Attachment Packet Interface**) The standard interface used for attaching CD, DVD and tape drives to a PC. ATAPI is a type of IDE connection (or EIDE, to be exact). See also *IDE*.

Attachment File included with an email or other form of message.

ATX A modern standard specification for PC cases, power supplies and motherboards that superseded the older AT standard in the mid-1990s. The ATX layout supports USB, as well as integrated audio and video. Old motherboards won't fit in new cases and vice versa.

AUTOEXEC.BAT A file used by Windows each time a PC is turned on or restarted, running specific commands to get everything up and running.

B

Background task A task, such as a file download, which takes place behind the scenes while the computer deals with a foreground task (generally whatever you see in the active window).

Backup A copy of data or program files made for safekeeping, usually stored on a different device.

Backward compatible A product – hardware or software – that will work with certain older products, formats or media.

Bad sector Physically damaged or defective segment of a disk, marked by the operating system as not to be used.

Bandwidth The rate at which digital data flows through a cable or over a connection, usually measured in bits per second (bps). In analogue systems the bandwidth is the range of frequencies transmitted and is measured in hertz (Hz).

Binary Number system that uses only zeros and ones. When data is converted into binary code it can be dealt with electronically, with the zeros and ones represented by electrical charges being on or off (or high/low).

Binary file Any file that contains more than plain text, such as a program or image.

BIOS (Basic Input Output System) Pronounced "bye-ose" or "bye-oss". Set of essential software codes stored in a ROM chip on the motherboard. The BIOS tests hardware upon startup, kick-starts the operating system and supports the transfer of data between hardware devices.

Bit (Binary digit) Abbreviated to b. Smallest unit of information that can be handled by a computer. One bit represents a 0 or 1 numerically, true or false logically, and opposing physical states in an electric circuit or magnetic disk.

Bitmap A picture file format that represents an image in the form of rows and columns of dots.

Bluetooth A short-range radio technology standard, designed to allow all types of desk-bound and portable devices, including mobile phones, to communicate with each other.

Bookmarks The Netscape equivalent of "Favorites" in Internet Explorer. The two terms are often used interchangeably.

Boot To start or reset a computer.

Boot disk A disk, usually a floppy, which is capable of launching an operating system. Also called a Startup disk.

Boot sector Space at the beginning of a diskette or partition reserved for the instructions that start the operating system.

bps (Bits Per Second) Basic measure of data transfer speed. Not to be confused with bytes per second (Bps), which is generally written with an upper-case B.

Bps (Bytes Per Second) Measure of data transfer speed often used in relation to PC components like hard drives. Not to be confused with bits per second (bps), which is generally written with a lower-case b.

Broadband High-speed information connection; most commonly refers to cable or ADSL Internet access.

Browser Web viewing program such as Internet Explorer.

Buffer A temporary data storage area.

Bug Logical, physical or programming error in software or hardware that causes a recurring malfunction.

Burner Device that can write to certain types of CDs or DVDs. See also *CD-R*, *CD-RW*, *DVD-R*, *DVD-RW* and *DVD-RAM*.

BurnProof (**B**uffer **U**nder **R**un-**Proof**) A trademarked technology that drastically reduces the likelihood of errors occurring while burning a CD-R or CD-RW. Many CD burners now ship with BurnProofing features.

Bus A data transmission path on the motherboard that links the processor to various other components, such as expansion cards and disk drives. Or a set of conductors used to transfer data between two hardware components. See also *ISA* and *PCI* (two types of bus for attaching expansion cards).

Byte (**B**inar**y** **Te**rm) Abbreviated to B. A small amount of memory consisting of eight bits. This is the amount needed to represent one character. Memory, file size and disk capacity are measured in bytes, kilobytes (roughly 1,000 bytes), megabytes (roughly 1,000,000 bytes) and gigabytes (roughly 1,000,000,000 bytes).

C

C: Letter normally assigned to the primary hard drive of a PC.

Cache Pronounced "cash". To cache data is to store it in a convenient place where it can be re-accessed quickly. The cache frequently mentioned in computer adverts is L2 (level 2) cache, a special piece of fast memory built into the processor. But operating systems also use system RAM for caching frequently used data, and when you visit a Website it may be cached on your hard drive.

Card See *Expansion card*.

CD burner A drive that can write, or "burn" data to CD-Rs or CD-RWs (most can write to both). Also called a "CD writer".

CD-R (**CD R**ecordable) A special type of CD that can be written to by a CD-R drive. Once a section of a CD-R disc has been "burned" it cannot be changed. Each disc has a capacity of around 700MB.

CD-ROM (**CD R**ead **O**nly **M**emory) Compact discs used for storing data. They can be read by a computer but not written to.

CD-RW (**CD R**e**w**ritable) A special type of CD that can be written to by a CD-RW drive. CD-RWs can be rewritten on again and again like floppy disks. Has a capacity of around 700MB.

CD writer See *CD Burner*.

Chip See *Microchip* and *Processor*.

Chipset Any collection of chips designed to function as one unit. The term is mostly used to describe the all-important chips and circuitry of a motherboard, which determine many things, including the speed that information can pass between the processor and the RAM.

Click To position the mouse cursor over a screen object such as an icon or Web link, and press down on the left mouse button.

Client/server A type of networking relationship where one computer (the server) manages resources and access to data, while other PCs (the clients) simply run applications, relying heavily on the server for access to files and peripheral devices. This is sometimes called a "two-tier architecture".

Clip art Collections of graphics for pasting into documents, usually categorized into themes such as Christmas or Music.

Clipboard Special memory resource that holds the last piece of data Copied or Cut so that it can be transferred using the Paste command. See also *Cut*, *Copy* and *Paste*.

Cluster A section of a disk surface, consisting of various sectors. See also *Lost clusters* and *Sector*.

CMOS (**C**omplementary **M**etal-**O**xide **S**emiconductor) Pronounced "see-moss". This is an energy-efficient battery-operated memory chip in a PC that stores fundamental system information relating to the system setup, time and date.

Code Passage written in a programming language.

Codec 1. (Compressor/Decompressor) Any technology – hardware or software – used for compressing and decompressing data. MPEG and MP3 are both examples of codec file formats. 2. (Coder/Decoder) A communications device such as a modem that translate analogue signals into digital and vice versa.

Combination drive A drive that combines functions usually served by two separate drives – most commonly a CD writer and a DVD drive.

Command line A line where you type instructions for your PC, such as the bottom line in a DOS window or the text input section of the Run box, launched via the Start menu.

Command prompt A string of characters (such C:\>) inviting you type a command into a PC.

COM port See *Serial port*.

Configuration The way that a system – hardware or software – is set up.

Context menu See *Mouse menu*.

Control key A standard key on PC keyboards, usually marked "Ctrl". It can be combined with other keys to create characters or commands outside the normal keyboard range.

Control Panel Special Windows folder that contains applets to configure and adjust the system. Found in the Start menu (under Settings in Windows Me and 98).

Cookie A small file placed on your hard drive by a Web server so that it can recognize your PC when you return to the site.

Copy To duplicate the selected text, image, file or folder to the Clipboard so that it can be Pasted elsewhere. The shortcut is Ctrl+C. See also *Cut*, *Paste* and *Clipboard*.

Core logic Another term for a motherboard's chipset. See also *Chipset*.

CPU (Central Processing Unit) The proper term for a PC's processor. See *Processor*.

CPU fan A little fan attached to a computer's processor to stop it from overheating.

Crack To break a program's security, integrity or registration system, or to fake a user ID.

Crash When a program or operating system fails to respond or causes other programs to malfunction.

CRIMM (Continuity RIMM) Pronounced "see-rim". A dummy RIMM module without any memory on it. Unused RIMM slots on a motherboard must always be filled with CRIMMs. See also *RIMM*.

CRT (Cathode Ray Tube) Glass vacuum tube that forms the basis of the standard desktop computer monitor.

Ctrl See *Control key*.

Cursor Special screen character that usually looks like a flashing "I". It indicates where typed text will appear.

Cut Remove the selected text, image, file or folder from its current location, but keep it on the Clipboard so it can be Pasted elsewhere. The keyboard shortcut is Ctrl+X. See also *Copy*, *Paste* and *Clipboard*.

CYMK (Cyan, Yellow, Magenta, Black) These are the four colours of ink found in most standard colour printers. CYMK, or CYMB as it's sometimes known, describes the inks as well as the system by which they're mixed to make other colours.

D

Daisy chain A set of computers or devices connected "in series" – each one connected to two others like a set of Christmas lights .

Data Information in a form suitable for a computer.

Database A file designed to collect, store and retrieve information.

Daughterboard An expansion card that connects to the memory and CPU directly instead of shunting data via the expansion bus.

DDR SDRAM (Double Data Rate SDRAM) Pronounced "dee-dee-are-ess-dee-ram", and often shortened to DDR RAM. A relatively new type of RAM that is twice as fast as normal SDRAM because it transfers data on both the rising and falling edges of each clock cycle. See also *SDRAM*.

Default The standard setting of an application or device.

Defragment Often shortened to "defrag". To rearrange the data stored on a hard drive so that it can be accessed more quickly.

Degauss To remove unwanted magnetic charge, usually from a monitor.

Delete 1. Remove a file or part of a document. Deleting a file in Windows normally sends it to the Recycle Bin 2. The key that does this.

Desktop 1. The background space in an operating system such as Windows 2. Any non-mobile computer – ie one that lives on a desk 3. A computer in a case that sits flat on a desk, generally with the monitor perched on top of it. Contrast with *Tower case*.

Device name The operating system's title for a PC component.

Dialog box A box – like a window – that appears on the screen to ask or tell you something.

Dial-up connection Temporary network connection between two computers via a telephone line and modem.

Digital A signal that varies in steps rather than smoothly, or a device that produces, records or stores such a signal. Computers only work with digital information. Contrast with *Analogue*.

DIMM (Dual Inline Memory Module) A type of strip-like circuit board that holds RAM. SDRAM and DDR SDRAM come on DIMMs. See also *SIMM* and *SODIMM*.

DIP switch (Dual Inline Package) Tiny switches built onto the circuit board of a computer component for configuring it to work with a certain piece of hardware or software. These days you will rarely need to worry about DIP switches thanks to Plug and Play technology.

Direct cable connection A means of connecting two PCs using just a cable (no network cards, hubs or other hardware). One machine is defined as the Host and the other as the Guest.

Directory 1. See *Folder* 2. Online guide that organizes Internet sites into categories.

DirectX A special system that allows programs to take full advantage of certain video and sound cards to improve multimedia capability.

Disk cache Area of a PC's RAM set aside for storing the data most recently transferred to and from the hard drive, so it can be quickly re-accessed by the processor if it's needed again.

Disk drive A device that reads and/or writes to magnetic or optical disks. The disks can be removable, as in the case of a CD-ROM, or fixed, as with a hard drive.

Display See *Monitor*.

Display adapter See *Video card*.

Display Properties Windows dialog box for configuring everything that relates to how things look on the screen, including the appearance of the Desktop and the resolution of the monitor. Found in the Control Panel or by right-clicking on the Desktop and selecting Properties.

DLL file (Dynamic Link Library) A set of software modules that can be used by a range of application programs to perform common tasks.

DMA (Direct Memory Access) A means of transferring data from a PC component, such as a hard drive, straight to the RAM, bypassing the processor. PCs with a DMA channel can transfer data faster than computers without, which is especially handy for fast backups, real-time applications, etc. See also *UDMA*.

DNS (Domain Name System) The system that translates Web addresses as used by humans (such as **www.roughguides.com**) into numeric IP addresses that computers understand (like 156.154.253.142). See also *IP*.

Docking station Device for connecting a portable notebook computer to a range of desk-bound external devices such as a printer, monitor and mouse.

Document A file (a letter, image, spreadsheet or anything else) that is created, saved and edited in a program.

Domain Part of an Internet address that specifies details about the host, such as its location and whether it's commercial (.com), governmental (.gov), etc.

DOS (Disk Operating System) 1. An abbreviation of MS-DOS, the forerunner of Windows. 2. Any operating system loaded by disk devices at startup, as opposed to the operating systems of early computers which were permanently stored in the circuitry.

DOS prompt A command prompt in MS-DOS, showing that the machine is ready for input. Typically, it looks something like C:\>.

Dot pitch A measure of the maximum image sharpness that a monitor can achieve. It describes the minimum size of a pixel in millimetres (though in some cases it is used to refer to the gap between the pixels). A smaller dot pitch normally means a sharper image.

Double-click To press and release the left mouse button twice quickly in succession. In Windows, double-clicking a file or folder opens it.

Download To copy files from a remote computer to your own. Contrast with *Upload*.

dpi (dots per inch) A measure of printer, scanner or monitor resolution, defined by the number of dots a device can print or display in a linear inch.

Drag and drop To move an object, such as a file, icon or passage of text, by selecting it and moving the mouse with the left button held down. Releasing your finger drops the object in its new location.

DRAM (Dynamic Random Access Memory) Pronounced "dee-ram". Family of RAM types, which need to be periodically topped-up to stop them "leaking" their electronic charges. There are many types, including EDO, FPM, SDRAM, DDR SDRAM and RDRAM.

Driver Small program that acts like a translator between a hardware device and the operating systems or programs that use that device.

DSL (Digital Subscriber Line) An "always on" data transfer system that allows high-speed transfer of digital data over standard phone lines. There are various types, such as ADSL and SDSL, sometimes collectively referred to as xDSL.

DTP (Desktop Publishing) Software, such as Quark Express, PageMaker or Publisher, used to produce documents containing positioned text and images – a brochure or book, for example.

DV (Digital Video) Video footage stored as digital code on tape or disk, or a camera that captures such footage.

DVD (Digital Versatile Disc or Digital Video Disc) High-capacity optical storage disc that looks like the CD and which is likely to supersede it. Currently used mostly for storing movies, DVDs can be only read by DVD drives, not standard CD drives.

DVD burner A DVD drive that can write information to one or more types of DVDs. See also *DVD-R*, *DVD-RW* and *DVD-RAM*.

DVD-R (DVD Recordable) A type of DVD that can be written to by a DVD-R drive.

DVD-RAM A type of DVD that can be written to again and again. It usually comes in a protective plastic case that slots into a DVD-RAM drive, or as a permanent internal unit. They cannot currently be read by standard DVD drives and players.

DVD-RW (DVD Rewritable) A type of DVD that can be written to by a DVD-RW drive. They cannot currently be read by most standard DVD drives and players. A newer, more compatible standard called DVD+RW is currently being developed.

E

eBook (Electronic Book) A "book" in the form of a file that can be bought and downloaded from the Web. There are various formats available that can be read on computers, notebooks or PDA devices with the appropriate software. See *eBook reader*.

eBook reader A program for reading titles saved in a particular eBook format. The two most commonly used programs – both downloadable for free – are the Adobe Acrobat eBook Reader (**http://www.adobe.com/products/ebookreader**) and Microsoft Reader (**http://www.microsoft.com/reader/download.asp**).

Edit To change the contents of a document.

EIDE (Enhanced IDE) A faster version of the standard IDE connection. Also known as Fast ATA. See also *IDE*.

EISA See *ISA*.

Email (Electronic Mail) A system of sending messages, sometimes with files "attached", from one computer to another.

Email address A unique private Internet address to which email is sent. Takes the form user@host.

EPS (Encapsulated PostScript) File format that can contain two versions of an image: a bitmap for displaying on the screen and a PostScript for high-resolution printing on a laser printer.

Error message A message displayed by a program or operating system reporting that a problem has occurred.

Ethernet Very popular type of local area network (LAN) that connects devices using coaxial cable. The protocol was developed by Xerox in the 1970s.

Ethernet card Expansion card that lets a computer hook up to an Ethernet network.

Expansion card A rectangular circuit board, usually with a back panel, that slots into a computer's motherboard to expand its features or add extra sockets. Examples include sound cards, video cards and SCSI interface cards.

Exit To quit a program. This option is normally found at the bottom of the File menu. The shortcut in Windows is Alt+F4.

Expansion slot A slot on a motherboard where expansion cards (video, sound, modems, etc) are inserted. The three types are AGP, PCI and ISA.

Explore An option in Windows when you right-click a folder or drive icon. If selected, the contents of the folder or drive are displayed in an Explorer window with the folder tree displayed on the left.

Explorer See *Windows Explorer* and *Internet Explorer*.

Extension See *File extension*.

External A computer device not housed within the PC's case, such as an external hard drive or external CD-ROM drive.

F

FAQ (Frequently Asked Questions) Document that answers the most commonly asked questions on a particular topic.

Fast ATA See *EIDE*.

Fast user switching A feature of Windows XP that allows users to switch between their accounts without having to close applications or documents.

FAT (File Allocation Table) A system that Windows and other operating systems use to keep track of exactly where each file on a disk is stored – quite complicated, as a single file can be spread across many locations. There are various versions of FAT. The term on its own is generally used to describe FAT16, the system used up until the first edition of Windows 95, which could only support tiny hard drives by today's standards (maximum 2GB). Windows XP, Me, 98 and later versions of 95 also support FAT32 (meaning the entries in the allocation table can be 32 bits long) – this allows bigger hard drives and uses disk space more efficiently. See also *NTFS*.

FAT32 See *FAT*.

Fatal error Program failure for which the only remedy is to restart the system.

Favorites A system in a Web browser such as Internet Explorer that allows you to store a list of Web pages you wish to return to again. (In reality it's a folder on the hard drive containing a file for each Website listed.) The term is used interchangeably with "Bookmarks", the equivalent in the Netscape Navigator browser.

Fax modem A modem capable of sending and receiving fax messages. Most modern modems are fax modems.

File A chunk of data stored on a computer, such as a program, image or document. Programs tend to be made up of many files, while a document is contained in a single file.

File attributes Certain properties of a file – such as whether it's read-only or editable, shared or private and visible or hidden. To view the attributes of a file in Windows, right-click its icon and select Properties.

File compression *Zip file*.

File extension Set of characters added to the end of a filename (after a dot) which identifies the file as a particular type. For example, the extension .txt identifies a text file. In recent versions of Windows, known file extensions aren't shown unless you unhide them in Folder Options (see p.122). For a list of extensions and their file types, visit: **http://www.webopedia.com/quick_ref/fileextensions.html**

File format See *Format*.

Firewall A security system – hardware, software or both – which restricts unauthorized access to a computer or network, especially from other computers connected to the Internet.

FireWire See *IEEE 1394*.

Firmware Operational software stored in the ROM (Read Only Memory) chips of a hardware device. This software is put in place by the manufacturer and can not be altered by the user.

Flash memory A special type of RAM that retains data even in a device that's switched off. It's often used on motherboards to store BIOS code or in digital cameras for holding image data, and can be bought on little sticks or cards for use with portable computers, MP3 players and other devices.

Flat panel See *LCD monitor*.

Floppy See *Floppy disk*.

Floppy disk A removable magnetic storage medium. The term is almost always used to refer to the 3.5" diskettes that have hard square plastic cases (they're floppy inside) and which are used in a standard PC A: drive.

Folder A container for files in a graphic user interface (GUI) system such as Windows.

Folder tree A graphic representation of the folders and drives of a PC, laid out as in the folder view of Windows Explorer.

Font A typeface, such as Times New Roman or Arial. Technically, the font includes factors such as size (in points), style (italic, outline, etc) and weight (bold).

Footprint The amount of space a PC system or device takes up. Most commonly used in relation to the depth of monitors.

Foreground task The activity or program displayed in the current active window. See also *Background task* and *Active window*.

Format 1. Every file is saved with a particular "file format", which determines which application or applications can be used to open, view and edit it. There are thousands of different file formats – simple text format, rich text format and JPEG being a few examples. See also *File extension*. 2. The structure or appearance of a document, font, paragraph, number or any unit of data. 3. To initialize a disk so that it can be used to store information. When a disk is formatted, all previously stored data is lost.

Freeware Copyrighted software that is available for free for your own personal use. Countless freeware utilities and programs are downloadable from the Internet.

fsb (frontside bus) The bus within a processor that connects it to the RAM, determining the speed at which data can be sent or received. See also *Bus*.

FTP (File Transfer Protocol) A standard for sending and receiving files over the Internet. FTP is commonly used for sending Web pages from the computer where they were created to the server where they will live and be accessible from the rest of the Internet. It is also used for downloading files. FTP sites are like Internet storage depots where people send files for others to download, thus avoiding having to send large files as email attachments.

Full duplex Capable of transmitting data in two directions simultaneously. A full duplex sound card can record and playback sound at the same time, for example.

Function keys Keys labelled F1, F2 and so on, running along the top of a computer keyboard. They do different things in different programs, though F1 nearly always activates Help.

Chapter 24

G

Game port Socket for connecting a joystick or other gaming device to a computer.

GB See *Gigabyte.*

GIF (Graphic Interchange Format) A compressed graphics format frequently used for images on the Web.

Gigabyte Abbreviated to GB. Roughly 1 billion bytes of data – 1,073,741,824 to be exact. This is the most common means of describing the capacity of a hard drive.

Graphics card See *Video card*.

Graphics tablet A special input device (an alternative to the mouse), which is favoured by illustrators. It uses a pen, or "stylus", and sensitive pad to duplicate the action of a regular pen or pencil.

GSM (Global System for Mobile Communications) The leading digital wireless communication system technology in Europe and Asia. It allows multiple calls to be made on a single radio frequency.

Guest 1. A type of Windows XP User account that allows an individual to use a PC without already being registered as a user. 2. The name given to a PC that accesses the resources of a host PC using a Direct cable connection. See also *Direct cable connection*.

GUI (Graphic User Interface) Pronounced "gooey". Any system with which you operate a computer using graphics rather than text. In Windows, for example, the GUI lets you enter instructions with a mouse pointer, icons, menus and windows.

Hacker A computer user who breaks into networks or servers by various means, such as decrypting user IDs and passwords. The term is also used in computer circles to describe a legitimate programmer.

Hard disk See *Hard drive.*

Hard disk controller An expansion card that controls one or more hard drives.

Hard drive The primary storage device in modern PCs. All PCs have at least one hard drive (usually labelled C: in Windows), though they can have two or more. Hard drives, which are also referred to as hard disks, consist of a stack of magnetic disks housed in a dust-proof shell. A modern hard drive's capacity is usually measured in gigabytes (GBs).

Hard reset Turning a computer off completely before restarting, as opposed to simply pressing the reset button. This gives the components a chance to discharge.

Hardware The physical components of a computer.

Hidden file A file not displayed in the normal listing (such as in Windows Explorer) to protect it from deletion or modification. See also *File attributes*.

Hi-Speed USB The successor of the original USB connection, this connection standard shifts data at up to 480 Mbps – 40 times faster than a standard USB. Also known as USB 2.

Home page 1. The page automatically loaded by your Internet browser when you start it up. 2. The entry page of a particular Website.

Host Computer that offers some sort of service to users via a network or a direct cable connection. See also *Direct cable connection*, *Client/server* and *Guest*.

HTML (Hypertext Mark-up Language) A programming language used to create Web documents. It's also a file format: behind most Web pages there's an HTML document that determines what it looks like.

HTTP (**H**yper**t**ext **T**ransport **P**rotocol) The Internet's communication protocol. Most Internet addresses begin with "http://", though you don't need to type this when entering Web addresses into a modern browser.

Hub A cable junction box: types include a USB hub (which turns one USB port into two or more), and a network hub (which each computer connects to in certain types of network).

Hypertext links Bits of text, often in blue and underlined, that when clicked take you to another Web page, window, etc.

I

Icon Small image used to represent an object (document, program, etc) in a graphic user interface system. Individual programs and file formats generally have their own unique icon.

IDE (**I**ntegrated **D**rive **E**lectronics) Also known as ATA. An interface for connecting disk drives and other devices (its name comes from the fact that IDE devices have their controller built-in rather than on a separate card, as with SCSI). Standard IDE was superseded by EIDI and Ultra ATA, but the term "IDE" is used to describe all these different standards. Most modern PCs have two IDE ports on the motherboard, each of which can take two devices. See also *EIDE*, *Ultra ATA* and *SCSI*.

IEEE (**I**nstitute for **E**lectrical and **E**lectronics **E**ngineers) 1. A body that classifies and promotes computer standards such as interface types, and gives them numbers like IEEE 1394. 2. An abbreviation for IEEE 1394. See also *IEEE 1394*.

IEEE 1394 High-speed type of computer connection developed by Apple and used for peripherals such as digital video cameras and external hard drives. It supports Plug and Play, lets you attach 63 devices to a single port, allows you to plug and unplug devices without turning the computer off (known as "hot swapping"), and transfers data at up to 400 Mbps (30 times faster than a regular USB connection).

Often abbreviated to IEEE, and also known as FireWire (Apple's name for it) and i.LINK (in Sony products).

i.LINK See *IEEE 1394*.

Infrared A type of wireless PC connection that uses a line-of-sight beam to transmit data in the same way as a conventional TV remote control. Though not commonly used on desktop systems, Infrared ports are often found on notebook PCs.

Inkjet printer The most commonly used type of home printer, which works by spraying tiny droplets of ink onto the paper. Contrast with *Laser printer*.

Insertion point See *Cursor*.

Input device Any device that allows a user to instruct a PC to perform tasks. Mice, keyboards and joysticks are all examples of input devices.

Install 1. To integrate a program into a computer's setup so that it's ready to be used. 2. To add a new piece of hardware, usually an internal component such as an expansion card or hard drive, to a computer.

Internal Any computer device, such as a disk drive, that lives inside the PC's case.

Internet A co-operatively run global computer network with a common addressing system.

Internet connection sharing Using one Internet connection for two or more PCs on a network.

Internet Explorer Microsoft's Web browser, which comes bundled with Windows. It's also downloadable for free from:
http://www.microsoft.com/ie

Internet Favorites See *Favorites*.

I/O (Input/Output) 1. The selection of ports on a computer. 2. Any devices or programs that send or receive a flow of data to the PC's core components. Two examples are the keyboard (an input device) and the monitor (an output device).

IP (Internet Protocol) Every computer connected to the Internet, including the servers where Web pages live, has a unique numeric IP address that allows computers to find each other. Whenever you request a Web page online, your PC's IP address is sent to the computer where the Web page is stored so it can send the page to your machine. See also *DNS*.

IP address See *IP*.

IRQ (Interrupt Request Line) The path that a PC device, such as a printer or expansion card, uses to send messages to the processor. If two devices try to share the same IRQ, a conflict may occur and neither device will operate.

ISA (Industry Standard Architecture) Pronounced "eye-sa" or as separate letters. A type of internal slot (technically a bus) used for connecting expansion cards to the motherboard. However, despite the development of EISA (Extended ISA), ISA has now been almost completely superseded by PCI and AGP. Many new PC motherboards, though, still feature one or more ISA slots. See also *PCI* and *AGP*.

ISDN (Integrated Services Digital Network) An international standard for sending digital data over telephone lines. Commonly used for Internet connections.

ISP (Internet Service Provider) Company that provides access to the Internet. When you connect to the Internet, you actually connect to your ISP's computer, which feeds the Web pages you request to your machine.

IT (Information Technology) Anything relating to computers and their development. People who work in computing are often said to work in IT.

J

Java A programming language often used to create applications for use on the Web, as the language is compatible with all major operating systems.

Jaz drive A type of high-capacity SCSI-connecting removable storage device built by Iomega (**http://www.iomega.com**). See also *Zip drive*.

Joystick A type of gaming device.

JPEG/JPG (Joint Photographic Experts Group) Pronounced "jay-peg". A compressed graphics file format often used in Web pages.

Jumper A small plastic and metal block used for configuring a piece of hardware. A jumper connects two metal pins, and can be removed or moved to change the setup of the device.

Justified Text which has each line expanded to fit the full width of a page or column.

K

Kbps (Kilobits per second) A standard measure of how fast data is transferred by cables, ports, connections, etc. 1Kbps is the same as 1000bps.

Kernel The underlying program code on which an operating system is based.

Keyboard One of the two main input devices of a PC, the other being the mouse. Various different types of keyboard are available, but almost all feature the traditional QWERTY key layout.

Kilobit (Kb) 1024 bits when referring to data storage and 1000 bits when referring to data transfer.

Kilobyte (KB) 1024 bytes when referring to data storage and 1000 bytes when referring to data transfer.

Chapter 24

L

LAN (**L**ocal **A**rea **N**etwork) Computer network that spans a relatively small geographical area, such as in a home or office. Contrast with *WAN*.

Landscape The view or print option for a document where the width of a page is greater than its height. Contrast with *Portrait*.

Laser printer High resolution printer that creates images by rolling a charged drum through a reservoir of toner and then over the paper. Contrast with *Inkjet printer*.

LCD Monitor (**L**iquid **C**rystal **D**isplay Monitor) The thin, light but expansive monitors used in notebook computers. They are also available for desktop systems as a thinner alternative to the CRT monitor. Most LCDs sold today are of the TFT (Thin Film Transistor) type.

Link Any clickable text (technically "hypertext"), icon, button or image in a Web page (and sometimes elsewhere) that takes you to either another Web page or another location within the same page. Links on Web pages are also sometimes used to trigger a download or play music and video clips. See also *Hypertext links*.

Linux A version of the UNIX operating system that is becoming an increasingly popular alternative to Windows for both home and business users. Unlike Windows, the source code for Linux is freely available, allowing programmers to tailor the OS for their individual needs. Many versions of Linux are available, either to buy or download for free.

Local Describes the drives and folders on your computer, as opposed to those on a computer connected via a network or the Internet.

Logical drive See *Partition*.

Log off To disconnect from a network or Website, or end a session on a computer to make way for another user. Contrast with *Log on*.

Log on To connect to a network or Website, or start a session on a computer as a particular user – generally the term implies entering a username and possibly also a password.

Lost clusters Small sections of a hard drive that have been labelled by the operating system as being in use even though they are not associated with a particular file. Lost clusters can be identified and reassigned for use in Windows using the ScanDisk utility. See also *ScanDisk*.

M

Macro A sequence of actions, within an application, that has been assigned either a keyboard shortcut or toolbar button so that the actions can be executed with a single click or keystroke.

Magnetic storage The collective term for storage devices that hold their data magnetically, such as hard drives, floppies and Zip disks. Contrast *Optical disc*.

Mainboard See *Motherboard*.

Mass storage Hardware and related media used for storing large quantities of data. Common examples are hard drives, Zip disks and optical discs such as CD-Rs.

Maximize See *Minimize/Maximize/Restore*.

MB See *Megabyte*.

Media Player 1. The built-in Windows utility for playing CD audio, sound files and video files. 2. Any media playback program.

Megabyte Abbreviated to MB, and often referred to as "meg". When used to refer to disk space, a megabyte is roughly 1 million bytes (1,048,576 to be exact); when used to refer to data transfer it describes exactly 1 million bytes. See also *Byte*.

Megahertz Abbreviated to MHz. A measurement of frequency, equivalent to one million cycles per second. Commonly used to describe the speed of computer processors and other components.

Memory Generally refers to system RAM, or the RAM on video cards and other components. But there are also various other types of removable and non-removable memory. See also *RAM*, *ROM* and *Flash memory*.

Menu bar A strip towards the top of a window that contains dropdown menus. Among others, these bars commonly house File, Edit and View menus.

MHz See *Megahertz*.

Microchip Dense electronic circuit fabricated on a single piece of silicon. A chip smaller than a thumbnail can contain millions of transistors. Also called an "integrated circuit", "microchip" or "silicon chip".

Microprocessor See *CPU*.

MIDI (Musical Instrument Digital Interface) A standard adopted by the electronic music industry for controlling devices such as sound cards and synthesizers. MIDI files contain synthesizer instructions rather than recorded sounds.

Minimize/Maximize/Restore Windows options for resizing and hiding windows. They can be executed in many ways, such as by using the buttons on the right-hand side of a window's Title bar.

Mobo Techie slang for Motherboard.

Modem (Modulator/Demodulator) Device that allows one computer to communicate with others, usually over a telephone line. It converts digital data into analogue signals and vice versa.

Monitor Computer screen.

Motherboard The PC's main circuit board that all the other components connect to.

Mouse One of the two primary PC input devices, along with the keyboard.

Mouse menu A useful little menu that pops up when you right-click screen items such as icons, Web links and the Windows Taskbar. Also called a "Shortcut menu" or "Context menu".

Mouse wheel See *Scroll wheel*.

MP3 (MPEG Audio Layer 3) A compressed music file format.

MP3 player A small portable Walkman-like device for playing compressed music files downloaded from a computer.

MPEG/MPG Pronounced "em-peg". A compressed video file format.

MS-DOS (Microsoft Disk Operating System) The forerunner of Windows. It's a single-tasking operating system where the user types in coded commands rather than clicking icons and menus with a mouse pointer. Usually referred to just as "DOS".

Multitasking An operating system such as Windows that can run many applications, and perform various tasks, simultaneously.

N

Net See *Internet*.

Network 1. To connect a computer to one or more others. 2. A set of connected computers. See also *LAN* and *WAN*.

Network card See *NIC*.

Newsgroups Internet-based message forums, or discussion groups, organized into subjects.

NIC (Network Interface Card) Expansion card that enables a computer to be linked to a network.

Notebook Portable computer. Used interchangeably with "laptop".

Notepad A very basic text editor built into Windows.

Notification area The right-hand end of the Windows Taskbar where system utility icons and the Windows clock reside. Sometimes called the "System tray".

NTFS (New Technology File System) A type of disk drive filing system favoured for its stability and security features. Windows XP is the first home version of Windows to use this system. Contrast with *FAT*.

Chapter 24

O

OCR (**O**ptical **C**haracter **R**ecognition) Software that enables a computer to read a scanned page of text, converting it from a bitmap to a text file.

Offline The state of being disconnected from a network, typically the Internet. Contrast with *Online*.

Online 1.The state of being connected to a network, typically the Internet (contrast with *Offline*). 2. Any resource located on the Internet, such as an online directory.

Operating system A special program – such as Windows, DOS or Linux – that acts as a bridge between the hardware of a computer and the software on it. Among other things, it allocates system resources to specific tasks and determines the way in which you view, move and open files and programs. Sometimes abbreviated to OS.

Optical character recognition See *OCR*.

Optical disc (or **disk**) Any disc – such as a CD or DVD – that is read or written to by means of a laser in an optical drive. Unlike magnetic storage media, optical discs have data physically burned onto them. Some are read-only, some can be written to once and others can be written to again and again. See also *CD-ROM*, *CD-R*, *CD-RW*, *DVD-R*, *DVD-RW* and *DVD-RAM*.

OS See *Operating system*.

Overburning A technology that allows you to squeeze a little more data or music onto a CD-R or CD-RW by burning beyond the official capacity of the disc.

Overclocking Setting a PC to run the processor faster than its theoretical maximum speed. This requires you to know what you're doing and involves an element of risk (processors fry if pushed too far). For more information; see:
http://www.tomshardware.com/overclocking

P

Palmtop A small hand-held PC with a stylus instead of a keyboard. Also called a "PDA".

Parallel port A type of PC input/output connection often used for printers or scanners. A PC's parallel port is often referred to as the "printer port".

Parent folder The folder that a particular file or folder is stored in.

Partition A hard drive (or other disk) can be divided into various sections called partitions that work as if they were separate physical drives. Partitions can be created to help organize data, or install more than one operating systems on a computer. A partition can also be referred to as a "logical drive" (as opposed to a physical drive).

Paste To insert text or graphics that have been Cut or Copied to the Clipboard. The standard shortcut is Ctrl+V. See also *Copy*, *Cut* and *Clipboard*.

Patch Temporary add-on to fix or upgrade software.

Path name The location of a particular file or folder on a PC expressed as the drive and folders you have to would go through to find it. For example: **C:\Documents and Settings\Bob\My Documents\My Music\Bach**

PC card See *PCMCIA*.

PCI (Peripheral Component Interconnect) A standard type of internal connection (technically a bus) for expansion cards such as modems, video cards, etc. PCI devices attach via PCI slots on the motherboard.

PCMCIA card (Personal Computer Memory Card International Association) A computer device about the size of a thick credit card used primarily for adding devices to notebook PCs. PCMCIA devices can be either self-contained components or external devices that attach via a cable with a card on the end. Also called a "PC card".

PDF (Portable Document Format) A file format frequently found on the Web. Can be viewed with Adobe Acrobat Reader, freely downloadable from: **http://www.acrobat.com**

Pentium Frequently updated CPU series produced by Intel. The Pentium superseded the 486 in 1993.

Peripheral device Any external hardware device attached to a computer, such as a printer, scanner, keyboard or mouse.

PIM (Personal Information Manager) An appointments and contacts management program.

Pirated Software that is illegally copied and distributed.

Pixel (pix – picture – element) Bitmap images and everything you see on a computer screen are made up of small squares of colour called pixels. The size and number of pixels displayed depends upon the resolution of the image and the screen.

Platform Another name for a computer operating system. The most common examples are Windows, Linux and Mac OS.

Plug and Play A system, often abbreviated to PnP, that simplifies hardware installation by having the PC detect the new device and configure it automatically.

Plug-in A small program or utility that adds additional features to a bigger program.

POP3 (Post Office Protocol 3) A standard email protocol. If you have a POP3 mail account, the messages are stored on a mail server until you download them to your machine (or someone else's).

Port A socket for connecting a cable. There are many different types, including serial, USB and PS/2.

Portal Web site that specializes in leading you to others via links.

Portrait The view or print option for a document where the width of a page is narrower than its height. Contrast with *Landscape*.

POST (Power-On Self Test) The self-diagnostic sequence that a PC runs when it's turned on to check that everything is working correctly.

PostScript An industry-standard language and file format for printing high-resolution text and images on compatible laser printers. Developed by Adobe, PostScript treats letters and images as scalable shapes rather than bitmaps.

PPM (**P**ages **P**er **M**inute) The maximum number of pages a printer can churn out in a minute.

Printer port See *Parallel Port*.

Print preview Shows how a program expects a document to look when it's printed. This option is normally found in the File menu.

Processor Also called the CPU or the "chip", this is the component that does most of the work in a PC and determines the system's maximum speed. The Intel Pentium and AMD Athlon are examples of PC processors.

Program A piece of software that tells the PC how to perform certain tasks, such as word processing or photo editing.

Protocol Agreed way for two devices to communicate.

Proxy server A computer that sits between a client, such as a home user, and the actual ISP server. Most often used to improve performance by delivering stored pages (in a similar way to browser cache) and to filter out undesirable material.

PS/2 A little circular port used for attaching mice and keyboards.

QuickTime A multimedia standard commonly used to preview movie clips online. You can download the QuickTime player from: http://www.quicktime.com

Chapter 24

R

RAID (Redundant Array of Inexpensive Disks) A type of hard disk setup that employs multiple drives running in combination – frequently used in servers.

RAM (Random Access Memory) Memory used for short-term data processing rather than storage. The term generally refers to the main system RAM, but sound cards and other components can also have their own RAM. Usually, when a PC is turned off the memory is drained of its data.

Rambus A company best known for producing RDRAM. See also *RDRAM*.

RDRAM (Rambus DRAM) Pronounced "are-dee-ram", and often referred to simply as "Rambus memory". A recently developed type of high-speed RAM capable of very high data transfer rates. Comes on RIMMs and SORIMMs.

Readme file A document included with a program that provides installation instructions or other information. Sometimes useful when things go wrong.

Read-only A file or piece of data that can be accessed (read) but not modified. See also *ROM*.

RealPlayer A program, downloadable for free from **http://www.real.com**, for playing streaming audio and video from the Web.

Recycle bin Special Windows system folder where deleted files are stored until you choose to delete them permanently. You can view the contents of the Recycle bin by clicking its icon on the Start menu or Desktop.

Refresh rate Generally refers to the rate at which a monitor renews its image, measured in Hz (number of times per second).

Registry A database in Windows where system and software configuration settings are recorded. It can be viewed and edited by typing **Regedit** in the Run command in the Start menu – but altering anything incorrectly can cause major problems.

Rename To assign a new name to a file or folder. In Windows, select an icon, click the nametag and type the new name; or right-click the icon and choose Rename from the mouse menu.

Reset To restart a computer, either via the operating system (in the Turn Off or Shut Down options in the Windows Start menu) or with the small button on the case.

Resolution 1. The degree of detail in a printed or displayed image, usually expressed in dpi (dots per inch). The resolution of an individual image can be altered using an image editing program – reducing the resolution should reduce the file size. 2. The number of pixels on a screen. See also *Pixel*.

Restore See *Minimize/Maximize/Restore*.

RIMM Pronounced "rim". A module of RDRAM. See also *RDRAM* and *CRIMM*.

ROM (Read Only Memory) Computer memory chip or disc on which data has been pre-recorded. Once data has been written onto a ROM chip, it can only be read, not removed or altered. Unlike RAM, ROM retains its contents even when the computer its in is turned off.

Save To transfer data from short-term memory (RAM) to a more permanent storage place such as a hard drive, floppy or tape drive. Found in the File menu of most applications.

Save As The same as Save, except this option lets you choose a different filename or file type. Found in the File menu of most applications.

ScanDisk A Windows built-in utility that checks the surface of a hard drive or floppy disk for errors and lost clusters. See also *Lost clusters*.

Scanner A peripheral device used to transfer "hard copy" such as photos and documents on paper into digital images in order to edit, save, print or send them with a computer.

Screen resolution See *Resolution.*

Screen saver Utility that blanks the computer screen, or displays an animated loop, after a certain period of user inactivity.

Scroll bar Horizontal or vertical bar at the side or bottom of a window allowing you to view parts of the document, Web page or list not currently displayed. Either click on the arrows at either end of the bar or drag the slider to scroll up, down, left or right.

Scroll wheel Small wheel positioned between the right and left buttons on some mice, useful for scrolling through Web pages, among other things.

SCSI (Small Computer System Interface) Pronounced "scuzzy". A type of high-speed connection for internal and external PC devices. Several devices can be attached to a single SCSI port, but you need a SCSI interface expansion card to get the port.

SDRAM (Synchronous DRAM) Pronounced "ess-dee-ram". A type of RAM found in most machines built in the last few years, though it's starting to be superseded by DDR SDRAM and RDRAM. See also *DRAM*, *DDR SDRAM* and *DRDRAM*.

Sector The smallest unit of disk space, usually 512 bytes.

Serial mouse Mouse that plugs into a serial port. Such mice can often also be plugged into in a PS/2 port with the aid of an adapter.

Serial port An old-school PC socket that allows data transfer 1 bit at a time. Can be used for many different peripherals.

Server Computer that makes services or files available on a network or on the Internet.

Shareware Software with a free trial period, generally downloaded from the Internet and often produced by a single programmer. Users are encouraged to send the programmer a token payment if they like and use the program.

Shortcut An icon that opens a program, folder or file that lives in another location on the computer. Shortcut icons generally have little arrows on their lower left corner to differentiate them from "real" files.

Shortcut menu See *Mouse menu*.

Shut down To close down a program, operating system or computer in a way that ensures no data is lost. Windows should always be shut down via the option on the Start menu (Turn off computer in Windows XP or Shut Down in earlier versions).

SIMM (Single Inline Memory Module) Pronounced "sim". A type of RAM memory module, typically containing FPM or EDO RAM. SIMMS have now been almost completely superseded by DIMMs and RIMMs. See also *DIMM* and *RIMM*.

Slot A long thin socket on a computer motherboard or elsewhere for inserting an expansion board or RAM module.

SODIMM (Small Outline Dual Inline Memory Module) Pronounced "so-dim". 1. A small type of DIMM memory module often found in notebook computers. See also *DIMM*. 2. A Mac user.

Software General term for the various kinds of programs used to operate computers and related devices. Software consists of coded instructions rather than physical ("hard") components.

SOHO (Small Office/Home Office) A category of computer users who run small and home offices – and any product designed for such users.

SORIMM Pronounced "so-rim". A smaller type of RIMM memory module sometimes found in notebook computers. See also *RIMM*.

Sound card Expansion card that allows a PC to play and record sound.

Spam Junk email or newsgroup postings.

S/PDIF (Sony/Philips Digital Interface Format) Pronounced "ess-pee-diff". Digital audio connection found on some sound cards, used for attaching surround-sound speaker systems, DAT players and effects racks.

Spreadsheet Document based on a grid of rows and columns, or a program that creates such documents. Spreadsheets are used for organizing information, manipulating numbers and producing graphs.

Start button The button on the left of the Windows Taskbar that launches the Start menu. See also *Start menu*.

Start menu The main Windows menu, which is accessed by clicking the Start button in the lower left hand corner of the screen.

Startup disk See *Boot disk*.

Storage A device that stores data. Sometimes storage is divided into "primary" (RAM, cache, etc) and "secondary" (hard drives, tape drives, etc), though generally the term is only used to describe mass storage devices. See also *Mass storage*.

Streaming A process that allows you to view movie files or hear audio files (generally on the Web) in real-time. Whilst you watch or listen to the first segment of a file, your computer is downloading and preparing the next segment, so you don't have to wait for the whole file to arrive before playback can begin.

Subwoofer Speaker specifically for dealing with low frequency sound, which often comes in a set with small "satellite" speakers for treble.

Surf Skip from page to page on the Web by clicking links.

Surge protector A device that stops surges in an electrical power supply from reaching a device such as a PC.

Swap file See *Virtual memory*.

System disk See *Boot disk*.

System RAM See *RAM*.

System tray See *Notification area*.

T

Tape drive A type of mass storage device that utilizes magnetic tape – often used for backing up data.

Taskbar The long thin strip that generally spans the bottom of the Windows Desktop, with the Start menu at one corner and the Notification area (or System tray) at the other.

TCP/IP (Transmission Control Protocol/Internet Protocol) The basic communication protocols that make the Internet possible.

Temporary Internet Files Special system folder used by Internet Explorer to store the content of Web pages for quick recall when backtracking.

Text file A simple document that contains nothing but plain text (ASCII characters, to be exact). Can be read or created with Windows Notepad.

TFT See *LCD monitor*.

Thumbnail A small preview image of an unopened image file. One of the View options for files and folders in Windows.

TIF or **TIFF** (Tagged Image File Format) One of the most popular bitmap image file formats.

Title bar The uppermost strip of a window, where you'll find the name of the program or document running within the frame.

Toner cartridge Disposable unit that supplies toner, the equivalent of ink, in a laser printer.

Toolbar A strip in a window – usually on one of the edges – that contains icons, dropdown menus and so on. It can sometimes be detached from the window to become an independent floating palette.

Touchpad The pointing device used in most notebooks. Operated by moving your finger around a small flat touch-sensitive pad.

Tower case A computer case that stands upright – is taller than it is wide. Contrast with *Desktop*.

Trackball An input device resembling an upside-down mouse. Instead of moving the mouse, you roll the ball around with your fingers.

Trackpad See *Touchpad*.

Trojan (**horse**) A malicious and destructive program that hides its true (usually sinister) intentions.

Troubleshooter In Windows XP this is a diagnostic tool that asks you various multiple-choice questions to try and locate, and help you fix, a problem.

TV card A type of expansion card that allows your PC to receive and display television signals. Equivalent external devices are also available.

TWAIN Standard interface protocol used to bridge software and image capture devices such as scanners. (From the saying "Ne'er the twain shall meet", not "Technology Without An Interesting Name", as is often claimed).

U

UDMA (**U**ltra **D**irect **M**emory **A**ccess) A high-speed interface protocol governing the flow of data to and from EIDE hard drives; it vastly improved upon the DMA standard. See also *DMA*.

Ultra ATA A high-speed IDE hard drive interface that supports the UDMA protocol. The three types are Ultra ATA/33, Ultra ATA/66 and Ultra ATA/100; the numbers represent the theoretical maximum data transfer rate expressed in megabytes per second, though most drives don't achieve the stated speed. These terms are often written differently – Ultra ATA/33 is the same as a UDMA ATA33, UDMA33, DMA33, etc. Ultra ATA devices can generally be plugged into standard IDE ports, though the speed will be limited.

Uninstall To remove all parts of an application from a PC.

Update To bring a program, operating system or data file up to date by installing a patch, revision or complete new version. See also *Patch*.

Upgrade To improve a computer system by adding hardware, or to update a program.

Upload To send files to a remote computer. Contrast with *Download*.

UPS (**U**ninterruptible **P**ower **S**upply) A power source incorporating a battery that kicks in when the mains supply is disrupted, providing at least enough power to shutdown the PC properly.

URL (**U**niform **R**esource **L**ocator) The technical name for a Web address.

USB (**U**niversal **S**erial **B**us) A popular type of connection that allows the connection of up to 127 devices to one port, supports Plug and Play and lets you "hot swap" devices – plug and unplug them without shutting down the computer. See also *Hi-Speed USB*.

USB 2 See *Hi-Speed USB*.

Usenet (User's Network) A collection of networks and computer systems that exchange messages, organized by subject into newsgroups.

Utility A small program which serves a specific function – usually as part of a bigger program or operating system.

V

Video adapter See *Video card*.

Video card An expansion card that sends signals to the monitor, though video capability is sometimes built into the motherboard. Also called a "video adapter", "video board" or "display adapter".

Virtual memory The concept of using part of a hard drive – called a "swap file" – as pretend RAM. When the real RAM is full, some of the data is temporarily moved to the swap file where it stays until it's needed or until there is some free RAM.

Virus A small program or piece of program code that finds its way onto a computer and then causes havoc. Viruses are most commonly spread from machine to machine via infected floppy disks or email attachments.

Voice recognition software Application that attempts to interpret the user's voice, either to turn spoken text into type or to respond to commands.

Chapter 24

Wallpaper Background image on the Windows Desktop.

WAN (**W**ide **A**rea **N**etwork) A network of geographically diverse computers connected via satellite or telephone. Contrast with *LAN*.

Warez Pronounced "wares" or "ware-ez". Slang for software, usually pirated. See also *Pirated*.

Web (or **World Wide Web**; the "**www**" in Web addresses) A globally spread collection of graphic and text documents published on the Internet that are connected by clickable links and which share a common programming language (HTML). A Web page is a single HTML document; a Website is a collection of related HTML documents.

Web authoring Designing and publishing Web pages.

Webcam A small digital video camera that perches on top of a PC monitor, primarily used for video conferencing and image capture.

Window A self-contained rectangular portion of the screen in which a particular document or program is dealt with.

Windows A series of GUI-based operating systems designed and published by Microsoft.

Windows CE A slimmed-down version of Windows designed to be run on handheld computers.

Windows Explorer The special Windows program that is used to browse through the files on a PC. My Documents, Control Panel and so on all open in Windows Explorer. Confusingly, it's sometimes used to describe only those windows with the folder tree showing, and it's sometimes muddled up with *Internet Explorer*.

Windows key A special key found on most modern PC keyboards, used for various shortcuts in Windows.

Wizard A special Windows program that walks you through the various stages of a particular task – installing a new printer, for example.

WMA (Windows Media Audio) A compressed file format supported by the Windows Media Player and many MP3 devices.

WordPad Simple word processor bundled with Windows. Found under Accessories in the Programs menu.

Word processor Software used for creating and manipulating text based documents such as letters. Some popular examples are Microsoft Word and Corel WordPerfect.

World Wide Web See *Web*.

Worm A type of virus that self-replicates and consumes system resources. They spread very quickly via emails and the Internet.

WYSIWYG (What You See Is What You Get) Pronounced "wiz-ee-wig". A program, such as a Web design package, that lets the user see what the finished document will look like, rather than forcing them to work in code and view the results later.

Z

Zip file A file compression format with the extension .zip. Files are "zipped" to reduce their size for transfer or storage, or to bundle numerous files onto into one archive file.

Zip drive Like a floppy drive, but takes disks that hold up to 250MB. Made by Iomega (**http://www.iomega.com**). See also *Jaz drive*.

25 Web directory

News and reviews

Anad tech

http://www.anandtech.com

Good techie site dealing with all kinds of hardware news and reviews. Includes weekly prices for memory, motherboards, etc.

CNet

http://www.cnet.com

"The source for computers and technology", as it calls itself, is a massive computer portal, containing everything from hardware reviews and downloads to how-to guides and an effective price comparison tool.

Dan's Data

http://www.dansdata.com

Contains in-depth reviews of all kinds of hardware, from heatsinks to DVD-RAM camcorders, as well as some good how-to articles. Dan really knows his stuff, but is a bit of a nutter and also reviews model tanks.

Maximum PC

http://www.maximumpc.co.uk

A nice-looking and user-friendly site with loads of reviews, downloads, links, tips, forums – definitely worth a click or two.

Motherboards.org

http://www.motherboards.org

You simply won't believe how much there is to know about motherboards until you visit this site. As well as reviews, it includes info on BIOS upgrades and overclocking, and the "Mobot", a huge tool for identifying and comparing motherboards.

Sharkey Extreme

http://www.sharkeyextreme.com

Very similar in layout to Tom's (below), and again a little on the techie side, this site is overflowing with articles and product reviews. Includes weekly CPU and memory price guide.

Tom's Hardware

http://www.tomshardware.com

This large but easy-to-navigate site has made Tom something of a living legend. Though techie in places, you'll find hundreds of informative articles about all things hardware.

ZDNet

http://www.zdnet.com

Another giant computer site, a bit like CNet, this covers pretty well everything. Includes loads of articles and reviews.

Magazines

Magazine sites are a great place to find out what's hot and what's not, and many offer downloads, tips, forums and links for purchasing the kit you've read about – though be sure the site you're using isn't an overseas one before you tap in your credit card details.

Computer Shopper http://www.computershopper.co.uk

PC Answers http://www.pcanswers.co.uk

PC Buyer http://www.pcbuyer.com

PC Format http://www.pcformat.co.uk

PC Magazine http://www.pcmag.com

PC Plus http://www.pcplus.co.uk

PC Pro http://www.pcpro.co.uk

PC World http://www.pcworld.com

Personal Computer World http://www.pcw.vnunet.com

What Laptop http://www.whatlaptop.co.uk

Reference

About

http://www.about.com/compute

About.com is a mammoth site where you can find resources – and links – relating to almost every subject. Their computing section is excellent, covering everything from downloads to computer history.

Webopedia

http://www.webopedia.com

This is a great reference tool, overflowing with easy-to-understand definitions with good links for most entries.

The PC Guide

http://www.pcguide.com

Though the presentation is a little cold, this is an unbelievably comprehensive PC site that offers information for both advanced and uninitiated PC users. The only problem is that there's simply too much here to read.

The PC Technology Guide

http://www.pctechguide.com

Similar to the PC Guide, this site offers in-depth info about all elements of PC components and operation. Contains lots of links and illustrations.

PC911

http://www.pcnineoneone.com

This good reference site is geared toward troubleshooting and tutorials for upgrading. There's also regular articles, usually focusing on hardware.

What Is?

http://whatis.techtarget.com

Probably the best definitions site around, What Is? provides in-depth but easily-digestible articles on everything from AAA Servers to ZV Ports.

PCs and components

Stores

Many online PC stores do more than just flog stuff – in fact it's becoming hard in some cases to tell the difference between stores and magazines – and now feature reviews, articles and product comparisons. Try a few out to see which company's style you prefer.

Dabs (UK) http://www.dabs.com
Insight (UK) http://www.insight.com/uk
Jungle (UK) http://www.jungle.com
The Laptop Shop (UK) http://www.thelaptopshop.co.uk
Widget (UK) http://www.widget.co.uk
Computers 4 Sure (US) http://www.computers4sure.com
Insight (US) http://www.insight.com
Insight (Canada) http://www.insight.com/canada
Outpost (US) www.outpost.com
PC Mall (US) www.pcmall.com
Aus PC Market (Aus) http://www.auspcmarket.com.au
Ozbuy.com (Aus) http://www.ozbuy.com
eCost (US) www.ecost.com

Auctions

Internet auctions are often a good place to pick up real bargains, but be warned: it's also easy to get your fingers burnt, so try to limit your bids to products that claim to be boxed or sealed, have a full description that you're happy with and which offer a picture of the goods. Many auction sites also offer vendor ratings if you want to check credentials before you buy. For the full story on Internet auctions, see *The Rough Guide to Shopping Online*.

Ebay (UK) http://pages.ebay.co.uk/computer-index.html
QXL (UK) http://www.qxl.com/uk
Yahoo (UK) http://uk.auctions.yahoo.com/uk
CNET (US) http://auctions.cnet.com
Ebay (US) http://www.ebay.com/computers
Yahoo (US) http://auctions.yahoo.com/computers
Sold (Aus) http://www.sold.com.au

Manufacturers

Here's a list of some manufacturers' sites worth looking at – for specification comparison, if nothing else. Many will sell to you direct, though you're unlikely to save any money by cutting out the middleman.

Acer http://www.acer.com
AJP http://www.ajp.co.uk
AMD http://www.amd.com
Carrera http://www.carrera.co.uk
Compaq http://www.compaq.co.uk
Creative http://www.creative.com
Dan http://www.dan.co.uk
Dell http://www.dell.co.uk
Dragon Systems http://www.dragonsys.com
Evesham http://www.evesham.com
Fujitsu http://www.fujitsu-computers.com
Gateway http://www.gw2k.co.uk
Golf http://www.golfplc.co.uk
Hewlett Packardhttp://www.hp.com
Hi-Grade http://www.higrade.com
Hitachi http://www.hitachi.com
IBM http://www.ibm.com
Intel http://www.intel.com
Iomega http://www.iomega.com
MBC http://www.mbc.co.uk
Mesh http://www.meshcomputers.co.uk
Packard Bell http://www.packardbell.com
Psion http://www.psion.co.uk
Samsung http://www.samsung.com
Simply Computers http://www.simply.co.uk

Sony http://www.sony.com
Texas Instruments http://www.ti.com
Time Computers http://www.timecomputers.com
Tiny Computers http://www.tiny.com
Toshiba http://www.toshiba.com
Umax http://www.umax.com
Watford Electronics http://www.watford.co.uk

Software

Where to buy it

Though most titles are available directly from the manufacturer (see below), you'll often find the best deals via a third party retailer, such as those listed here.

Amazon (UK) http://www.amazon.co.uk/software
Jungle (UK) http://www.jungle.com
Amazon (US) http://www.amazon.com/software
Beyond (US) http://www.beyond.com/software.htm
Software Warehouse Australia (Aus) http://www.software-warehouse.com/cgi-bin/store/nph-frameset

Software companies

For information about, updates for, and trial versions of a specific software title, try visiting the page of the manufacturer. Here are a few popular titles and the relevant addresses.

Ability Office http://www.ability.com
Acid and Vegas http://www.sonicfoundry.com
Cakewalk http://www.cakewalk.com

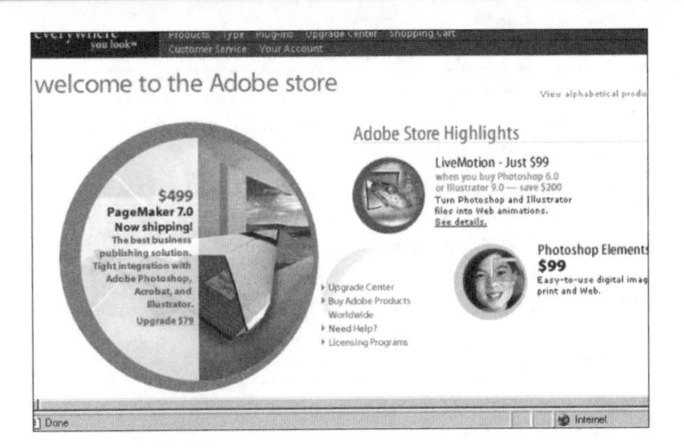

Cool 3D http://www.ulead.com
CorelDRAW http://www.corel.com
Cubase http://www.steinberg.com
Dreamweaver, Flash and Fireworks http://www.macromedia.com
FileMaker http://www.filemaker.com
Final Draft http://www.finaldraft.com
Finale http://www.codamusic.com
Lotus Smart Suite http://www.lotus.com/smartsuite
Microsoft Office http://www.microsoft.com/office
Microsoft Works http://www.microsoft.com/works
Photoshop and Illustrator http://www.adobe.com
PhotoSuite http://www.mgisoft.com
Quark Xpress http://www.quark.com/products/xpress
Sibelius http://www.sibelius.com
Star Office http://www.sun.com/staroffice
WebDraw http://www.jasc.com
WordPerfect http://www.corel.com

Chapter 25

Free software and downloads

Most people don't realize quite how much free software is available online. Check out the following for everything from tiny utilities to whole applications.

Nonags http://www.nonags.com

PC Plus Downloads http://www.pcplus.co.uk/downloads

ZDNet Downloads http://www.zdnet.com/downloads

StuffALL.com http://www.stuffall.com/software/winutils.shtml

Stroud's CWSApps http://www.cws.internet.com/menu.html

Shareware

There's some brilliant shareware around. It's inexpensive and can be tried out for free.

The Shareware Directory http://www.sharewaredirectory.com

Shareware Solutions http://www.sharewaresolutions.com

Review Now Shareware Directory
http://www.reviewnow.com/links

Handy utilities to download

Of the thousands of free downloads available, the following are definitely worth getting hold of.

Adobe Acrobat Reader http://www.acrobat.com

QuickTime player http://www.quicktime.com

Power Archiver http://www.powerarchiver.com

Shockwave and Flash Players http://www.macromedia.com

Google Toolbar http://www.google.com/options/toolbar.html

Windows

Microsoft

http://www.microsoft.com

Home of the all-powerful Microsoft, the creators of Windows. Once you've cut through the corporate spin, there are loads of useful resources to be had: downloads, updates, forums, tips, troubleshooting, links and loads more.

Paul Thurrott's SuperSite for Windows

http://winsupersite.com

This very stylish site is sure to help you find your way around the Windows environment. It's frequently updated and features loads of tips and info about all Windows versions, both current and future.

Toejumper

http://www.toejumper.net

Though the address suggests that you're about to enter some strange foot-fetish Website, you are in fact presented with a good troubleshooting and resource guide for Windows, full of sound, well-written advice and easy-to-follow troubleshooting instructions.

Win Drivers

http://www.windrivers.com

Great site containing every Windows driver you ever needed as well as tips, troubleshooting, news and reviews.

Web stuff

The List

http://www.thelist.com

The best way to find an ISP is to read up-to-date reviews in magazines. But if you just want to know what companies offer what services, try this site.

Top Search Engines

There are loads of search engines around, but some are better than others. Try the following.

AltaVista http://www.altavista.com

Deja (Newsgroup entries) http://www.deja.com

Fast Search http://www.alltheweb.com

Google http://www.google.com

Raging Search http://www.raging.com

Web-based email

Hotmail http://www.hotmail.com

Twigger (UK) http://www.twigger.co.uk

Yahoo Mail http://www.mail.yahoo.com

PC books online

If your local bookshop doesn't stock all the computer books and manuals you want, try one of these.

Computer Manuals Online Bookstore (UK)

http://www.compman.co.uk

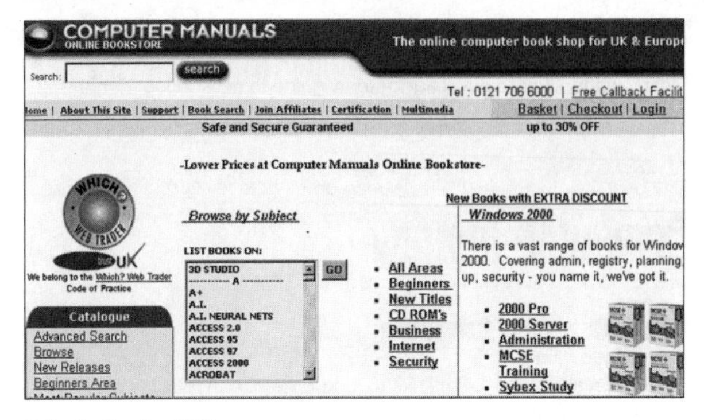

Brian's Books (US) http://www.briansbooks.com
Bookware.com (Aus) http://www.bookware.com.au

Networking

Home PC Network

http://www.homepcnetwork.com
The place to find out all you'll ever need to know about home networking. The site offers help with hardware, software, gaming, and much more.

World of Windows Networking

http://www.wown.com
An extremely detailed (if not very pretty) guide to networking with Windows. Covers everything from the basics to customizing your own cables.

Dan's Data Network Pages

http://www.dansdata.com/network.htm

Clearly written what-you-need-to-know guide to networking from the man down under.

Computer history

Virtual Museum of Computing

http://vmoc.i.am

An unbelievably huge list of links to, and reviews of, Websites relating to the history of computing.

Old Computers

http://www.oldcomputers.freeserve.co.uk

One for nerds trying to rediscover old computing flames. Maintained by a chap called Brian, this site will help to put everything in perspective – a work of genius. Please pay Brian a visit.

The Commodore 64 is built round the 6510 Processor at a clock speed of 1 MHz with a 20k ROM and 64k of RAM of which a maximum of 54k is available to the user. The colour display is capable of displaying 40 characters on 24 lines in16 colours as well as graphics of up to 320 x 200 pixels. The covers 3 voices, 6 octaves.

Interfaces include, Cassette, TV, ROM Slot, Monitor, RS232 and user port.

Miscellaneous

PC Music Guru

http://www.pc-music.com

A brilliant site, covering all aspects of PC music-making. These pages show you both what's possible and what you need to achieve it. There's loads of hardware and software reviews and a list of free music software and plug-ins.

Desktop Publishing.com

http://desktoppublishing.com

A large site dealing with – you guessed it – desktop publishing. There's loads of hints, tips and reviews as well as template downloads and more.

The Elvis Presley Theme Page

http://www.xs4all.nl/~mouwen/elvis

If your regular Windows themes and icons seem dull, why not transport The King into your Windows environment? Wallpapers, screen savers and entire themes are available to download.

Chapter 25

Online directories

If you can't find what you need in our directory, then try one of these comprehensive online directories of PC-related links.

The Open Directory http://dmoz.org/Computers

Yahoo http://www.yahoo.com/computers

101 Hardware Links

http://www.sharewareplace.com/101/101hard.shtml

Looksmart http://www.looksmart.com

Google http://directory.google.com/Top/Computers

Yahoo http://dir.yahoo.com/Computers_and_Internet

Index

As well as references to equipment, people and other subjects, this index contains important functions and features of Microsoft Windows. These appear capitalized, and can also be found under the entry for Windows.

a

Index

b

c

d

e

Index

f

g

h

i

j

l

m

n

o

q

r

s

U

V

Index

X

Z